Issues in Technology, Learning, and Instructional Design

In *Issues in Technology, Learning, and Instructional Design*, some of the best-known scholars in those fields produce powerful, original dialogues that clarify current issues, provide context and theoretical grounding, and illuminate a framework for future thought. Position statements are introduced and then responded to, covering a remarkably broad series of topics across educational technology, learning, and instructional design, from tool use to design education to how people learn. Reminiscent of the well-known Clark/Kozma debates of the 1990s, this book is a must-have for professionals in the field and can also be used as a textbook for graduate or advanced undergraduate courses.

Alison A. Carr-Chellman is Dean of the College of Education at the University of Idaho.

Gordon Rowland is Professor of Communications at Ithaca College.

Issues in Technology, Learning, and Instructional Design

Classic and Contemporary Dialogues

Edited by
Alison A. Carr-Chellman
and Gordon Rowland

NEW YORK AND LONDON

First published 2017
by Routledge
711 Third Avenue, New York, NY 10017

and by Routledge
2 Park Square, Milton Park, Abingdon, Oxon, OX14 4RN

Routledge is an imprint of the Taylor & Francis Group, an informa business

© 2017 Taylor & Francis

The right of Alison A. Carr-Chellman and Gordon Rowland to be identified as the authors of the editorial material, and of the authors for their individual chapters, has been asserted in accordance with sections 77 and 78 of the Copyright, Designs and Patents Act 1988.

All rights reserved. No part of this book may be reprinted or reproduced or utilised in any form or by any electronic, mechanical, or other means, now known or hereafter invented, including photocopying and recording, or in any information storage or retrieval system, without permission in writing from the publishers.

Trademark notice: Product or corporate names may be trademarks or registered trademarks, and are used only for identification and explanation without intent to infringe.

Library of Congress Cataloguing in Publication Data
A catalog record for this book has been requested

ISBN: 978-1-138-89788-5 (hbk)
ISBN: 978-1-138-89789-2 (pbk)
ISBN: 978-1-315-70891-1 (ebk)

Typeset in Sabon
by Apex CoVantage, LLC

Contents

List of Contributors   x

Introduction   1

PART I
The Nature of Design and Instructional Design   5

1 Instructional Design as Design   7
PATRICK PARRISH

Response by Harold Nelson 12
Rejoinder by Patrick Parrish 16

2 Toward Understanding the Nature of Design   18
BRENDA BANNAN

Response by Andrew S. Gibbons 22
Rejoinder by Brenda Bannan 24

3 Guerrilla Design: How Can We Accommodate Against-the-Grain Thinking in Our Practice?   26
BRENT WILSON

Response by Barbara L. Martin 28
Rejoinder by Brent Wilson 30

4 Design Beyond Content: Extending the Value of Educational Technology: An Examination of the Role or the Anti-role of Content in Educational Technology   32
BRAD HOKANSON

Response by Peter Samuelson Wardrip 35
Rejoinder by Brad Hokanson 37

5 The Systems Approach to Instructional Development   39
MICHAEL MOLENDA

Response by Thomas Argondizza 44
Rejoinder by Michael Molenda 46

6 Instructional Design Models and the Expertise Required to
Practice True Instructional Design   48
ROBERT MARIBE BRANCH

Response by Lloyd P. Rieber 50
Rejoinder by Robert Maribe Branch 53

PART 2
Preparing Instructional Designers   55

Introduction to Part 2   55

7 Developing Design Expertise   57
KATHLEEN FORTNEY

Response by Elizabeth Boling 60
Rejoinder by Kathleen Fortney 62

8 Design Education as a Site for Educating Disciplines   64
KENNON M. SMITH

Response by Atsusi Hirumi 68
Rejoinder by Kennon M. Smith 71

9 Necessary Ingredients for the Education of Designers   73
IRENE VISSCHER-VOERMAN

Response by Monica W. Tracey 77
Rejoinder by Irene Visscher-Voerman 79

10 Teaching the Complex Performance of Instructional
Design: Why We Cannot Use the (Existing) Tools
of Instructional Design   81
ELIZABETH BOLING

Response by M. David Merrill 84
Rejoinder by Elizabeth Boling 86

11 My Hope for the Future of Instructional Technology   88
M. DAVID MERRILL

Response by Tonia A. Dousay 92
Rejoinder by M. David Merrill 94

12 Preparing Instructional Designers 95
MONICA W. TRACEY

Response by Brad Hokanson 98
Rejoinder by Monica W. Tracey 100

PART 3
Contexts of Learning, Design, and Technology 101

Introduction to Part 3 101

13 Education Is Completely Broken 103
ROGER C. SCHANK

Response by Kyle Peck 106
Rejoinder by Roger C. Schank 108

14 Paradigm Change: Its Time Is Now 110
CHARLES M. REIGELUTH

Response by Roger C. Schank 114
Rejoinder by Charles M. Reigeluth 115

15 The Unbalancing of Corporate Systems: The Neuroscience of Intellect vs. Wisdom 117
ANTHONY MARKER

Response by Rob Foshay 120
Rejoinder by Anthony Marker 122

16 Women in Educational Technology 124
AUDREY WATTERS

Response by Rose Marra 128

PART 4
Technology 131

Introduction to Part 4 131

17 The Learner-Centered Paradigm of Instruction 133
CHARLES M. REIGELUTH

Response by Stephen W. Harmon 137
Rejoinder by Charles M. Reigeluth 139

18 Learning From and With Media and Technology 141
THOMAS C. REEVES

Response by Wilhelmina C. Savenye 145
Rejoinder by Thomas C. Reeves 148

19 Building Educational Technologies to Scale in Schools 150
    ROB FOSHAY

    Response by MJ Bishop 154
    Rejoinder by Rob Foshay 156

20 For the Foreseeable Future, Instructional Technology Devices
    and Products—No Matter How Well Designed—Will Not
    Eliminate the Need for Human Teachers 158
    WARD MITCHELL CATES AND THOMAS C. HAMMOND

    Response by Sugata Mitra 163
    Rejoinder by Ward Mitchell Cates and Thomas C. Hammond 164

21 What's Next for E-learning? 166
    JOHN SAVERY

    Response by Clark Quinn 169
    Rejoinder by John Savery 171

22 Any Time, Any Place, Any Pace . . . 173
    KATHRYN KENNEDY AND JOSEPH R. FREIDHOFF

    Response by Victoria Raish 177
    Rejoinder by Kathryn Kennedy and Joseph R. Freidhoff 179

PART 5
Learning Science 181

Introduction to Part 5 181

23 Points of Contact: Educational Technology and the Learning Sciences 183
    ANDREW S. GIBBONS

    Response by Jason Yip 190
    Rejoinder by Andrew S. Gibbons 192

24 Bring Design to Design-Based Research 194
    GORDON ROWLAND

    Response by Heather Toomey Zimmerman 197
    Rejoinder by Gordon Rowland 200

25 Participatory Design   202
JASON YIP

Response by Thomas C. Reeves 206
Rejoinder by Jason Yip 208

Conclusion   210

Index   211

Contributors

Thomas Argondizza
argondizza@gmail.com
Pennsylvania State University

Brenda Bannan
bbannan@gmu.edu
George Mason University

MJ Bishop
mjbishop@usmd.edu
University System of Maryland

Elizabeth Boling
eboling@indiana.edu
Indiana University–Bloomington

Robert Maribe Branch
rbranch@uga.edu
University of Georgia

Ward Mitchell Cates
ward.cates@lehigh.edu
Lehigh University

Tonia A. Dousay
tdousay@uwyo.edu
University of Wyoming

Kathleen Fortney
kfortney@judge.com
The Judge Group

Rob Foshay
rfoshay@foshay.org
The Foshay Group

Joseph R. Freidhoff
jfreidhoff@mivu.org
Michigan Virtual Learning Research Institute

Andrew S. Gibbons
andy_gibbons@byu.edu
Brigham Young University

Thomas C. Hammond
tch207@lehigh.edu
Lehigh University

Stephen W. Harmon
swharmon@gatech.edu
Georgia Institute of Technology

Atsusi Hirumi
Atsusi.Hirumi@ucf.edu
University of Central Florida

Brad Hokanson
brad@umn.edu
University of Minnesota

Kathryn Kennedy
kkennedy@mivu.org
Michigan Virtual Learning Research Institute

Anthony Marker
anthonymarker@boisestate.edu
Boise State University

Rose Marra
rmarra@missouri.edu
University of Missouri

Barbara L. Martin
barbaram1605@gmail.com
Darryl Sink & Associates

M. David Merrill
professordavemerrill@gmail.com
Utah State University

Sugata Mitra
sugata.mitra@newcastle.ac.uk
Newcastle University

Michael Molenda
molenda@indiana.edu
Indiana University–Bloomington

Harold Nelson
nelson.group@frontier.com
Advanced Design Institute

Patrick Parrish
pparrish.alt@gmail.com
World Meteorological Organization

Kyle Peck
kpeck@psu.edu
Pennsylvania State University

Clark Quinn
clark@quinnovation.com
Quinnovation

Victoria Raish
vrc112@psu.edu
Pennsylvania State University

Thomas C. Reeves
treeves@uga.edu
University of Georgia

Charles M. Reigeluth
reigelut@indiana.edu
Indiana University–Bloomington

Lloyd P. Rieber
lrieber@uga.edu
University of Georgia

Gordon Rowland
rowland@ithaca.edu
Ithaca College

Wilhelmina C. Savenye
Willi.Savenye@asu.edu
Arizona State University

John Savery
jsavery@uakron.edu
University of Akron

Roger C. Schank
roger@socraticarts.com
Socratic Arts

Kennon M. Smith
kennsmit@indiana.edu
Indiana University–Bloomington

Monica W. Tracey
mwtracey@gmail.com
Wayne State University

Irene Visscher-Voerman
j.i.a.Visscher-Voerman@utwente.nl
University of Twente

Peter Samuelson Wardrip
psw9@pitt.edu
Children's Museum of Pittsburgh

Audrey Watters
audrey.watters@gmail.com
Independent Scholar

Brent Wilson
Brent.Wilson@ucdenver.edu
University of Colorado–Denver

Jason Yip
jcyip@uw.edu
University of Washington

Heather Toomey Zimmerman
haz2@psu.edu
Pennsylvania State University

Introduction

Welcome to *Issues in Technology, Learning, and Instructional Design*. This has been an amazing journey with more than fifty colleagues to best represent the essential elements of current debates and discourse in our field. Weaving together issues from the nature of design and instructional design, to the role of learning sciences in the field generally, we have devoted the past several years to nurturing this dialogue to the point where we are now ready to launch it into the world.

> Now you could say that our ordinary thought in society is incoherent—it is going in all sorts of directions with thoughts conflicting and canceling each other out. But if people were to think together in a coherent way, it would have tremendous power. That's the suggestion. If we have a dialogue situation—a group which has sustained dialogue for quite a while in which people get to know each other, and so on—then we might have such a coherent movement of thought, a coherent movement of communication. It would be coherent not only at the level we recognize, but at the tacit level, at the level for which we only have a vague feeling. That would be more important.
> (D. Bohm, *On Dialogue*, ed. L. Nichol [NY: Routledge 1996], p. 4)

We hope that you will also engage in this dialogue with us and further build the discipline. The book is laid out with the following five sections:

The Nature of Design and Instructional Design
Preparing Instructional Designers
Contexts of Learning, Design, and Technology
Technology
Learning Science

Within each section there are several dialogues that we feel are connected to one another and to the larger dialogues in the field. Naturally, another editor might consider a different organization for the contributing pieces in the text, but we felt that each of these pieces was connected to others in some overarching fashion based on the connecting theme. Others will likely see other connecting themes than we did and might find their own organizational scheme works better for them.

Each of the dialogues themselves has at least two and typically three parts. First, there is a position statement. In this case, we approached authors who we felt had important things to say about a particular area. We sought balance and thoughtfulness as well as a strong ability to write about a topic that we had the need to illuminate. David Bohm points out that the best way to forward a dialogic agenda is through knowledge of each other.

A true community is most able to reach levels of new understanding when people know one another well, and so we did indeed select authors for position statements that we felt were connected in a variety of ways to the larger community. Each position statement is then followed by a response. We encouraged the respondents to look for both agreements and disagreements from their own perspectives within the position statement to which they were asked to react. We encouraged informal thoughtful language and simple, direct reflection without too much jargon or exclusive language. The idea was to make this dialogue as accessible to the novice as the professor. The responses were then cycled back to the original position holder for a rejoinder. In almost all cases, a rejoinder was forthcoming, bringing the dialogue to a strong initial conclusion. Again, we hope that you will join in the dialogue, and so, for us, each dialogue is never altogether concluded.

Why did we seek to undertake this arduous challenge? After all, asking our colleagues and friends to write courageous position statements was a difficult request, and one that we then invited other friends to criticize. Needless to say this opens us up, as editors, to a great deal of criticism ourselves. For some readers, we will have selected the wrong contributors, or the wrong respondents; we will have identified the wrong major categories or organized the sections wrong-headedly. There are many potential pitfalls for such a publication, but we have been inspired by one of the all-time great dialogues in our field—the Clark/Kulik/Bangert-Drowns "mere vehicles" debate with which most readers will be familiar. If you happen not to know this debate, please do take some time now, before going further in this book, to learn about one of the most influential and critical discussions in our field. Many dialogues that we have engaged in through the years have come back to this original "mere vehicles" debate. If, we reasoned, we could create even one such important exchange, we would certainly feel that our contribution to the field was significant.

With this in mind, we start our journey with the nature of design. This section is made up of six contributions of dialogues with responses and rejoinders. Design itself can be seen as the cornerstone of our field; it is indeed a central activity without a doubt. The nature of design itself, however, has been debated for decades, and the term "design" has been reshaped and reconceptualized over and over by different fields and different theorists. The basic notions of design have tended, however, toward a scientific/engineering perspective (CITE) that we find to be insufficient for our own field. We believe that perspectives from other design fields may prove helpful.

Patrick Parrish initiates our exploration by considering the possibilities of aligning ID with applied science, aggrandizing design, drawing connections to art, and aligning ID with the natural order. He argues for including all in a definition of design as a "cross-cutting life-embracing activity" and suggests instructional design is an exemplar. Nelson focuses his critique on distinguishing design, art, and science.

Bannan continues the exploration, and both she and Gibbons (in his response) call attention to the great complexity of contemporary learning environments. They offer significant potential insights that can be gained by studying design cognition.

Highlighting the need to challenge conventional approaches in this complex world, Wilson proposes "guerrilla design," an idea that Martin suggests might be promoted through planned change.

Initiating one such challenge, Hokanson examines the role or anti-role of content in educational technology. Wardrip suggests that content agnosticism is a possibility in co-design, while Hokanson counters that his challenge goes beyond who brings what to design practice, to an expansion of what we believe constitutes learning.

Returning to the conventional approaches that others have criticized, Molenda defends the systems approach to instructional development. Argondizza responds by debating the historical origins and, consequently, what is meant by the "systems approach."

Branch concludes this section by returning to the implications of complexity. He asserts that respecting complexity is central to the nature of "true instructional design." Rieber responds with questions of applicability and appropriateness, and he brings us back to what we mean by design and instructional design.

We believe that you will find this section of the text particularly meaty and full of important and deep reflections of the nature of design and instructional design. This is contested territory, and currently this territory is increasingly confusing. These positions on design offer an especially rich and healthy dialogue on the nature of our field.

Part I

The Nature of Design and Instructional Design

Chapter 1

Instructional Design as Design

Patrick Parrish

> Over the years I have learned that what is important in a dress is the woman who is wearing it.
>
> —Yves St. Laurent

The relationship of instructional design (ID) to the other design disciplines is to a large extent one of envious outsider. What we produce is not as elegant as a penthouse living room, as majestic as the modernist high-rise hosting it, as sexy as the evening dress worn by the woman living there, or as clever and influential as the iPhone inside the Hermès purse she carries. Our designs lack glamour (Postrel, 2013).

We produce little of lasting utility or global impact. Our designs are typically ephemeral and often intended only for local or narrow use. No consumer magazine is devoted to ID—people do not care to fuss over their learning experiences as much as their gardens or their clothing. Very few awards are given to IDs. IDs rarely, if ever, appear as characters in novels. The profession does not creep into the list of the one hundred best jobs.

We frequently have to explain our discipline even to those on our work teams, and the results are often unconvincing. The content experts we work with sometimes see what we do as window dressing. What we do is not just nonintuitive; to many, it is also nondescript.

How Do We Respond to Such an Unenthusiastic Response to Our Work? One Approach Is to Align ID with More Respected, Nondesign Disciplines, Like Science

Instructional design has long teetered on a figurative edge between design and applied science. At times it is subjected to a game of tug of war between two loosely organized but vocal camps with seemingly incompatible goals: (a) the goal to create prescriptions for replicable and reliable designs of "effective and efficient" instruction, based on rigorous scientific research (the applied science camp), and (b) the goal to develop reflective practitioners capable of finding situated, crafted, or artistic approaches to the task of creating "good" instruction (the design camp) (Smith & Boling, 2009; Wilson, 2005), instruction that serves the purposes at hand well, and does so ethically. Put extravagantly, the goal on the one hand is teacher- and ID-proof design strategies and decision-making tools, and, on the other hand, independent, confident, and creative practitioners willing to shun prescriptions and focus on a unique solution for the situation at hand. The discipline can be seen tottering forward in this pushmi-pullyu state, where both sides feel compelled to make proclamations to claim their ground. But in the end, it is as applied science that an explanation of ID is easier to swallow for those outside the discipline. And if you connect to advances in the popular neurosciences, you are seen as especially well connected.

The same teetering is reflected in (a) the push of technology and its inexorable progress, which defines the parent discipline of educational technology, and in (b) the subtler pull to remain "humane" and egalitarian. These are not mutually exclusive, of course, and may in fact reinforce one another. Still, the mindsets created by these foci generate tension. While we often say, "technology in the service of design," the reverse is often what we follow as we quickly look for applications of the newest technological offerings.

Another Approach to Raise the Appreciation of ID Is to Aggrandize Design

Aggrandizing design rarely works except among the already devoted, since most people do not possess a very broad concept of design, and they see its connection to ID as superficial, perhaps even grasping.

Nelson and Stolterman (2012), speaking for the devoted, see design at work in just about every activity that does not claim to be either science or art. Indeed, in their book, humans designed fire rather than discovered it. In other words, design is a process not just of invention but of appropriation. Their definition of design would not exclude products like the periodic table that depicts the elements, the institution of marriage, or the to-do-list sitting unattended on my office desk. And maybe this is not a bad thing.

Design is indeed a grand tradition, and older than science by several billion years, yet there is still plenty of room for theorizing and improvement. Unfortunately, Nelson and Stolterman (2012) depict design as a privileged perspective (in the same manner as those who privilege science), calling it "the first tradition," and also calling it the thing that makes us human. Such anthropocentric statements are unhelpful. This one ignores the design accomplishments of societies of chimpanzees and other primates, and also the constructions of ant colonies, bees, and other social insects. Design is clearly a response of life to the world it occupies, from microbes that chemically alter their environment, to beavers that dam streams to make homes and fertile feeding grounds, and to whales that offer songs to one another for who knows what reasons, and not something unique to *Homo sapiens*. That humans use their human faculties to achieve their designs does not make them unique. Beavers use their beaver faculties to achieve their designs, after all. Design is the response of life to the challenge of living.

Yet Another Approach to Raise Enthusiasm for ID Is to Draw Connections to Art

Indeed, there are many connections to art, since both artists and IDs are in the business of creating experiences to change perceptions and conceptions, to raise curiosity, and often to generate emotional response. Both aim to prime us to experience the world in new ways. Some propose art as one of the prevailing perspectives of practitioners in the discipline, but at times with the intentional or unintentional pejorative connotation of selfishness—self-expression at the expense of providing service to learners. But art as self-expression is a false lead; it is more accurate to view art as striving for shared meaning through exploration of personal experience. This viewpoint suggests more alignment with ID. But artists and instructional designers ultimately have different intentions, even if they sometimes share means. Serious artists often aim for ambiguity as an expression of the world they live in. IDs can use ambiguity as a strategy for stimulating engagement, but rarely aim to leave a learner in that state. An artist, in particular an actor or writer, may take on a persona to explore perspectives and to understand and reveal alternative truths. IDs may do this in the process of analysis, and they often ask learners to take on personas, but as a step toward more permanent change.

Some design professions lean much more toward art. A fashion designer might even thwart the purpose and practicality of a garment to make an artistic statement, which would be condemning to an instructional design. But such designs rarely reach a large user audience beyond a few gala parties (although one could argue that high heels are such a phenomenon, and some forms of body art nearly cripple their wearers). The line between art and design is at times even more blurred than that between design and science.

Yet Another Approach Is to Align ID, and Design in General, with the Natural Order

Design is a natural, adaptive response for meeting life's needs and challenges by taking advantage of native faculties and the tools and resources within the environment we are given. It is the reasonable (not overly rational) approach for negotiating one's needs, with respect for the social and natural environment. It represents a successful strategy for living within a complex natural system, living within natural constraints, and using one's full capacity for achieving useful outcomes.

Design is pervasive, not privileged. It should be a respected tradition not because it is special or because it represents an ability exclusive to human beings but because it is the most natural approach. Design focuses on good and useful outcomes, and not so much on ideals like efficiency and effectiveness except as they reflect a reasonable response. Design also embraces aesthetics, if only in its broadest, pragmatist sense (Dewey, 1934/1989).

But even though design is natural and exemplified throughout nature, this does not make design easy. In fact, in human societies, behaving naturally is a rare skill. The effort that design theorists make in defining design and design processes is essential to our progress. This effort is as important as the work to understand how to seek a good life and achieve happiness, goals that are equally as difficult as achieving good designs.

I suggest that IDs should embrace as potential models all practices in the family of disciplines we designate as design. This includes not just architecture and industrial design but the culinary arts and fashion design. But, in a way, even science is just a specialized form of design, a more rigid and incredibly successful form perhaps, but still a natural response. Because it is even closer, art and its practices provide even more useful models, even if art has its own purposes.

ID *is* a design discipline, but it is more, just as any design discipline is more. It includes science and engineering and many other traditions, including art. For some instructional designers, the "design" association has been a tentative one—but remembering that ID has roots in design makes its inherent complexity more navigable, not fuzzier, because we bring more to bear. Nelson and Stolterman (2012) work to distinguish design from science and art, but in the end it is more prudent to view them merely as domains of activity along a spectrum of inquiry methods, since all three do in fact work to make "the invisible visible" (Buchanan et al., 2013, p. 41). But if inquiry is a spectrum, along what dimension does it lie? Or is inquiry just a collection of lenses, or epistemological stances, for viewing our connections to the world, lenses that include not just science, design, and art, but criticism, social debate, philosophy, craft, and many others. Do they differ fundamentally (essentially), or are the differences only the result of constructed disciplinary knowledge and shared traditions and practices? Nelson and Stolterman use the degree of focus on the "particular" as a promising dimension, but one that does not do so well at distinguishing art and design. Perhaps a better dimension to define the spectrum is the degree of uncertainty acceptance. In this case, art lies at one extreme by embracing uncertainty (from the Mona Lisa smile to Rothko) and science at the other by making uncertainty its nemesis (stochastic mathematics and complexity merely embrace the enemy to keep it closer). Design lies near the middle, allowing plenty of room for the push and pull of its practitioners.

So let us try to define this middle. Let us look at design in a way that does not aggrandize but also does not limit it artificially. Let us also try to uncover the source of the joy that IDs find in their work, despite the inattention they might experience.

Since it is fruitless to imagine what it is like to be a chimpanzee, beaver, or whale, let alone a microbe, I will inevitably, sensibly, and very quickly move into the human domain.

Design is the process of modifying the environment for use and/or enjoyment through physical effort, as well as both intuitive and rational faculties. Design roots are shared by a broad array of disciplines, from architecture, graphic design, interface design, and organizational development, to even more diverse disciplines like urban planning, politics, culinary arts, and fashion design. Design disciplines may vary widely in terms of their materials and products, but their processes and the impacts of their products reveal commonalities. In very general terms, the phases in their processes typically include the following.

- Yearning, or desire, based on dissatisfaction or need. Instructional designers specify goals or needs to emphasize that they do not design frivolously, but underlying any design is a yearning for change, success, enjoyment, or improvement.
- Gathering. In ID, this phase is usually encapsulated in needs assessment and analysis, but many things are gathered to move a design forward—data, information, opinions, materials/resources, sources/examples, and templates, for example.
- Envisioning. Both rational and intuitive, envisioning is a process of imagining and choosing what specifically could and should be created. An internal process, envisioning is sometimes labeled "instinct."
- Depicting/forming. In this phase, the emphasis is on making representations or descriptions that make the final product more tangible to the designer and others so that planning and development can proceed with confidence and shared vision. This is the one step that is negotiable but ill advised to skip in large efforts. As far as we know, only humans perform this step.
- Transforming. Design decisions, becoming more refined and detailed, continue during the stage in which materials are transformed into the shape of the envisioned product. Most often transformation also involves negotiation—with others, and between the design and the affordances of the materials used.
- Learning. Design products are to be used and enjoyed, and we learn to improve them and future products by watching how, how well, and for what purposes they are used and enjoyed. We also learn about the world by watching how it resists or accommodates our designs.

This definition of the design process is certainly very close to the list of fundamentals offered by Nelson and Stolterman (2012), but it merges things differently and implies a sequence. The definition is more closely aligned with the theory of inquiry offered by

Dewey (1938/2008), which provides a basis for many of the ideas expressed here, which can be regarded as a pragmatist stance on design. It also suggests that the design process can become an aesthetic experience (Dewey, 1934/1989), which is the source of that joy felt by all designers, including IDs.

Designs cannot be fully appreciated outside the context of their use. Different cultures might reject or cling to the same design. Moreover, designs reach their full potential only in use. Yves St. Laurent recognized this and diminished his own world-renowned reputation as a fashion designer by telling us that the woman wearing his dress (firstly a model in his case) made a greater difference than he did to an appreciation of its quality. In addition to the quote that opened this statement on design, he was also famous for saying that "a good model can advance fashion by ten years." Can a good set of learners do the same for an instructional design model? In the end, who is the ultimate guarantor of the quality of a design? (Wryly labeled "g.o.d." by Nelson and Stolterman, 2012.) It is the wearer, of course.

In truth, design is more than the collection of disciplines that share processes—it is a cross-cutting life-embracing activity, wherein our imaginations meet reality to create new possibilities. It is how we shape reality to our needs and desires, reshaping ourselves in return when our designs assume their place in the new reality. The final products of all designs are our reshaped selves. For this reason, one could argue that ID is an exemplar among the design disciplines, perhaps the one most explicitly aimed at changing people. There is no reason for envy.

References

Buchanan, R., Cross, N., Durling D., Nelson, H., Owen, C., Valtonen, A., . . . & Visscher- Voerman, I. (2013). Design. *Educational Technology, 53*(5), 25–41, Special Issue, Innovation over the edge, Rowland, G. (Ed).
Dewey, J. (1934/1989). *Art as experience* (Vol. 10). Carbondale, IL: Southern Illinois University Press.
Dewey, J. (1938/2008). *Logic: A theory of inquiry* (Vol. 12). Carbondale, IL: Southern Illinois University Press.
Nelson, H. G., & Stolterman, E. (2012). *The design way*. Cambridge, MA: MIT Press.
Postrel, V. (2013). *The power of glamour: Longing and the art of visual persuasion*. New York: Simon & Schuster.
Smith, K., & Boling, E. (2009). What do we make of design? Design as a concept in educational technology. *Educational Technology, 49*(4), 3–17.
Wilson, B. G. (2005). Foundations for instructional design: Reclaiming the conversation. In J. M. Spector, C. Ohrazda, A. Van Schaack, & D. A. Wiley (Eds.), *Innovations in instructional technology: Essays in honor of M. David Merrill* (pp. 237–252). Mahwah, NJ: Erlbaum.

RESPONSE BY HAROLD NELSON

It is good to see a discussion about design coming from a profession with the term design in the descriptive title of its field. The final paragraph of the chapter points to good dialogues to come in the future: "In truth, design is more than the collection of disciplines that share processes—it is a cross-cutting life-embracing activity, wherein our imaginations meet reality to create new possibilities."

Because of time and space limitations, I will limit my specific thoughts here to the argument that design should emulate science—not because it is the most significant among the four arguments presented, but only as an example of a detailed critique of one of the four.

There are several reasons design cannot emulate science, or be treated as a form of art. Design cannot be treated as a form of science or art because the focus on the process of inquiry and outcome is dramatically different from that of design (see Figure 1.1).

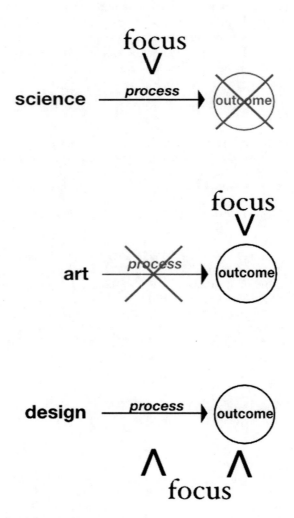

Figure 1.1 Primary Focus on Process and/or Outcome of Inquiry

For science, the focus is on controlling the *process* of inquiry—not controlling for the outcome. For art, the focus is on *outcome* and is indifferent to which kind of process is utilized. However, for design the inquiry is for *action*: the focus is on both the process and the outcome. For example, an architect comes to know what kind of building the client expects and endeavors to assure that it will be built as intended.

The architect follows specific processes (creative, legal, professional, and technical) in order to assure that design specifications and construction documents are accurately produced and effectively used—facilitating the timely and efficient construction of the desired building as an outcome.

It is often suggested that design needs to be more scientific, or design needs to be more humanistic and artistic. Many graduate design programs at major universities approach design scientifically and ask students to engage in "design research." Other universities try to combine science and art into a design kluge.

This relationship between inquiry and intentional action is not always well understood by academics or professionals. Description and explanation (science) do not prescribe action. That is why people are sometimes slow to follow the suggestions that scientists have derived from their research. Human actions are based on values, not data. To paraphrase Hume,[1] you cannot create an "ought" or a "desiderata" from an "is."

Design needs good science but, although good science is necessary for design, it is not sufficient. There is a chasm between rational inquiry and action (see Figure 1.2).

Design inquiry needs to include a bridge between inquiry and action (see Figure 1.3).

A schema for showing the multidimensional nature of *design inquiry* shows different types of inquiry formulating design inquiry (see Figure 1.4). Scientific inquiry (research) is just one part of a complex process of design inquiry.

More generally, in following the four arguments presented in the chapter,[2] it is important to stay alert for assertions that are not proofs. The assertion "Design is the response of life to the challenge of living" may or may not be useful for understanding design's relationship to ID, but it cannot be taken as true. Also, the assertion that *the* common design process among design disciplines is inclusive of six specific phases may be useful as a schema but should not be treated as a fact in support of an argument.

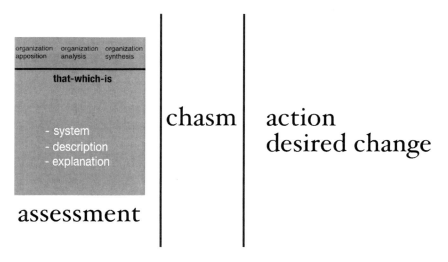

Figure 1.2 Chasm Between Rational Inquiry and Action

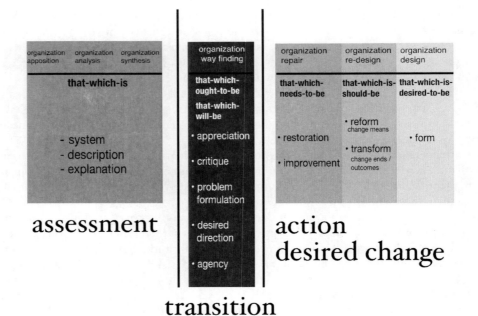

Figure 1.3 Bridging Between Rational Inquiry and Action

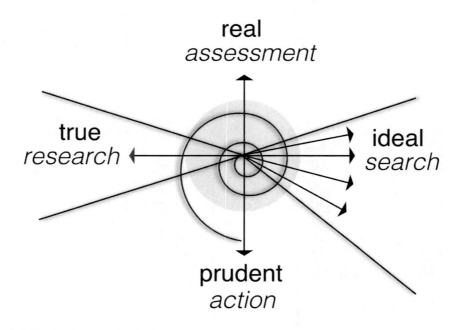

Figure 1.4 Design Inquiry for Action

The four arguments presented in this chapter for how design ought to be approached have been made and acted upon in the past. The arguments for design being treated as a science, or that design is a form of art, or merely a midpoint between science and art/humanities are all common. The argument that design is nothing really exceptional—just common behavior among all animals—is also frequently heard.

Other arguments concerning the nature of design that would be interesting to explore include divergent possibilities beyond the familiar four presented—for example, approaching design as a form of rhetoric and coercion, or design as crafting and making, or design as composing functional assemblies, or design as a means to participate in the ongoing genesis of the real world. These are just a few suggestions for inquiry that could lead to a deeper and richer understanding of designing and designers.

Finally, the issue that is conspicuous by its absence is that of the relationship between agents and clients of designed change. When scientific research dominates design inquiry, a dangerous precedent is set—that it is acceptable to impose change on people if done objectively. Such inchoate issues as this should be included in any dialogue around the relationships of ID to design.

Notes

1. *A Treatise of Human Nature* is a book by Scottish philosopher David Hume, first published at the end of 1738.
2. ". . . align ID with more respected, non-design disciplines, like science . . . raise enthusiasm for ID is to draw connections to art . . . align ID, and design in general, with the natural order . . . view them merely as domains of activity along a spectrum of inquiry methods . . ."

REJOINDER BY PATRICK PARRISH

Conversation, like design, can be a process of clarifying, refining, debating, negotiating, and ensuring good outcomes. It is a privilege to be engaged in this one.

There are many important points of agreement between the opening statement and the response:

- that design is a fascinatingly complex phenomenon, and one deserving of study
- that design is not the same as science or art, even though many find the comparisons and distinctions useful to think about
- that design is a cross-cutting discipline that requires a variety of faculties, and therefore offers many avenues for exploration
- that design is about creating desired states through interaction between the world, users, and the designer

But some differences of opinion are clear as well, and some of the concerns raised may stem from misinterpretation created by the structure and slightly irreverent tone of the statement. To be clear, no argument was made to view design as science or art—just the opposite. The following structure was used:

1. Instructional designers differ in their opinions about the relationship of ID to other design disciplines, and sometimes prefer allegiances to disciplines outside design.
2. Applied science offers a limited and disputable stance for instructional design.
3. Posing design as above nature, and more holistic than other forms of inquiry, is also ungrounded.
4. Art reveals similarities to design but is also an ill-chosen direction of allegiance.
5. Viewing design as a natural process might be a more useful stance.
6. Finally, a generalized, typical design process model depicts design in a holistic and inclusive way—one that includes design agents, clients, and the worlds they inhabit.

Where we seem to disagree most is on HOW design differs from science and art. When one considers them not as distinct disciplines but as modes of thinking or forms of inquiry that pervade one another, their similarities emerge.

Design is not the only activity focused on both *outcomes* and *process*. This claim (and the accompanying diagrams) may seem appealing if one is a designer, because it suggests a privileged position. But it is highly questionable and might be taken as offensive.

For most of the scientists I have worked with, it is the potential of good and useful outcomes that motivates them to choose their fields of study and research questions (a "controlling for the outcome"). Scientists do not care only for equations, test tubes, and the scientific process. They are compelled by how their work contributes to society. Consider the following:

- A biologist works to identify genes responsible for vulnerability to disease.
- A biochemist searching for a medicine to cure a disease.
- Climatologists working to ascertain global warming, and to identify causes in order to mitigate its impacts, including droughts, flooding, and heat waves.
- Atmospheric scientists using models and radar data to identify the mechanisms of tornado formation so that early warnings can save lives.
- Learning scientists seeking ways to improve learning.

In all these cases, scientists seek their "desiderata" (Nelson & Stolterman, 2012) through scientific means, which asserts objectivity above all, unlike design.

Artists as selfish entertainers concerned only with appearance (outcome) is also a stereotype. Artists also care deeply about process, and indeed it can be process that is the work of art:

- Tibetan sand paintings take days to construct and then are destroyed immediately upon completion. The process of creation, a form of communal meditation, is the work of art. The final outcome obviously is not.
- The 1960s offered Happenings to produce random outcomes up to the participants.
- The development of a baroque fugue (and twentieth-century serialist music) was about process and rules. There was faith that beautiful outcomes would result.
- Impressionist paintings capture a moment, but stress the act of seeing.
- Jackson Pollack and other abstract expressionists aim to make a work that allows for the recreation of the process of creation in the viewer.
- Andy Goldsworthy creates ephemeral art works in natural settings—leaves on water, gently intertwined twigs, molded ice crystals—that stimulate awe in the effort, sensitivity, and patience they embody.
- Reader interaction theories of literature, such as Ingarden's and Eco's, point to the empty spaces filled in during the process of reading (c.f., Julio Cortazar's randomized-chapters novel, *Hopscotch*, as an extreme example).

The creation and experience of art is a process, not an instantaneous appreciation of an object (Dewey, 1934/1989). The work is a medium between the artist, the artist's experience, and the appreciator's experience. When it resonates, it changes how we experience the world, and, therefore, how we respond to it.

The differences between science, art, and design are not "dramatic." All are forms of inquiry. Design is not more complete, addressing more concerns and using more input to achieve its outcomes. All three forms have changed the real world in almost miraculous ways. But there are differences. (For a definition of "real," see Nelson and Stolterman, 2012.)

- Science seeks to avoid uncertainty by applying a rigorous, objective method of attempting to disprove a hypothesis.
- Art explores experience often without attempting to prove anything—uncertainty is embraced from the start to finish.
- Design reaches its conclusions in collaboration, avoiding uncertainty by consensus, for example, which is only part way. Part way is often best to generate useful outcomes.

Upon reflection, I can agree that the statement "Design is the response of life to the challenges of living" is carelessly constructed. In fact, there are many other useful responses, including art and science, as well as craft, philosophy, and play, just to get started. This and other statements are offered not as facts or truths but as assertions, warranted with examples. Their ontological weight will be determined by the reader as he or she tries them on and decides their utility.

References

Dewey, J. (1934/1989). *Art as experience* (Vol. 10). Carbondale, IL: Southern Illinois University Press.
Nelson, H. G., & Stolterman, E. (2012). *The design way*. Cambridge, MA: MIT Press.

Chapter 2

Toward Understanding the Nature of Design

Brenda Bannan

Capturing and representing the true nature of design is elusive, and, therefore, the assertion that the process of instructional design is clearly defined is problematic especially given the complexity of our practice and related research today. Our field has relied upon broad and reductionist stage models that work toward framing the design problem and constraining the solution space but may also overlook the true complexity of the act of design itself. Some design theorists purport that the act of design involves the creation of a unique particular design and involves interpretive design thinking and judgment rather than a definitive, abstract process and absolute truths (Nelson & Stolterman, 2012). The challenge of applying abstract and systematic design processes to learning situations may be similar to the limitations and inherent complexity of a physician's diagnostic process. The type of process that relies solely on clear, clinical algorithms for common diagnoses and treatments may "quickly fall apart when symptoms are vague or multiple or confusing, or test results are inexact. In such cases—the kinds of cases where we most need a discerning doctor—algorithms discourage physicians from thinking independently and creatively. Instead of expanding a doctor's thinking, they can constrain it" (Groopman, 2007, p. 5). The same might be said for the practice of instructional designers in relying on limited design models and prescriptive approaches without deep, experiential knowledge of the intellectual activity of design. Reliance on learning principles or broad, prescriptive models can quickly prove less useful without full acknowledgement of the current complex, vague, and confusing environments that we attempt to orchestrate for learning. Confronting today's ambiguous and complicated learning environments is also just when we most need innovative designers; however, we may be ultimately constraining their design thinking and creativity through our approach and limited understanding of design itself.

Current learning environments demonstrate an extremely high level of complexity often incorporating multiple target audiences, multiple learning goals, and the use of multiple devices across different settings to exponentially expand the design problem space, decision-making, and potential design paths. Friedman (2012) presents these issues as the major challenges that the design professions collectively face today, including (1) increasingly ambiguous boundaries between artifacts, structures, and processes; (2) increasingly large-scale social, economic, and industrial frames; (3) an increasingly complex environment of needs, requirements, and constraints; (4) information content that often exceeds the value of physical substance; (5) a complex environment in which many projects or products cross boundaries of several organizations, stakeholders, producers, and users; (6) projects or products that must meet the expectations of many organizations, stakeholders, producers and users; and (7) demands at every level of production, distribution, reception, and control (p. 150). These challenges that intersect with designing for learning environments are not addressed through a "right" answer or "correct" instructional design pattern but do provide an opportunity for deep understanding of the problem context, divergent and convergent creative thinking, and an expressed intention for change through the act of design. In contrast to today's multi-layered, complex challenges, the models and processes of the instructional systems design field seem to be woefully inadequate to combat the intricacy of today's learning environments with a surface-level, more algorithmic view of the act of design. To combat this issue, perhaps it would require the field to more fully acknowledge, embrace, and integrate what has been conceptualized about the nuances of design process in other fields and to integrate an interdisciplinary as well as cross-disciplinary view of the act of design.

The question is, can we actually represent and teach the nature of design? Much can be learned from other disciplines involved in design theory and research that has not yet migrated into our practice and research to progress our work forward—for example, recognizing that design is much more than problem solving but a distinct human intellectual activity with multiple inputs involving synthesis that is neither "objective nor subjective but is both at different moments" (Kolko, 2011, p. 12). Deeply considering the multiplicities inherent in the act of design acknowledges the tenuousness defining this creative act and highlights the added challenge of attempting to integrate the act of design with research (e.g., in the popular, but only beginning to be defined, education design research).

Some design theorists and researchers believe there are commonalities or meta-processes that cross design fields or domains and attempt to identify similarities as well as differences. Gero (personal communication, October 27, 2014), for example, begins with the premise that design is any intentional activity that results in some kind of change involving a specific set of requirements, purpose, or function and expected behavior as well as generating structure. The act of design typically also involves some type of analysis, description, documentation, and evaluation; however, these may manifest differently in different domains. Gero, Kannengiesser and Williams (2014) believe that there is "some common cognitive designer behavior that is independent of domain and task" (p. 2). Investigating the cognition of design through observable acts and verbal protocol analysis as evidenced in Gero et al.'s (2014) research begins to set the stage for identifying regularity in design processes and cognition for the benefit of many fields who practice, teach, and conduct research on this complicated, nuanced process.

In our own field, an interdisciplinary appreciation of design theory has begun to take root in the literature evidenced by Gibbons' (2013) work aligning our practice with architectural design process that begins to unpack this perspective, but much more is needed to enrich our understanding of our own practice. Outside our field exists an appreciation of cross-disciplinary perspectives on design process and research (e.g., see Cross, Christiaans & Dorst, 1996, who attempt to analyze design activity with similar protocol across design domains and purposes). These efforts are largely not fully recognized or considered in our models or processes and could contribute more to our understanding of our own work about the important and challenging intellectual activity of instructional design.

Instead of us relying on simplistic models or algorithmic solutions to complex, vague, and confusing instructional design problems, perhaps our efforts would be best used to increase our understanding of the nature of design through the above type of design research and toward further understanding of how designers actually derive solutions creatively in-situ. The resulting improved understanding of the nature of design would benefit our conceptualization of design expertise and guide experiences for teaching design in our field. Friedman also speaks to the role of design education, broadly, in the world today and against the backdrop of challenges of the current economic context. In Friedman's view, "design professionals now require a broad range of analytical, conceptual and creative skills related to the social and economic context of design along with advanced skills in a design specialty" (2012, p. 150). The current challenges require a higher level understanding of human-centered research, human motivation, and engagement to address increasingly complex environments than are incorporated in current design education efforts. Friedman states that past environments were more rudimentary and that, today,

> professional design practice involves advanced multi-disciplinary knowledge that presupposes interdisciplinary collaboration and a fundamental change in design education. This knowledge isn't simply a higher level of professional education and practice. It is a qualitatively different form of professional practice. It is emerging in response to the demands of the information society and the knowledge economy to which it gives rise.
>
> (p. 151)

Enacting learning design in complex environments as well as teaching or researching instructional design contexts today requires a higher level skill and an enhanced sensitivity to the act, cognition, and complexity of the intellectual challenge of design than ever before, requiring moving beyond simplistic models and approaches. Design and demonstration of design expertise is inherently a social, complex, interactive, and activity-based endeavor; and, as encouraging work begins to emerge in this direction, our processes need to integrate, reflect, and embrace this complexity of the challenges at hand. As an example, Rapanta, Maina, Lotz and Bacchelli (2013), who recently wrestled with attempting to unpack complex team-based design processes in our field, came to this conclusion:

> Prescriptive ID models, as presented in most of the literature, refer to conceptual frameworks that claim to guide design practice. Although they offer a general overview of an idealized ID process, detailed insights into the dynamic and often changing nature of interdisciplinary team design practice cannot be sufficiently represented by a stage model.
>
> (p. 602)

There is a continued level of frustration within our field regarding the perceived simplicity and constraints of current models and approaches, and their inability to fully address the complexity of current learning environments and aligned design approaches. We need to more fully embrace what is postulated about the theory and practice of design in an interdisciplinary and cross-disciplinary manner in order to move forward to confront the challenges of today and tomorrow without constraining creativity. Perhaps we need to study the "science of design" as researchers are attempting to study the "science of love," with all its complexity and nuance, as applied behavioral scientists (Gottman, 2014). It is becoming increasingly important that we more fully explore the nature of design, design cognition, and design process to attempt to promote the enhanced analysis, synthesis, and creativity that our field, practice, and research currently demand in today's challenging economic, interconnected, and dynamic learning landscape.

References

Cross, N., Christiaans, H., & Dorst, K. (1996). *Analysing design activity*. New York: John Wiley & Sons.

Friedman, K. (2012). Models of design: Envisioning a future design education. *Visible Language*, 46(1/2).

Gero, J., Kannnengiesser, U., & Williams, C. B. (2014). Does designing have a common cognitive behavior independent of domain and task: A meta-analysis of design protocols. *Proceedings from the International Conference on Human Behavior in Design*. Ascona, Switzerland.

Gibbons, A. S. (2013). *An architectural approach to instructional design*. New York: Routledge.
Gottman, J. M. (2014). *Principia amoris: The new science of love*. London: Routledge.
Groopman, J. (2007). *How doctors think*. Boston, MA: Houghton Mifflin Company.
Kolko, J. (2011). *Exposing the magic of design: A practitioner's guide to the methods and theory of synthesis (Human Technology Interaction)*. Oxford: Oxford University Press.
Nelson, H. G., & Stolterman, E. (2012). *The design way: Intentional change in an unpredictable world*. Boston, MA: The MIT Press.
Rapanta, C., Maina, M., Lotz, N., & Bacchelli, A. (2013). Team design communication patterns in e-learning design and development. *Educational Technology Research and Development, 61*, 581–605.

RESPONSE BY ANDREW S. GIBBONS

Bannan describes design as "complicated" and "nuanced," giving much-overdue credit to design's complexities. Her noting of the shared interdisciplinary interests in design is a heartening sign that instructional experience designers may find a channel for moving beyond emphasis on design models, toward a more robust conception of design practice by studying design in other fields. Such a move could be characterized in terms of the Einsteinian assimilation of Newtonian physics—in which earlier conceptions (such as systematic design models) and their usefulness were not destroyed but rather placed in proper perspective, opening up new horizons for exploration and discovery.

But in my own thinking, I have found it harder and harder to look at design—in all of its complexity—as an activity separate from everyday cognition. In their book *Everyday Cognition* (1984), Lave and Rogoff gathered several tradition-challenging chapters, each illuminating some aspect of cognition in everyday life settings. The net effect of these historical pieces was to draw back the veil of priestly mystique from cognitive psychology and connect the study of thinking processes to the flow of common life events. This made it easier to examine cognition introspectively and made every person, in a sense, a cognitive psychologist. The effect of the work was to bring cognition to life rather than isolating it from life.

I have wondered if there is not a similar volume in the wings that will bring design into the everyday realm, so that it can be studied by everyone who designs—which I believe is everyone. This would move us in the direction of finding the "true nature" of design that Bannan places in the foreground. Would it not be ironic if we came closer to the heart of design by examining daily design events and were able to scale up our thinking to the industrial level described by Friedman, as quoted by Bannan. Dwelling on these industrial-scale concerns at first may mask a simple cognitive core of activities that lies at the heart of designing. Surely they have to be dealt with, but at the proper time, after we have looked into the heart of designing.

Dorst (2015) examines the nature of designing practice by examining the *logic* of designing in terms of Pierce's concept of abduction (Weiner, 1958, pp. 368–375). According to Dorst, "deduction and induction are not enough if we want to *make* something" (p. 48, emphasis in the original).

In normal abduction, we know the result, the value we want to achieve through the desired outcome, and also the "how," a pattern of relationships that will help achieve the value we seek. The missing element is the "what" (an object, a service, a system), which still needs to be created (p. 48).

Having established the idea that abductive reasoning may be involved in design, Dorst further suggests the notion of "design" abduction:

> In design abduction, the starting point is that we *only* know something about the nature of the outcome, the desired value we want to achieve. . . . Thus we have to create or choose both a 'how' and a 'pattern of relationships'. As these are quite dependent on one another, they should be developed in parallel. This double creative step requires designers to devise proposals for both the 'what' and the 'how', and test them in conjunction.
>
> (p. 49)

This account of the core logic of design corresponds with a description by Klir (1969) of general systems theory and its underlying relationship to both scientific investigation and design exploration. Klir explains that in scientific investigation the "what" and the "how" are fixed and that the outcome (and its value) is to be determined; in engineering design, the outcome (and its value) is fixed, and the activity consists of determining the "what" and the "how." In this account, both activities—science and engineering, or design—are different aspects of humans exploring the properties of systems.

This approach to describing the core activity of designing adds weight to Bannan's argument for the interdisciplinary nature of design and the study of design cognition—whatever the field. Mechanical designers deal with physical systems and their properties; likewise, instructional experience designers deal in experiential systems and their properties. In the case of instruction, the systems are somewhat more complex because they are more abstract, probabilistically determined, and immaterial. It is worth contemplating that studying the logical processes of abduction—described by one author as making "an intelligent guess" in the absence of a complete body of evidence (Walton, 2004)—may be the key to a better understanding of what some have referred to as "the science of design," whether in mechanical designs or in educational designs. Nature may have a sense of humor after all.

References

Dorst, K. (2015). *Frame innovation*. Cambridge, MA: The MIT Press.
Klir, G. J. (1969). *An approach to general systems theory*. New York: Van Nostrand Reinhold.
Lave, J., & Rogoff, B. (1984). *Everyday cognition: Development in social context*. Cambridge, MA: Harvard University Press.
Walton, D. (2004). *Abductive reasoning*. Tuscaloosa, AL: University of Alabama Press.
Weiner, P. P. (Ed.) (1958). *Charles S. Pierce: Selected writings*. New York: Dover Publications.

REJOINDER BY BRENDA BANNAN

In response to Gibbons' insightful commentary, I will offer a few brief thoughts. Einstein also stated, "Look deep into nature and then you will understand everything better." Similarly, looking deep into the act of design, as Gibbons points out, may potentially open up new horizons in our field to help us better understand and address current societal challenges through design.

Gibbons continues to enlighten our field with his insights into design practice and cognition and how we study them to promote a more robust conceptualization of design itself. What most struck me in his thought-provoking response, however, was studying the process of design in everyday life. Everyday life, indeed, our in-situ systems and processes, now manifest themselves in such complex forms across multiple disciplines, practices, and technologies that they may benefit from a design mindset. The types of challenges that design is currently being leveraged to address include an expansive range of societal problems that are taking advantage of processes such as design thinking (for example, to fight poverty), or service design to improve medical care, or other design techniques to attempt to combat different multilevel organizational problems requiring the integration of expertise from various fields of study. I believe we are at a crossroads in our own practice that demands acknowledging and integrating an interdisciplinary perspective on design process.

This perspective is also evidenced by Gibbons in his description of design as involving abductive processes. Abduction is described as a type of reasoning that propels designers from a desired result, purpose, or function to form and use, often described as a creative leap (Roozenberg, 1993). Most scholars agree it involves something more than inductive or deductive algorithmic and logical processes and may, in fact, include intuition and serendipity as well as often provoking unexpected consequences, particularly when a given design is deployed in the real world. This view that design is incredibly complex and encompasses much more than logic or structured processes seems to permeate across many disciplines of practice outside of our own (Gero & Hanna, 2015). Conceptualizing design as abductive, everyday cognition conducted by everyday citizens, as Gibbons notes, is an excellent start to begin to uncover the complexity, multidisciplinarity, and nuances of the act of design. Jane Fulton Suri in her work in experience prototyping and observing the use of everyday objects that are reinvented for purposes they were not originally intended for in what she calls "thoughtless acts" demonstrates this heightened sensitivity in how we interact with the designed world as a form of inquiry (Suri, 2005). Her approach connects to Gibbon's point to examine daily design events exploring properties of objects and systems to begin to synthesize and make sense of our world. Regularly conducting this type of design inquiry across the many facets and functionality of the objects and systems in our lives would enhance this interdisciplinary design mindset in multiple contexts and for all.

If these observational, creative, and abductive thinking processes could be represented, harnessed, and regularly leveraged to address current societal challenges (e.g., via new designs for products and systems in finance, government, healthcare, etc.), then we might advance quickly beyond the level of an "intelligent guess" toward systematically and progressively improving these objects and systems as well as our understanding of the "science of design." For example, improving our understanding of design through enhanced sensitivity to everyday design cognition and interdisciplinary processes can also be seen in the so-called "in-the-wild" evaluation and testing. Hutchins (1996) describes "in-the-wild" cognition as depicting distributed individual and team actions as cultural, interdisciplinary, cognitive, and computational systems that are best studied outside the laboratory or—"in the wild." Similarly, Gibbons and I agree on advocating for an "in the wild" study of design cognition and everyday activity to learn from and integrate multiple perspectives and investigate the full complexity of our continually evolving learning systems with a focus on the in-situ nature and process of design.

Viewing design as an interdisciplinary and significant act of inquiry is important because our field is expanding beyond instructional design and is propelling our practice into the everyday realm of not just designing learning software solutions but also configuring interconnected systems of smart hardware, devices, people, things, and cities (e.g., see the National Science Foundation's recent focus on Cyberlearning and Smart Cities efforts). We find ourselves as a field moving toward addressing novel and expansive learning and performance problems in the intersection of the physical and digital worlds through emerging technologies such as the Internet of Things and the realization of new forms of ubiquitous computing related to sensor-based technologies and learning/behavioral change. The significant challenges for the future of learning technology design in the networked devices world is that we need to expand our conceptualization of design as an interdisciplinary act to begin to integrate the physical *and* the abstract or the mechanical *and* the educational (instead of separately as Gibbons implies), connect it to real-world experiences, testing, and everyday cognition, to gain insight into an expanded view of design process and evolve new types of learning systems. This would involve expanding our perspectives on traditional ISD systems thinking approaches to potentially integrate other types of systems and systematic approaches into instructional and learning design from fields such as organizational psychology, computer science, and hardware and software engineering. A future path for instructional designers may include the integration of these multiple perspectives on design to more fully address the complexity, abductive thinking, and systematic and humanistic aspects that both Gibbons and I see as necessary for our field. This expanded focus is sorely needed as our world and our profession is progressing rapidly into the realm of interconnected human and technology ecosystems that will demand an enhanced understanding of design, design processes, and design research to fully address future learning environments designed for smart, connected citizens and communities.

References

Gero, J., & Hanna, S. (2015). *Design computing and cognition '14*. New York: Springer International Publishing.
Hutchins, E. (1996). *Cognition in the wild*. Cambridge, MA: Bradford Books.
Roozenburg, N. F. (1993). On the pattern of reasoning in innovative design. *Design Studies*, 14(1), 4–18.
Suri, J. F. (2005). *Thoughtless acts? Observations on intuitive design*. San Francisco, CA: Chronicle Books.

Chapter 3

Guerrilla Design
How Can We Accommodate Against-the-Grain Thinking in Our Practice?

Brent Wilson

The domain of instructional design and technology (IDT) brings people together through shared ideas, methods, and practices as we address needs encountered in the use of technology for learning. Systems planning models, instructional theory, constructivist learning principles, and computer-based and Web-based learning environments—each has played a role in guiding the use of technology for learning over the years and bringing a sense of coherence to the field. A problem arises though: sometimes our common-sense, conventional wisdom becomes a barrier to innovation and fresh thinking. We cling to old models beyond their usefulness. Every generation of professionals needs to *reinvent the field* as they cast aside certain ideas and practices, reinterpret others, and develop new ones based on emerging technologies and advancing knowledge.

To encourage this process of reinvention, I posit the need for *guerrilla learning / instructional design*—that is, design practice based intentionally on premises and models that challenge the status quo. Guerrilla design seeks to address present needs (of clients, curriculum, students, setting), but in a way that is inspired by radical or subversive thinking about core models and practices that may go unchallenged by others. Guerrilla design offers *principled resistance* to certain ideas that are seen as negatively impacting the profession. Guerrilla designers need to specify which conventions are under attack and why. They must persuade clients and teams and stakeholders to engage in a subversive exercise to test the merits of an alternative way of doing the work. Guerrilla design goes against the grain of conventional practice, but in a way meant to contribute knowledge and understanding to the field—uncomfortable in the short run, but playing a critical role to strengthening the field in the long run.

Guerrilla design looks for binaries and dualities and tries flipping them around to find new valances. What is held as perfectly natural and commonsensical comes into question, in a way that would lead to new practices or ways of thinking about work. Here are some sacred cows that may benefit from a challenge:

- *Learning theory—owned exclusively by psychology.* Contenders to psychology's claim include critical theories of various kinds, other social sciences, and other change theories.
- *The academic tenure system—good for knowledge advancement in the field.* The pressure is growing on aspiring academics to pursue "safe" research agendas that will lead to top-tier refereed journal publications—yet the ever-growing field of practice is crying out for actionable knowledge and wisdom to help them address pressing and messy problems encountered in their daily work. The mismatch between academic incentives and professional needs is wide and growing.
- *Progressive pedagogies—the only way to go.* The academy is enamored with a particular class of instructional strategy—namely, progressive or constructivist or authentic

learning, even in settings where conditions might dictate another solution. Open, connectivist, constructionist, experiential approaches using problem- and project-based learning exclusively do not have the research evidence to back up their strong claims. The field needs to make and keep room for a variety of pedagogies, progressive and traditional, to address the wide variety of conditions and needs found in schools and other learning settings.

- *Advancing knowledge—the realm of academic journals and programs.* Universities are dedicated to advancing knowledge, and refereed review has the same intent—yet academic discourse forms hold no monopoly on knowledge generation. A strong case can be made, especially in our field, that the most exciting advances typically come from the field—new technologies open up huge new avenues of promising practice; the blogosphere seizes a barely noticed idea and memes it out to the world; an innovative, over-achieving professional is constantly sifting through new ideas and applying the best ones to his or her work.

These are from my list of vulnerable icons—your list will vary. The point is, we need safe places where people can challenge assumptions and try out new ideas. Guerrilla designers will work from a conviction about needed change and then frame a design project in terms of a fresh understanding that is shared by the design team and sponsors. The success (or failure) of their work will serve in part as a proof-of-concept of alternative assumptions, which itself advances knowledge and can be shared within the profession.

RESPONSE BY BARBARA L. MARTIN

What is not to love about Brent Wilson's section on guerrilla design? Every field needs to shake it up a bit. Sometimes, a little change is needed; sometimes, a lot. Sometimes, change comes in intervals; other times, continuous redevelopment is needed. The concept of guerrilla design as "radical or subversive thinking about core models that may go unchallenged" coupled with *principled resistance* to certain ideas that are seen negatively impacting a profession" is appealing. As Wilson states, all of us can think of ideas that would fit into our definition of sacred cows that need to be revisited.

The literature on planned change may give us some perspective on guerrilla design. It might not provide answers but may offer a framework. Planned change can be addressed from multiple perspectives—e.g. organizational, individual and/or system change, the change agent role, and the adoption and diffusion of innovations—and in a variety of fields including education. If we want to promote radical or subversive thinking coupled with principled resistance, what does the planned change literature say? Here are a few things to consider.

Radical Ideas: When Is an Idea New, When Is It a Paradigm Shift, and When Is It a Bastardization of a Previously Good Idea?

While definitions of innovation abound, let us adopt one for this discussion: a deliberate, novel, specific change that is thought to be more efficacious in accomplishing the goals of the system. In general, innovations have a core set of principles, practices, and philosophical/theoretical underpinnings that define them. They can also be scrutinized and tested, praised or debunked, on their merits or lack thereof. Innovations, whatever their genesis, must hang together conceptually and be more worthwhile than what exists.

Whether or not the term "bastardization" is actually in the change literature escapes me. Colloquially, the term applies to dissecting an innovation, using pieces and parts, without maintaining the integrity of the whole. Bastardization applies less to "conceiving" an idea and more to establishing a change. Taking individual chunks of an idea without attention to its whole can lessen its impact and effectiveness.

Defining paradigm shift as "a time when the usual and accepted way of doing or thinking about something changes completely," it begs the question, what are the parameters of accepting radical changes? Guerrilla designers need to analyze and test paradigm shifts, including the core set of foundations, then ask the question, does the new idea accomplish the goals of the system?

Undesired, Undesirable, and Unanticipated Consequences: Radical Ideas Come with Baggage

If all the kinks had to be worked out for every new idea or practice before acceptance, nothing would ever get done. The old saw "it's better to live with the problems you know, than with new ones you don't" can prevent us from challenging the status quo. Like old ideas, new ideas come with consequences. By their very definition, unanticipated consequences cannot be foretold. Undesired and undesirable consequences can cause diffusion efforts to stall or fail. Change researchers say that unanticipated, undesired, and undesirable consequences usually come together.

As guerrilla designers tackle radical ideas, it behooves them to think carefully about unplanned consequences. These can include social, financial, and technological consequences that result in a variety of changes—e.g., practices. In education, all the sacred cows listed can be defined by their good and bad consequences; new ideas will be no different. While we hope that the desired, desirable, and anticipated consequences will outweigh the others, guerrilla designers need to prepare. Start with small-scale testing before rollout with the intent of identifying and planning for the inevitable consequences.

Attitude Change: The Workhorse of Individual Change

Individual acceptance of innovations, including radical changes, has often been compared to how learning occurs: the acquisition of cognitive information and the development of attitudes. For example, when behavioral objectives were initially introduced, in-service teacher training was focused primarily on the cognitive aspects of writing and using objectives. Subsequent research data, however, showed that teachers learned the cognitive skills, *but they saw little or no value in using objectives.*

Of course people can be forced to adopt new ideas. But take away forced use and couple it with negative attitudes and you have rejection brewing. Whenever one is introducing new ideas, acceptance will be improved when potential adopters have positive attitudes about the change.

As the field embraces guerrilla design, diffusing new ideas will likely be as important as the specific ideas. Keep in mind what we know about successful diffusion: (1) carefully frame the idea and have data of all kind to support it, (2) prepare for unplanned consequences, and (3) make attitude change a priority.

REJOINDER BY BRENT WILSON

Thank you Dr. Martin for responding and moving the ideas forward! A lot can be learned from the research and thinking about planned change. Let me respond to your three summary points, in order.

Problem Framing and Range of Evidence

Guerrilla design, as I envision the construct, is based on *seeing* things differently, and then engaging in projects and activities based on those differing visions. Like design-based research, we do not know quite where a given design might go. It is more like a journey or adventure, and less like an execution of a predefined plan. A guerrilla design initiative would start with extra attention at the front end—the visioning or grounding of the journey in a set of alternative values or principles. Then follow the evidence as you go along, using diverse indicators of success (or warning signs of trouble).

Expect the Unexpected

Again—something we know but do not use enough in our daily practice! This points to a tension, or even a paradox, in our practice: we say everything is systemically interconnected, but our prescriptively procedural tools (e.g., ADDIE, training needs/performance gaps, models for planned change, etc.) treat issues and problems as if they were technical, linear, and isolatable. Almost by definition, our models lead us to those unplanned consequences. But what is the alternative—sitting on our hands? Like many continuing tensions, I believe this one propels us forward to be better professionals, always looking for solutions while acknowledging the complexity.

Attitudes and Beyond

I endorse your discussion of attitudes but want to raise you one—to issues of identity. The distinctive element of guerrilla design, in my judgment, lies in the *existential concern and passion* of the designers. Guerrilla designers are not sure they fit in a field dominated by ideas they want to challenge. They look around and are not sure they identify as full-fledged citizens of this particular community. They are acutely aware of their differentness. They worry that their heterodoxy may be too severe to qualify as full-fledged citizens. Their status and stake in the field is at risk. By engaging in a guerrilla design project, an IDT professional can reclaim a place in a field that feels dangerously alien.

The term *radical* derives from "the root"—meaning, starting over and rebuilding from scratch, back to the root of the problem or issue. My initial description hints at being radical, but only in a limited way, I confess. True radicals look at what passes for theory and research in IDT and just leave—they go and form their own club with different theories and research assumptions. Look at the number of research communities with a stake in learning technologies and the count is staggering—dozens and dozens of self-citing groups, many with their own journals, professional organizations, and edited book collections. Examples in IDT's own past are the people attached to postmodern, poststructuralist ideas in the 1990s—most simply left after being frustrated in their struggles against IDT's positivist tendencies. Because of our complex and nested interests, history, practices, and settings, the use of technology in education is as splintered as any established field in education.

My faux radical attitude is in fact more loyal and moderate. The pose is radical—like a college sophomore with a Che Guevara poster on the dorm wall—but the essence is more like trying to fit in and contribute. I, too, am often frustrated by the narrow framing of the field in terms of ADDIE and instructional strategies; sometimes I wonder what I am doing here! But then I remember: it's the shared pursuit of creating truly good instruction that works, and everything that goes with that (good assessment, support for learners and instructors, particularly good use of technology). That is where my eyes are fixed, and that is the ultimate goal for most IDT researchers and theorists.

The idea of change is about as fraught as learning—in fact, the two constructs are nearly identical. Beyond traditional change/adoption theories, helpful metaphors include the following:

- *Organization learning*—how organizations learn and adapt to changing conditions
- *Organizational culture*—how organization develop a culture through rites, symbols, and language
- *Communities*—how communities form around shared practices and interests and how they develop means to support learning, growth, and adaptation
- *Activity systems*—how people live within systems of shared activity and meaning
- *Political activism*—how community organizing at the local level can leverage and effect broader change
- *Social movements*—how people come together to respond to changing conditions
- *Pressure politics*—how deliberate tactics to be noticed and attended to can have an impact
- *Systemic/transformational change*—how principles of systems can lead to substantive change and transformation in individuals and organizations
- *Open adaptive systems* (crowd/Web)—how widely distributed agents can work in concert to achieve designs and solve problems
- *Political and religious affiliation*—how people's deep sense of identity and affiliation can evolve and change over time

The list may at first glance seem too long and far-reaching. But remember Barb's point about problem framing and diversity of evidence. Each metaphor for change on the list could lead to productive conversation and tie-in for how the field of IDT could profitably grow and move in positive directions—and how we each can find a way to contribute and stay connected.

Chapter 4

Design Beyond Content

Extending the Value of Educational Technology: An Examination of the Role or the Anti-role of Content in Educational Technology

Brad Hokanson

How we create, how we design instruction, how we design *learning*, is based on the challenges we choose to address, and on our epistemology. Those choices and ways of thinking and learning have developed over years but still retain much of their orientation from the history and evolution of our field. For innovation to occur, it is important to significantly shift our outlook and redirect our efforts.

The central focus of our work in educational technology over the past thirty years has been on developing the ability for learners to retain information—a direction rooted in the famous Clark/Kozma debates on competing media use.

That debate centered on the idea that media made "no significant difference" in retaining information or content. Clark noted, "media are mere vehicles that deliver instruction but do not influence student achievement any more than the truck that delivers our groceries causes changes in our nutrition" (1983, p. 445). In spite of our ardent denials, that commentary focused the field of instructional design by setting the criteria for evaluation and success. The focus, defined by our assessment methods, was based on retention of content. In the field of educational technology, media was removed from the equation, and the field centered on the retention of information. And so we have spent the most time working on delivering content, driving, as it were, the grocery truck, seeking to make the deliveries faster and more efficient.

Building on that analogy, effectiveness is judged only on the volume of groceries delivered. In other words, we test to see if the grocery truck actually delivered the groceries, not if they were nutritious, or if they rotted on the front porch, or if they were eaten. Those, metaphorically, are more critical aspects of the process, and should lead us to more broadly examining learning. Currently, success in education is narrowly defined as the quantity delivered or retained; validity of evaluation that is based solely on information retention is not questioned. (Did you remember to order rutabagas?)

It is clear many educators think "covering the content" is the most important part of the educational process, and so—in the midst of the present high-stakes testing environment—our research, discussions, and design efforts center on information retention and retrieval. This focusing on content is not a *valid* pursuit, for it is not the most important component of education.

Of course, this is a relatively narrow view of content—i.e., that of information transmitted and declarative knowledge, and not skills or character traits developed. Instructional design may focus on information-based content because of the ease of instruction, ease of evaluation, or a tendency toward quantitative analysis within the field. By experience, delivery and evaluation based on informational content is considerably simpler than a complex form of learning or skill; memorizing the poem is simpler than writing or analyzing; identifying a historical artist is simpler than creating a drawing; teaching about creativity is easier than developing creativity in the learner. It may also detract from true learning, through a "poverty of attention": "What information consumes is rather obvious: it consumes the attention of its recipients" (Simon, 1971).

Seeking more for our learners, what we must do is go beyond content and address other skills and capabilities. In reality, *content is a dead end*. It develops the false premise that learning is complete when the information is known—and not when learners seek more: their own directions, answers, and ideas. The capabilities to synthesize and generate ideas are not based on specific content; they are based on some content . . . but we focus on solely teaching the content. Within instructional design, there is a tacit understanding of the separation of content from the learning experience, through the use of a subject matter expert. Content, per se, can be separated from the learning process.

This is a problem not just within the field of instructional design but throughout education. Our educational work should build deep learners—those that can use and apply knowledge, but with a drive to finish their work, with the curiosity to find out more, and with the creativity to do something completely different. We give lip service to Bloom's Taxonomy and other descriptors of higher-level learning (Anderson et al., 2001; Bloom & Krathwohl, 1956), but we focus most of our effort on content and the lower levels. In a rush to content, the aspects that have been shown to be essential to the long-term success and development of students are forgotten or neglected—traits such as curiosity, creativity, and persistence. Teachers understand this and feel constrained by being pushed to "teach for the test."

This challenges our choice of educational goals and meaning: What should people learn? Why?

If, then, you could teach a child only one thing, what would you teach the child? One set of facts, or one set of skills, or how to learn? Or to be curious, persistent, or creative, to move forward and be self-motivated? The positive attributes we must develop in our learners are skills and character traits, and not the content of information. These are traits that will last for lifetime, a lifetime past the crap that is on the test.

Clearly, this is theoretical argument; we never get to choose one specific aspect of learning—and even not the ironic, default choice of "content." But this question seeks to illustrate the richness that can develop in successful learning. And it begins to create both a set of goals for learning and, perhaps, heuristics for choices in instructional design.

And this is why I have come, after a lifetime in design, to call myself a *content agnostic*: one who is looking beyond content toward more essential goals.

Design, a life of problem seeking and solving, can be described as curiosity applied and formalized. It works with content, but the development of a designer is centered on finding and solving problems; cognitively, it is more complex, and the learning deals more with *using* content instead of *knowing* content, the capabilities to synthesize and generate ideas and knowledge—i.e., knowing in action (Schön, 1983). Design begins without a set destination or answer, and, through discovery, it creates a solution and, often concurrently, an understanding.

It builds value not from the details that one knows, and not through a rigid process that is developed to a preordained end result. Most design education focuses not on content but rather on the process, the end results, how everything works, and the thinking and innovative nature of the work. Design is not a simplistic way of making something "look" better, or of solving a given problem; it is an epistemology and a belief system, a form of living. To be less is to simply manufacture results.

Using this deeper orientation for learning, one that is design or problem-based, may lead to better models of education. We could begin to view simplistic content as a medium, as something that can be used to support stronger forms of learning. If we view content as that which is helpful in developing skills of synthesis, logic, creativity, and curiosity, it does have value. Content could become a medium for education.

This does occur, in ways with which we are familiar. For example, memorizing a poem is not highly valuable for the content of the poem—that is, the specific words—but may be valuable for the considered, deeper examination of what is truly being said, as well as for the discipline of the act of memorization. Similarly, practicing the piano provides little new experience with melodies and notes, no new notes or "content," but rather it is an activity that supports the development of expertise and the dedication and persistence needed in many fields. Debussy recognized this in characterizing music as "the space between the notes."

Understanding that "space," within information/content, is where we will find the higher qualities of education. Somehow there must be more value in education than solely assessing education by how much people remember. That view, the simplistic understanding that learning can be measured by information retained, is a fallacy.

In the end, the field that is educational technology has the responsibility to improve all education, by the expansion of the use of technology and by the innovative nature of the field. And we know there is value beyond the simple information content. For instructional design, that means we need to reorient our methods. We need to embrace, as our role, the broader values of education, and separate content from the focus of our work.

References

Anderson, L. W., Krathwohl, D. R., Airasian, P. W., Cruikshank, K. A., Mayer, R. E., Pintrich, P. R., . . . & Wittrock, M. C. (2001). *A taxonomy for learning, teaching, and assessing: A revision of Bloom's taxonomy of educational objectives, abridged edition*. White Plains, New York: Longman.

Bloom, B. S., & Krathwohl, D. R. (1956). *Taxonomy of educational objectives: The classification of educational goals. Handbook I: Cognitive domain*. New York: Longmans, Green.

Clark, R. E. (1983). Reconsidering research on learning from media. *Review of Educational Research*, 53(4), 445–459.

Koomey, J. (2008). *Turning numbers into knowledge: Mastering the art of problem solving*. Oakland, CA: Analytics Press.

Schön, D. A. (1983). *The reflective practitioner: How professionals think in action* (Vol. 5126). New York: Basic books.

Simon, H. (1971). *Computers, communications and the public interest. Computers, communications, and the public interest*. Baltimore, MD: Johns Hopkins Press, 40–41.

RESPONSE BY PETER SAMUELSON WARDRIP

In Hokanson's piece, "Design Beyond Content: Extending the Value of Educational Technology: An Examination of the Role or the Anti-role of Content in Educational Technology," the author puts forth the idea that as a learning and technology designer, he is agnostic to the content he is designing for and more focused on the broader values of education. This position is similar to Barab and colleagues who contend that learning scientists and instructional designers have the opportunity to disrupt "existing practices and structures" with the potential of empowering learners beyond the academic content (Barab, Dodge, Thomas, Jackson & Tuzun, 2007, p. 264). I would like to extend his thought and take it in an additional direction. Ultimately, I see Hokanson's piece as an acknowledgement that learning designers[1] do not operate individually and therefore play a role in collective design efforts to improve teaching and learning.

Learning designers can afford to be content agnostic when they are working as co-designers. Working with subject-matter experts—as Hokanson points out—distributes the onus of content knowledge away from the designer. Teachers can often serve as these subject-matter experts. There have been numerous arguments for involving teachers and other relevant stakeholders into the design process. Some have argued that teachers are uniquely positioned as decision makers to be involved in curricular-related design activities (Remillard, 2005). Some have noted that involving teachers and other relevant stakeholders also ensures the utility of the products designed (Roschelle, Penuel & Shechtman, 2006; Kwon, Wardrip & Gomez, 2014). No matter the insight that educational partners bring to the design process, they lessen the need for learning designers to be steeped in expertise beyond their foundation in learning research and the design process.

When learning designers work within a collaborative environment, content knowledge becomes one of several types of knowledge that are important for robust educational technology tools designed for use in schools and other similar learning environments. For sure, some have rightly acknowledged the necessary role of content in the design and development of tools and curriculum, such as the role of content in the design of formative assessment tools (e.g., Coffey, Hammer, Levin & Grant, 2011). However, collaborators such as teachers, administrators, parents, and students can provide additional elements of knowledge and expertise that are important to the design of useful tools. Knowledge of instruction, district policies, and the school and classroom context are significant and influential in the design and development of successful educational tools.

Ultimately, a form of knowledge—if you can call it that—that learning designers may not be able to be agnostic about is the know-how to collaborate and partner with others in the design process. These partnerships can be complicated and reveal different expectations and roles for the work (Penuel, Allen, Coburn & Farrell, 2015). In short, by having teachers and learning designers engage in design, the group can simultaneously engage in theory development, create useful products, and attempt to improve teaching and learning in the classroom (Edelson, 2002).

While viewing learning designers as agnostic to content, the point is not to downplay the role of content in the learning design process. Instead, the role of learning designers as researchers, designers, developers, and change agents is a broad role. By co-designing with relevant partners in the process, we can hope to create more effective designs, and richer learning experiences.

Note

1. For the sake of brevity, I am using the term "learning designer" as short-hand for designers who design learning/educational technologies, tools, and materials.

References

Barab, S. A., Dodge, T., Thomas, M., Jackson, C., & Tuzun, H. (2007). Our designs and the social agendas they carry. *Journal of the Learning Sciences, 16*, 263–305.
Coffey, J. E., Hammer, D., Levin, D. M., & Grant, T. (2011). The missing disciplinary substance of formative assessment. *Journal of Research in Science Teaching, 48*(10), 1109–1136.
Edelson, D. C. (2002). Design research: What we learn when we engage in design. *Journal of the Learning Sciences, 11*, 105–121.
Kwon, S., Wardrip, P. S., & Gomez, L. M. (2014). Co-design of interdisciplinary projects as a mechanism for school capacity growth. *Improving Schools, 17*(1), 54–71
Penuel, W. R., Allen, A. R., Coburn, C. E., & Farrell, C. (2015). Conceptualizing research–practice partnerships as joint work at boundaries. *Journal of Education for Students Placed at Risk (JESPAR), 20*(1–2), 182–197.
Remillard, J. T. (2005). Key concepts in research on teachers' use of mathematics curricula. *Review of Educational Research, 75*, 211–246.
Roschelle, J., Penuel, W. R., & Shechtman, N. (2006). Co-design of innovations with teachers: Definition and dynamics. In S. A. Barab, K. E. Hay, & D. T. Hickey (Eds.), *Proceedings of the 7th International Conference of the Learning Sciences* (pp. 606–612). Mahwah, NJ: Erlbaum.

REJOINDER BY BRAD HOKANSON

Past the idea of separating informational content from the responsibilities of the instructional designer, this writing, *Design Beyond Content: Extending the Value of Educational Technology*, is meant as a call to examine a broader range of learning in our work as academics, teachers, designers, and researchers. Initially, this has been written to advocate for a systemic change in the field of instructional design. As leaders in how education is created, there is a need to advance our standards and change our focus; this is not a case for a redefinition of roles but one of conceptual change, truly changing our outlook in education. The field of educational technology in specific and education as a whole should develop a more broadly based model for the evaluation of learning.

From our understanding of design practice, we know there are recognized different forms of knowledge that are needed for success, including collaboration and communication. These desired skills are often evident, but often are generally not included as explicit learning goals.

We understand from critical theory, per Barab et al., that inherent in any instructional activity is a set of beliefs, both explicit and tacit, that shape learners. Education can support social values or character traits as well as privileging forms of learning such as information retention.

Learning that focuses on information retention, or on content, concentrates on that form of results and that type of knowledge. Similarly, *research* that focuses on the measurement of information content honors that form of learning, and implicitly encourages that goal of instruction, directing the subsequent generation of instructional design efforts with the same goal.

In higher education, as teachers, we often see the results of students having an education centered on information, with learning that is literal, positivistic, black and white, and immature. It is a dichotomy of facts, either known or not, right or wrong, and not one that adjusts to human nature and achievement, or one in which one sees the complexity of human experience.

There is value in "knowing how" as opposed to "knowing that," an understanding that skills, ranging from writing to collaboration to creativity to critical thinking, are more valuable than a detailed understanding of the facts. They are more difficult to evaluate and to teach, and specifically more difficult to present to learners. But they remain the most essential aspects of learning.

This conceptual redirection is similar to the current shifting of economic theory toward a more behavioral understanding of behavior, away from assumed rational and analytical behavior (Kahneman, 2011; Thaler, 2015). Behavioral economics has begun to look at how humans respond to the world, in purchasing, investing, and other choices—with all the real-life divergence from perfect economic behavior. People making economic decisions, like learners, do not always act rationally, and changing behavior, much like learning, is more challenging than simply presenting them with the facts.

Similarly, learning cannot be defined by the simplest forms of measurement, those of information retention. Our learners are humans, with a need to apply skills and engage others, not to simply be able to recall forms of information.

The field of educational technology should seek to support this broader understanding through more research of subjective topics, as has developed in the field of creativity research, for example, or in other traits such as curiosity or perseverance.

More research should be conducted dealing with online presence, motivation, and engagement; these can be examined through self-reported or observed data gathering, and will prove more transformational than information retention.

It is not just about accepting the need to utilize content experts as a part of a well-organized design team (that way is incremental) but rather a rethinking of how we should teach and how technologically we should help others learn, and, specifically, *how we should research*.

This is a call for more focus on skills, character, and quality of thought developed by the learner. The idea of *beyond content* as proposed here is meant not only as a form of design practice but as a revision of the epistemology of the domain, to extend our understanding of learning to other forms, including the social capability for collaboration and engagement, as well as the character traits of passion, initiative, and curiosity.

References

Barab, S. A., Dodge, T., Thomas, M., Jackson, C., & Tuzun, H. (2007). Our designs and the social agendas they carry. *Journal of the Learning Sciences, 16*, 263–305.

Kahneman, D. (2011). *Thinking fast and slow.* New York: Farrar, Straus, and Giroux.

Thaler, R. H. (2015). *Misbehaving: The making of behavioral economics*. New York: WW Norton & Company.

Chapter 5

The Systems Approach to Instructional Development

Michael Molenda

The claim asserted in this paper is that the systems approach is a valuable and productive framework for creating instructional materials and teaching-learning systems. For the purposes of this paper, the construct will be referred to as instructional systems development (ISD). Its hallmarks are, according to McCombs (1986),

> the use of analytical, problem-solving, and decision-making skills in an iterative and cybernetic process which begins with an analysis of system (or training) requirements and culminates in a fully evaluated instructional system (or set of training materials) that performs to specified standards and requirements.
>
> (p. 67)

What Are the Strengths of ISD?

Robust Intellectual Roots

First, ISD has robust theoretical grounding. A detailed account of the historical evolution of ISD and of the theoretical perspectives that came to be incorporated in it can be found in Molenda (2010). For present purposes it is enough to focus on two quite separate intellectual developments that happened to be progressing at the same time—the systems approach and programmed instruction.

The first root of ISD is planted in the U.S. military in the years right after World War II as the armed forces were striving to improve their operations by incorporating the principles of systems analysis. Systems analysis was a method of deconstructing complex problems (e.g., hunting enemy submarines) into their component parts, then constructing a mathematical model of the situation in order to discern ways of optimizing particular functions of the model. Mathematical modeling yielded precise results when used for the "machine" side of human-machine interactions, but, due to the vagaries of the human element, a looser "soft science" version evolved to deal with the human-machine combination. It was known as "the systems approach": "a much more general and hence less definitive idea. It is simply the idea of viewing a problem or situation in its entirety with all its ramifications, with all its interior interactions, with all its exterior connections and with full cognizance of its place in its context" (Mood, 1964, p. 1).

Each of the armed services developed its own interpretation of a systems approach to the design of training programs. In the 1970s, researchers at Florida State University collaborated with army researchers on a unified approach—the Interservice Procedures for Instructional Systems Development (IPISD), a visual-verbal model with accompanying texts, outlining detailed procedures clustered around five major functions: analyze, design, develop, implement, and control.

Another branch of the systems-approach root comes from academia. In the late 1960s, several universities cooperated in a project to generate and test home-brewed systems approach models for use in college instruction. Their report (Barson, 1967) included a unified procedural model with heuristic guidelines. It is unlikely that any other instructional planning framework has been subjected to as rigorous a program of development and testing as these systems-approach models.

The other root is planted in behavioral psychology where researchers, led by B. F. Skinner, were experimenting with procedures for improving human learning. One teaching-learning framework they developed was programmed instruction. After extensive product development and testing, some researchers realized that what was powerful was not the programmed instruction format but rather the *process* used to create the lessons. This process was codified by Markle and Tiemann (1967)—a procedural flow chart consisting of analyzing learners and learning tasks, specifying performance objectives, requiring active practice and feedback, and subjecting prototypes to testing and revision. This proto-model was highly congruent with the systems-approach models of that time. Educators and trainers with backgrounds in educational psychology brought the empirically oriented behaviorist mindset with them, which fit quite comfortably within systems-approach models.

Evolution through Real-World Testing

Second, ISD is resilient, having undergone modification through use in innumerable venues across a wide range of teaching-learning problems without losing coherence. Throughout the 1970s and 1980s, hundreds of individuals and organizations created diverse ISD models adapted to different contexts—colleges, corporate training, executive development, medicine, nursing, vocational training, special education, and more. Despite the local adaptations, there remained a consensus on the essential qualities of ISD:

- heuristic—asking incisive questions in a logical order, rather than simply following algorithms
    - "Step-by-step procedures exist for certain activities (e.g. for task analysis) but these are only at the level of collecting or organizing information. What to do with the information is not governed by an immutable algorithm. Creative solutions pop up as sudden flashes of insight" (Romiszowski, 1981, p. 24).
- systemic—viewing problems within the context of the supra-system and in relation to the internal components of the system of interest
- systematic—methodical in following a procedural plan, often represented as an ISD model, with the major phases being analyze, design, develop, implement, and evaluate (colloquially referred to as "ADDIE" models)
- empirical—committed to making decisions on the basis of evidence
- iterative—committed to recycling through stages of the process guided by evaluation data at each stage

ISD captured a large following, in the first place, because it offered a standardized procedure and vocabulary for working on training issues. In the second place, organizations are always under pressure to cut costs of training—time of development, delivery costs, and employee time away from the job. For hundreds, if not thousands, of organizations, ISD helped them do that.

Supported by Formal Research

Although it is difficult to conduct formal research on a process as broad as ISD, the studies that have been done tend to yield positive findings. In addition to the developmental testing described above, early dissertation studies strove to demonstrate the comprehensiveness and usability of specific ISD models (e.g., Stowe, 1971; Belmore, 1973; Holsclaw, 1974). Hundreds of other dissertation studies focused on one or another of the elements of the ISD model.

By the mid-1980s, at least two authoritative researchers found sufficient evidence to make some summary judgments about ISD in general. Psychologist Douglas Ellson (1986) in his exhaustive review of comparison studies of instructional methods identifies a handful of techniques that yielded learning outcomes at least *twice* as good as control treatments. Among them was "performance-based instructional design," his term for ISD, a concept new to him.

Barbara McCombs (1986) surveyed a broader range of research literature on ISD, concluding, "One thing that most, if not all, persons . . . can agree upon is that the basic ISD model and its underlying systems approach to instructional development is sound" (p. 68). However, she found that there was a widespread perception, especially in the military, of deficiencies in the ISD model. She attributed this perception to the users' "failure to maintain a total systems perspective" (p. 71). She reiterated that ISD must be treated as a complex, creative process applying higher-order analytical skills. Reduced to mere routine procedures, the model loses its effectiveness.

More recently, a large meta-analysis of research on corporate training (Arthur, Bennett, Edens & Bell, 2003) discovered a medium-to-large effect size associated with several training features—"the training method used, the skill or task characteristic trained, and the choice of training evaluation criteria" (p. 243)—all of which are key features of ISD.

Expert Embrace

Today, ISD continues to enjoy widespread support, not only from practitioners but also from professional thought leaders. Prominent consultants (such as Darryl L. Sink & Associates and Handshaw Inc.), leading textbook authors (such as Morrisson, Ross, Kalman & Kemp, 2013, and Dick, Carey & Carey, 2014), and the major performance standards organization IBSTPI (Koszalka, Russ-Eft & Reiser, 2013) all continue to champion ISD as the standard for instructional design.

Contemporary Critiques: Theoretical

No doubt, ISD presents numerous targets for criticism, from the standpoint both of theory and of practice. The literature of educational technology is rife with criticism of the behaviorist perspective that is one of the contributing theories to ISD, primarily in the form of advocacy for "constructivism" as an alternative paradigm. Constructivism may be viewed as a challenge to ISD either at the level of selecting instructional methods or at the broad philosophical level (Dick, 1997). At the instructional methods level, constructivism is a label for a learner-centered pedagogy based on widely accepted principles from cognitive psychology. There is nothing in ISD doctrine to preclude incorporating such methods where appropriate. In fact, one of the classic works in ISD (Reigeluth, 1999), contains a vast compendium of instructional strategies and tactics available for use at the "design" stage of ISD, the majority coming from the cognitive perspective. Responding to the constructivist critique at the paradigm level is beyond the scope of this paper; Dick's (1997) response can stand in the meantime.

Also, it can be argued that systems theory provides a poor foundation for dealing with the complex human activities involved in education. It must be admitted that putting education under the "systems" lens has limitations. The systems approach requires clearly defined ends and objective assessment of the attainment of those ends. This is attainable in some venues, such as corporations, military services, and other work settings. But in American public education, both the ends and the criteria for measuring them have always been contested, making public education a venue poorly suited to any but the "softest" of "soft science" versions of ISD.

A more recent theoretical challenge proposes an alternative paradigm—SAM, the Successive Approximation Model (Allen & Sites, 2012). This model envisions an iterative process, beginning with a rough prototype modified through cycles of evaluation and revision. SAM rejects the "waterfall" analog, in which the output of each step is the input for the subsequent step in a lockstep manner, ending with evaluation. However, no textbook on ISD advocates such a lockstep or "waterfall" approach, and, as with SAM, the notion of iterative progression toward a more finished product is central to ISD, as is the notion of evaluating decisions all along the line. These ideas are evident in the earliest ISD textbooks but even more so in one of the most recent, Handshaw (2014)—in which the element "prototype" appears at the center of the model. Another popular contemporary ISD textbook—Morrison, Ross, Kalman and Kemp (2013)—presents a model in which evaluation and revision surround every step in the process.

Contemporary Critiques: Corporate Practice

One of the most publicized critiques from the corporate domain (Gordon & Zemke, 2000) laid out a broad array of attacks of an anecdotal nature. After a vigorous debate about the supposed deficiencies laid out in the original article, Zemke and Rossett (2002) concluded the discussion by suggesting that the flaws attributed to ISD lay more in how the process was executed, rather than flaws in ISD as a theory. For example, one of the major Gordon and Zemke criticisms is that some practitioners follow their favorite ISD model in a lockstep manner, ignoring commonsense boundaries of time and expense.

Another source of missteps is the level of detail depicted in a given ISD model. Too little detail: visual models of the ISD process have to be simplified to fit onto a page; they cannot be expected to represent the full complexity of real-world circumstances. Too much detail: elaborate flowchart models that attempt to portray every step in detail can lead to a drawn-out slog or give the false impression that ISD can be reduced to algorithms.

Conclusion

ISD has proven to be theoretically robust, coherent, resilient, adaptable, and efficacious. It can be comprehended by novices, helping them attain good results while they garner the experience necessary to make decisions based on their own expertise. One might ask whether any *other* structured approach to instructional planning is applied more rigorously or more successfully. We must avoid the temptation to compare ISD to some imagined ideal and instead compare it with its real rival, improvisation. As Rosenberg (2002) says, "ISD is the best thing we have, if we use it correctly" (p. 34).

References

Allen, M. W., & Sites, R. (2012). *Leaving ADDIE for SAM: An agile model for developing the best learning experiences*. Alexandria, VA: ASTD Press.

Arthur, Jr., W., Bennett Jr., W., Edens, P. S., & Bell, S. T. (2003). Effectiveness of training in organizations: A meta-analysis of design and evaluation features. *Journal of Applied Psychology, 88*(2), 234–245.

Barson, J. (1967). *Instructional systems development. A demonstration and evaluation project: Final report*. U.S. Office of Education, Title II-B project OE 3–16–025. East Lansing, MI: Michigan State University. 125 p. (EDRS: ED 020 673)

Belmore, W. E. (1973). The application of a cost analysis methodology to the design phase of instructional development. *Dissertation Abstracts International, 33*, 5996.

Dick, W. (1997, September–October). Better instructional design theory: Process improvement or reengineering? *Educational Technology, 37*(5), 47–50.

Dick, W., Carey, L., & Carey, J. (2014). *The systematic design of instruction*, 8th ed. Chicago: Scott, Foresman.

Ellson, D. G. (1986). Improving productivity in teaching. *Phi Delta Kappan, 68*(2), 111–124.

Gordon, J., & Zemke, R. (2000, April). The attack on ISD. *Training, 37*, 43–53.

Handshaw, D. (2014). *Training that delivers results*. New York: ASTD, AMACOM.

Holsclaw, J. E. (1974). The development of procedural guidelines for the systematic design of instruction within higher education. Unpublished doctoral dissertation, University of Southern California.

Koszalka, T. A., Russ-Eft, D. F., & Reiser, R. (2013). *Instructional designer competencies: The standards*, 4th ed. Charlotte, NC: Information Age Publishing.

Markle, S. M., & Tiemann, P. W. (1967). Programming is a process. Sound filmstrip. Chicago: University of Illinois at Chicago.

McCombs, B. L. (1986). The instructional systems development (ISD) model: A review of those factors critical to its successful implementation. *Educational Communications and Technology Journal, 34*(2), 67–81.

Molenda, M. (2010). Origins and evolution of instruction systems design. In K. Silber & W. Foshay (Eds.), *Handbook of improving performance in the workplace: Vol. 1. Instructional design and training delivery* (p. 53–92). San Francisco, CA: Pfeiffer.

Mood, A. (1964, April). *Some problems inherent in the development of a systems approach to instruction*. Paper presented at Conference on New Dimensions for Research in Educational Media Implied by the Systems Approach to Education, Syracuse University, Syracuse, New York.

Morrisson, G. R., Ross, S. M., Kalman, H. K., & Kemp, J. E. (2013). *Designing effective instruction*, 7th ed. Hoboken, NJ: John Wiley & Sons.

Reigeluth, C. M. (Ed.) (1999). *Instructional-design theories and models, Volume II: A new paradigm of instructional theory*. Mahwah, NJ: Lawrence Erlbaum Associates.

Romiszowski, A. J. (1981). *Designing instructional systems*. New York: Nichols.

Rosenberg, M. (2002). Quoted in R. Zemke & A. Rossett (2002). A hard look at ISD. *Training, 39*, 27–34.

Stowe, R. A. (1971). Investigation of a mathematical model for managing instructional development time. *Dissertation Abstracts International, 31*, 3185.

Zemke, R., & Rossett, A. (2002, February). A hard look at ISD. *Training, 39*, 27–34.

RESPONSE BY THOMAS ARGONDIZZA

Molenda gives a historical look at the development of instructional systems development (ISD). He offers facts of how ISD came from research in academia and the U.S. Armed Services. There appears to be a common belief that World War II spawned modern day ISD. The systems approach may have been more documented, researched, and analyzed at that time, but, if training soldiers for war is a catalyst to create a learning focused system, it could very well have roots far past World War II.

From Romiszowski (1988) we learn "a system exists because someone has defined it as such" (p. 5), meaning other military training techniques of perhaps Rome, which reigned in one form or another from 27 BC to 1453 AD (Roman Empire-Wikipedia, 2015). Whatever training techniques their armies may have used in Rome, for example, may also have been deemed instructional systems. Romiszowski also describes a system as black box inputs and outputs (Romiszowski, 1988). From this I believe an instructional system can exist as show in Figure 5.1. In my opinion, the black box model provided for an instructional system that offers (a) inputs, (b) a black box representing the instructional system or intervention, and finally (c) a box representing the output.

The input may sound like a learning goal, and it is; however, why would one create a system for no reason? Must there not be some catalyst (a performance deficiency, or a learning mandate) for anyone to design and create an instructional system?

I have also long believed universities to be instructional systems inherently. The oldest continually operating and the first degree-awarding university is University of al-Qarawiyyin founded in 859AD (University of al-Qarawiyyin-Wikipedia, 2015). Determination of goals, curriculum creation, design of educational materials, assessments, and necessary adjustments should have been done at thousands of universities since 859AD. Indiana University, founded in 1820 (Indiana University, 2015), states its mission "to create, disseminate, preserve, and apply knowledge" (Indiana University, 2015). I would argue at the very least that the dissemination and application of knowledge require some kind of instructional system to accomplish. If Indiana University has been working toward this mission since 1820 and is still present, it may have had a strong grasp on ISD long before World War II.

Another example of ISD in a form is vocational education or training. The trade guilds were the guardians of standards in profession as diverse as silversmiths, shoemakers, and law. The trade apprenticeship was the process almost universally adopted: "instruction by the 'master' or 'sitting next to Nellie' are alternative names for this process, mirroring different points of view as to its effectiveness. Outputs were never lost from view" (Romiszowski, 1988, p. 36–37).

As I take a look at that last sentence, that the outputs were never lost from view tells me assessment, evaluation, and improvements were part of their systems of instruction. As mentioned above, even outside of the military and in formal education, instructional systems development can be seen professional development giving it deeper roots.

Figure 5.1 An Instructional Systems Model With Input, Black Box, Output

Taking a look at the beginning of an instructional design model, one can define an educational goal, which Carr-Chellman (2015) calls the lifeblood.

Perhaps it is safer to say ISD was newly defined and documented during World War II. I believe that to say "the first root of ISD is planted in the years right after World War II" ignores centuries of organized well-grounded, and perhaps systems-based, learning history.

Molenda brings up the newer SAM model, Successive Approximation Model, as an example of more recent thinking. Less of a lock-step approach, it uses a more iterative approach allowing for adjustments along the way. This is similar to rapid prototyping as newer software tools allow instructional systems designers to design and develop materials synchronously.

When describing characteristics of instructional theories and models, Reigeluth (1999) lists "compatibility with a theory of learning and explicit linkage of learning theory" (p. 48). Molenda mentions B. F. Skinner but offered nothing more recent as a vital part of ISD. It may have been helpful to put more emphasis on how learning theories support a sound instructional system.

Finally Molenda suggests ISD models offer too little detail: visual models of the ISD process have to be simplified to fit onto a page, and understand they cannot be presented in their full complexity. But these one-page images of ISD models can be accompanied by detailed explanation elsewhere, perhaps in a book in an instructional designer's desk. The one-page ISD model can be a useful job aid, as job aids are used for infrequent (Romiszowski, 1988), yet important, tasks.

I believe Molenda put forward great points—for example, that the theory of ISD is vital and can be seen through different ISD models. The recent documentation and research of ISD has brought us into a deeper understanding of teaching and learning.

References

Carr-Chellman, A. A. (2015). *Instructional design for teachers: Improving classroom practice* (2nd ed.). New York: Routledge.

Indiana University. (2015). Indiana University. Retrieved from http://trustees.iu.edu/resources/mission-statements/iu-bloomington-mission-statement.shtml.

Reigeluth, C. M. (1999). *Instructional-design theories and models: A new paradigm of instructional theory* (Vol. II). Mahwah, NJ: Lawrence Erlbaum.

Roman Empire-Wikipedia. (2015). Roman Empire. *Wikipedia, the free encyclopedia.* Retrieved September 26, 2015, from https://en.wikipedia.org/wiki/Roman_Empire.

Romiszowski, A. J. (1988). *Designing instructional systems: Decision making in course planning and curriculum design.* New York: Kogan Page.

University of al-Qarawiyyin-Wikipedia. (2015). University of al-Qarawiyyin. *Wikipedia, the free encyclopedia.* Retrieved September 26, 2015, from https://en.wikipedia.org/wiki/University_of_al-Qarawiyyin.

REJOINDER BY MICHAEL MOLENDA

I am pleased that Argondizza agrees with the overall claim of my original paper: that "ISD has proven to be theoretically robust, coherent, resilient, adaptable, and efficacious."

He criticizes primarily my claim about the historical origins of ISD—that the construct was created after World War II. Although this is a minor point in my argument, it is worth debating because it is critical to clarify just exactly what construct I am talking about under the label of ISD. Based upon the historical examples he brings up, Argondizza may have quite a different—and very amorphous—construct in mind.

Argondizza argues that ISD predates modern times, supporting this argument with four claims: (1) that the Roman Empire must have used systematic instruction; (2) that universities are "instructional systems inherently"; (3) that early forms of vocational education are evidence that ISD must have existed in earlier times; and (4) that if education is directed toward a goal, it must be systematically developed.

I stand by my original claim and will show the falsity of Argondizza's argument. He first claims to find roots of ISD in Roman military training. The Roman Empire indeed had well organized training programs for its legions. In *De Re Militari* (a book still read by military trainers), Vegetius (*fl.* fourth or fifth century AD) describes Roman training for marching, physical fitness, and weapons handling. Training was rigorous, clearly specified, and highly organized—all traits of orderly instruction. However, there is no evidence that Roman trainers actually followed any sort of *prespecified design process*. More likely, the military drills were learned by young men as soldiers and then repeated by them as they became officers. Organized education in the Roman civilian realm was typically tutorial, one-to-one instruction by a mentor. There is no evidence of a design process at work in that venue either, just learning by example, memorization of text, and oral transmission, with each generation repeating the patterns given by the preceding one.

He supports this claim by quoting Romiszowski regarding how to define a system of interest. Romiszowski is arguing that there is a certain amount of arbitrary judgment involved in drawing boundaries around a cluster of human activities and dubbing it a "system"—that is, defining a system of interest. Romiszowski most certainly is not asserting that we can infer that a *systematic development process* exists because we observe organized training going on. Argondizza further supports his claim by showing a "black box" model, again asserting illogically that we can infer that if something happens inside the black box, there must have been a systematic development process in the box. The claim is simply empty and fallacious on its face.

Argondizza's second claim about historical origins is that universities appear to represent "instructional systems." We can agree that universities have survived for a remarkably long period and have had considerable success in creating, storing, and disseminating knowledge. We can agree that some of the ingredients of systematic instruction can be found in some university settings—goal-setting, curriculum creation, testing, and adjustments over time. But again, as with the Roman Empire, these elements were not consciously ordered into an explicit planning process meeting the criteria of ISD at any institution prior to World War II. Early twentieth-century psychologists such as William James (1842–1910) advocated a more scientific approach to instruction, but those ideas were not instantiated in American higher education in their times. On the contrary, universities have long thought of themselves first as a community of scholars, or what Thomas Jefferson envisioned as an "academical village," not as an industrial-type venue for systematic instruction.

A better example to support Argondizza's argument might be the individualized instruction programs created for K-12 education early in the twentieth century, such as the Winnetka Plan. Schools following such plans instantiated prespecified objectives, materials created for individual use, self-paced learning, and criterion-referenced testing—all traits of systematic instruction. However, the innovators who developed these programs did not pass along design procedures for future generations to follow either, so even this case does not succeed in supporting Argondizza's claim.

Argondizza's third historical case is the medieval guild system, a precursor to vocational education. Although the guilds did have an organized, even ritualized, procedure for training apprentices, the essence of that training was its secrecy. The "tricks of the trade" were closely held secrets, purposely wrapped in mystery, in order to maintain the guild's monopoly grip on its trade. Nothing of a systematic design procedure has been handed down to us as residue of the guilds' training methods.

Argondizza takes a fourth run at his claim of "ISD everywhere in history" by noting the importance of goal-setting in ISD. He again refers to Roman education, in which he believes there must have been goals set because there was organized instruction. And if goals were set, we can infer that a systematic development process was being used. No, we cannot. Possessing any one trait of ISD, no matter how important that one trait is, does not prove that *all* the traits of ISD were present.

Argondizza might have made a better case by citing historical figures whose work is actually known, accessible, and relevant to instructional technology. For example, Comenius (1592–1670) developed a robust set of principles of message design, admirably displayed in *Orbis Sensualium Pictus* (Molenda, 2008); but even Comenius, in his many admirable volumes on pedagogy, never proposed anything like a systematic development process. Coming closer to modern times, Edward L. Thorndike (1874–1949) proposed a robust theory of learning and took large steps toward explaining how his theory might be applied in instructional practice, even foreshadowing the format of programmed instruction (Saettler, 1990, p. 56), but he never proposed any sort of specific instructional planning process.

In short, anyone seriously interested in pursuing the intellectual history of ISD would do well to start with Saettler's (1990) encyclopedic history (which finds no ISD roots in Roman or medieval history).

Argondizza's other criticism is that I claim that "ISD models offer too little detail." This is a misunderstanding. I claim that others criticize ISD models for offering both too little detail and too much detail. I agree with Argondizza's explanation that "low detail" models are meant to be used with job aids that flesh out the details.

Argondizza concludes by agreeing with the thrust of my original argument about the value of ISD, which is gratifying.

References

Molenda, M. (2008). Historical foundations. In J. M. Spector, M. D. Merrill, J. Van Merriënboer, & M. P. Driscoll (Eds.), *Handbook of research on educational communications and technology* (3rd ed., pp. 3–20). New York: L. Erlbaum Associates.

Saettler, P. (1990). *The evolution of American educational technology.* Englewood, CO: Libraries Unlimited.

Chapter 6

Instructional Design Models and the Expertise Required to Practice True Instructional Design

Robert Maribe Branch

There appears to be a rise in the number of people who identify themselves as an instructional designer but rarely practice true instructional design. Instructional design is a complex process that requires more than writing objectives, publishing training manuals, and placing lesson plans online. Many so-called instructional designers lack a degree of expertise to practice true instructional design. The focus of this dialogue is that an effective instructional design model will have a high correlation between the amount of complexity contained within that instructional design model and the amount of complexity contained in the learning space being addressed by the instructional design process. Spaces dedicated to intentional learning are extremely complex, and any process used to satisfy the needs of intentional learning spaces must be equally complex. This idea is consistent with the law of requisite variety, which contends that in order to properly facilitate the quantity and diversity of a situation, you must have an equal quantity and diversity of responses. Requisite variety offers a rationale for matching the complexity of an end result with the complexity of means used to accomplish a goal. The learning product that is developed is the end. The means used to accomplish a goal is the process. Therefore, it becomes imperative that people who offer their professional moniker as instructional designer truly have the expertise to effectively practice the inherently complex process of instructional design.

Instructional design is a complex process. Complexity describes phenomena that produce increasing amount of information, energy, hierarchy, variability, and relationships, which, then, increase the possible outcomes and reduce certainty and predictability. This certainly describes the nature of instructional design processes whereby data and information about performance discrepancies are collected in order to determine possible solutions, while variables associated with people, content, context, and expectations are verified with some degree of measurability—process being defined as a series of actions, procedures, and functions that lead to a product. Processes occur either naturally or created artificially by people. Complexity also implies that natural and social systems are nonlinear and dynamic. Instructional design definitely qualifies as a nonlinear, dynamic system that is both natural and social. This position reinforces several tenets of instructional design. Specifically, instructional design models need to sufficiently address the complexities of the actual events that occur during the instructional design process. Further, instructional design models should be portrayed as cyclical, iterative, and multilevel processes, which are contextualized in order to reflect the values and complexity of a particular learning space.

Instructional design is an applied product development process, which only exists to respond to needs that are identified in spaces dedicated to intentional learning. There are several skills required to apply complex instructional design processes that distinguish an expert instructional designer from a typical educational technologist. Educational technologists can arrange classrooms in various configurations, schedule mutually agreeable meeting times, and prepare and sequence instructional materials to satisfy a linear order of events, but even educational technologists cannot guarantee the same linear order of a student's learning experience nor interaction patterns among peers, teachers, media, and context. The expertise required to practice true instructional design will include minimum competencies, such as those promoted by the International Board of Standards for Training, Performance and Instruction (IBSTPI) but also other skills that distinguish an expert instructional designer from a typical educational technologist. While instructional design is a domain of practice within the broader field of educational technology, instructional designers require more in-depth skills in the learning sciences and should possess more social design expertise than a general educational technologist. There is even less formal preparation required to qualify as an educational technologist than to be a certified instructional designer.

Another reason the practice of true instructional design is complex, and may be beyond the scope of skills of an educational technologist, is because instructional design is a social construction of independent and complex entities, such as schools, subject matter, students, and teachers. The typical educational technologist does live in similar environments, but unlike an instructional designer, who is required to manage those same interacting entities, which are interrelated, are interdependent, and function in nonlinear ways. Admittedly, there are similarities between the roles of the general educational technologist and the instructional designer, such as both are commonly involved with clients who are seeking educational goals. However, educational technologists usually have educational goals provided for them, whereas instructional designers are often intimately involved with a client in order to generate goals. Further, instructional designers must be astute enough to address the independent and codependent effects of arranging external teaching events to support internal learning events. External teaching events are things like curricula, courses, teaching units, and single lessons. Internal learning events are things like individual processes of constructing knowledge and skill.

Because instructional design is an educational product development process that involves organizing cognitive, biological, and epistemological events, complexity theory is invoked. Complexity theory is predicated on a phenomenon possessing five attributes: (1) it contains independent complicated entities, (2) multiple entities are contained within, (3) the entities within the phenomenon perform interrelated functions, (4) the phenomenon seeks a common goal through a process of adaptation, and (5) uncertainty is generated because of unpredictable interactions within itself and between itself and the environment. True instructional design models are endowed with these same five attributes. First, authentic instructional design models account for several independent complicated entities, including, but not limited to, the students and their peers, content, delivery systems, time, goals, and the teachers. Second, instructional design models provide opportunities for relevant entities to enter and exit the instructional design process at various points depending on a particular task or procedure. Third, the overwhelming majority of instructional design models are systemic and systematic, where the entities function in ways that are interrelated and synergistic. Fourth, instructional design models display resilience by satisfying the many stakeholder expectations by employing multiple paths to success. Fifth, instructional design models are characterized by cybernetic attributes that permit instructional designers who use them to treat the diversity associated with uncertainty and unpredictability as assets in the instructional design process. Therefore, consistent with complexity theory and the law of requisite variety, instructional design processes must possess a degree of complexity and diversity commensurate with the environment in which it is being applied.

RESPONSE BY LLOYD P. RIEBER

First of all, it is important to realize that Rob Branch understands instructional design very well. So, to paraphrase an old television commercial, when he speaks about instructional design, people should listen. I, on the other hand, have long had a like–not like[1] relationship with instructional design. I appreciate its analytic, systematic, and systemic nature, while at the same time I have been very frustrated by how limiting it can be and how unsatisfying a process it is for those seeking creative design. My point of view is also very much informed by play theory, which is probably the antithesis of the tenets of instructional design. This point of view is based on the assumptions that learning is always occurring and that most of learning is tacit or incidental. That is, most learning is not derived from another's intentional design.

So, my own point of view is that there are many paths to learning, with instruction being only one. Furthermore, I believe that providing instruction at the wrong time is quite detrimental to learning. Put another way, I am interested in those times that instruction is unnecessary, as well as identifying those times when it is most needed. This is a very difficult distinction to make, but also a fascinating one, which continues to keep me interested in the enterprise of educational technology.

But there is much to agree with in Rob's essay. I agree that instructional design is not merely a complicated process but a complex process. I think Rob does a great job of distinguishing the two. As Rob points out, design of instruction is not linear but a cyclical, iterative, and multilevel process. One cannot simply identify all of the variables, line them up, and then apply a formula that outputs an appropriate design. I think Rob is pointing out that many people do this and also think they are practicing instructional design. I agree that they are not.

But what is the route to understanding complexity? Good design (of any sort) always reminds me of what it takes to write a good story. It is one thing to know what are the elements of a story—such as knowing that a story should have a plot, character development, a narrative arc that develops some tension or unresolved conflict, resulting in a climatic ending—but it is quite another to practice this so as to write a good story, at least as judged by the reader. Where does that "special something" come from that distinguishes a good story from a poor one? Likewise, what triggers or informs those critical decisions that distinguish good from poor instructional designs? I am afraid that the formal instructional design process has never been the source for this creative "secret sauce." Instead, I think it comes from the creative and idiosyncratic capabilities and experiences of the designer and the task at hand. There is a literature about creative and innovative design, such as the work and writing that has come from IDEO (e.g., Kelley & Kelley, 2013). There are characteristics and traits that good designers seem to have, and we can at least expect creativity design to occur, but these are not fundamental outcomes that will result from only following the instructional design process.

Rob also seems to want to pick a fight with "educational technologists." I realize that the term has been appropriated by some to mean only K-12 educational technology and often times just a person who handles only technical support, but Rob does not make that too clear. But, even using a somewhat narrow definition of an educational technologist, I would argue that the best people to make instructional design decisions in a K-12 environment are still educational technologists, at least those who have teaching credentials and experience. The traits they have are likely more important than those outlined by the IBSTPI.[2] For example, I suspect these educational technologists are chock full of empathy for their learner audience. I believe that empathy is a very much neglected, yet essential, skill (or is it a trait?) that IBSTPI has unfortunately overlooked. For example, here are three of the twenty-two competencies for instructional designers by IBSTPI that address these issues:

- Identify and describe target population and environmental characteristics.
- Design instructional interventions.
- Develop instructional materials.

It is one thing to "identify and describe" the "population," but it is quite another to understand what it feels like to try to learn something from the point of view of the learner. Likewise, stating that design and development competencies are important does nothing to help a designer figure out how to achieve a creative design idea. This is why I think so much of instructional design continues to be based on content-heavy and content-centric models based on "present, practice, and test" strategies.

So I think instructional design is good at some things and poor at others. For example, I think a fundamental question for Dr. Branch is whether he views instructional design as an algorithm, a heuristic, or something in-between. Clearly, Rob does not see it as merely an algorithm, but nor do I think he sees it purely as a heuristic, as I do. That is, I believe that the instructional design process offers some general principles for initiating and managing a complex process, but it never leads far to the kinds of specific decisions that all designers ultimately have to make. As Michael Streibel (1991) long ago pointed out, instructional design is ultimately a situated act that depends "on the specific, concrete, and unique circumstances of the project" (p. 122).

Yes, when it comes to instructional design, Rob is a true believer. He understands its principles at a level that few others will ever attain. But, I do not think this understanding will be achieved by having people learn about complexity theory or the law of requisite variety as part of their instructional design education (ideas that are also not part of the IBSTPI's minimum competencies). Instead, this understanding will come from the thoughtful and reflective practice of instructional design, which I dare say is the same path Rob took to achieve his understanding. Like Rob, others will also need to continue their reading and study of the literature to see how the thoughtful ideas of others inform or align with their practice, necessitating at times shifting or changing one's practice accordingly. By doing so, they too will come to resonate with certain ideas and points of view, while deciding to leave other "tenets" by the wayside.

In my case, the design of learning environments will include some instructional design, but not that much. For Rob, it will likely all be about instructional design. But I worry that Rob will spend the rest of his career trying to explain to people what "true instructional design" is, but with very limited success. This reminds me of the joke by the comedian Steven Wright where he had invented the perfect business training game, but unfortunately it takes twenty-five years to play. Likely, it will take many years of experience, reflection, and study to master any design process that reliably helps people to learn or perform well and be inspired to do so.

Notes

1. I avoided the phrase "love-hate"; it is both trite and not accurate.
2. See http://ibstpi.org/.

References

Kelley, T., & Kelley, D. (2013). *Creative confidence: Unleashing the creative potential within us all.* New York: Crown Business.

Streibel, M. (1991). Instructional plans and situated learning: The challenge of Suchman's theory of situated action for instructional designers and instructional systems. In G. Anglin (Ed.), *Instructional technology: Past, present, and future* (p. 122). Englewood, CO: Libraries Unlimited.

REJOINDER BY ROBERT MARIBE BRANCH

Lloyd Rieber is perfect for this dialogue. His arguments are astute, yet modest, and he is an extraordinary instructional designer in his own right. Lloyd is extremely qualified in an extraordinary variety of areas within educational technology. His in-depth professional awareness of my instructional design philosophy and practice is accurately articulated throughout his reply. Dr. Rieber has firsthand knowledge of my approach to instructional design because he has actually observed me teaching a course on the introduction of instructional design, a course that I have taught for more than twenty-five years. I consider Professor Lloyd Rieber a consummate colleague and friend.

I maintain that true instructional design is a complex, yet creative, process. Indeed, professionals who practice true instructional design are required by the instructional design process to solicit input from the broadest range of stakeholders for whom the learning product will affect. Yes, "learning is always occurring," as we are reminded by Lloyd's comments, and, in fact, I agree that learning is omnipresent. Such learning can occur unintentionally, informally, through unplanned activities, and can be as valuable as any event in life that requires us to constantly process new information. While learning is a constant, instructional design is a process reserved for learning that has a specific goal or objective, and, thus, intentional. In other words, I believe there is a distinction between unintentional learning and intentional learning. While both are essential to learners of all ages throughout all stages of life, instructional design works best for spaces dedicated to intentional learning.

I concur with Dr. Rieber that "there are many paths to learning, with instruction being only one." There are also many paths to developing instruction other than instructional design. However, I think there is a distinction between instruction and instructional design. Instruction is one way to learn. Instructional design is one way to develop opportunities to learn. I agree with Lloyd "that providing instruction at the wrong time is quite detrimental to learning," and that is why instructional design is not appropriate for all teaching and learning situations. Indeed, the first step in any true instructional design process is to determine if instruction is the most appropriate approach for a particular educational situation.

While the instructional design process may be complex, the procedure for determining the need for instructional design is simple. Do not engage in instructional design if:

1. There is a performance discrepancy attributable to something other than a lack of knowledge or skill.
2. The performance discrepancy can be resolved by valid alternatives.
3. There is no need for measureable outcomes.

There are other similar conditions, but I believe these are essential to consider before attempting any instructional design process. I concur with Lloyd that sometimes "instruction is unnecessary." Formal instruction may not be the best approach to learning certain knowledge or a particular skill. This is particularly true when learning can be accomplished by alternatives to instruction, such as filling an information void, providing appropriate documentation, crafting effective job aids, offering timely feedback, modifying expectations, clarifying standards, and explaining consequences.

I wholeheartedly concur with Lloyd that "[t]here are characteristics and traits that good designers seem to have, and we can at least expect creativity design to occur, but these are not fundamental outcomes that will result from only following the instructional design process." However, I hope that creativity is an aspiration among all instructional designers and should be considered essential as instructional designers articulate the correlation between objectives, activities, and outcomes.

The purpose for mentioning educational technologists in a dialogue about instructional design is to indicate that one is part of the other, but the other is not part of the one. An instructional designer is an educational technologist, but an educational technologist may not necessarily be an instructional designer. Lloyd's right: I view instructional design as neither an algorithm nor a heuristic, but something in between. I regard instructional design as a structured problem-solving process. Yes, instructional design should be regarded as a situated act of initiating and managing the complexity of the variables associated with intentional learning spaces.

I stipulate that at a deep level of instructional design "understanding will come from the thoughtful and reflective practice of instructional design" as pointed out by Lloyd. My resolve, however, is that people who identify themselves as instructional designers are aware of the plethora of instructional design models and possess the expertise required to practice true instructional design. Instructional design is a complex endeavor where you are limited only by your creativity.

Part 2

Preparing Instructional Designers

INTRODUCTION TO PART 2

Based on a better sense of the nature of design from the prior section, our attention can turn to how we prepare instructional designers, learning technologists, and scientists. Included here are six contributions starting from the basic question of whether we start from the novice/expert gap or organize our preparation around simple versus complex activities. These dialogues address the nature of ill-structured complexity and how we foster expertise in responding to it with design, as well as the future of instructional technology as an avenue for understanding preparation programs.

Underlying these dialogues is the concern as to whether typical educational methods in ID/IT match the complexity of real-world ID problems or the basic identity of a designer. Those taking this view argue that ID preparation often focuses on models and linear processes that are effective for well-defined problems, while design problems are by nature ill-defined and ill-structured—what some would call "wicked" problems. This often results in under-conceptualization and over-specification (Weick) and fails to meet many client expectations or desires.

Fortney suggests teaching the basic thought processes of design prior to teaching explicit instructional design. As we consider how to prepare instructional designers, Fortney's suggestion is to help instructional designers focus on the emotional as well as cognitive needs of learners, introducing complexity instead of simplifying it and allowing novice instructional designers to begin to understand the real-world constraints under which ID is conducted. Boling responds with general agreement but adds that things in this direction are already happening, such as studio teaching and generation of precedent material, direct observations, and increased expert guest speakers.

Smith argues that we should move beyond educating with the express purpose of closing the expert/novice gaps in our learners, and instead focus on design education as a potential site for surfacing and challenging, even remaking the discipline itself. Hirumi supports this notion of ID preparation with a connection to preparing physicians and the struggles to encourage significant creativity among learners in both fields.

Visscher-Voerman proposes ingredients for future programs, such as emphasizing boundary-crossing competencies of "T-shaped professionals" and immersing students in the complexity of real-world problems. Tracey responds with agreement on the ingredients and adds suggestions regarding how to help students think as designers and develop their professional identity.

Boling argues that design is a complex performance, contrary to what is implied by the common approach of simplifying and teaching instructional design as a process of following models and prescriptive theories, as so many of us do. Merrill counters this position with the suggestion that closer examination of recent models shows them to support a progression of increasingly complex tasks rather than simplifying instructional design.

Merrill then articulates hopes for the future of instructional technology, particularly as it may relate to undergraduate programs, emphases on the science of instruction, and restructuring master's programs to prepare students to manage designers-by-assignment and to create ID tools. Dousay counters Merrill's suggestions particularly around the undergraduate programs by pointing out that such programs have existed for decades and considers implications for curriculum compression.

The final dialogue for this section on instructional design preparation comes from Tracey, who revisits the possibility of making stronger connections between ID and other design fields and argues that we need to focus on helping our students develop their full professional identities—that we need to go beyond a focus on "what," that is, on teaching design processes, and instead focus on "who," that is, educating designers. Hokanson cautions that this position should not be taken simply as a call to embrace "design thinking."

Chapter 7

Developing Design Expertise

Kathleen Fortney

As a practitioner who leads instructional design teams that create custom solutions for corporate learning and performance problems, one of the more vexing problems that I frequently face is how to foster design expertise in my less-experienced colleagues and, in some cases, my clients. My experience has been that many instructional designers view the problems that they face as well-structured problems for which a single correct solution can be found. Jonassen (2000), however, classified design problems as being among the most ill-structured problems. Design problems tend to have multiple possible solutions, and the criteria used to evaluate solutions is often unclear at the outset of instructional design projects. Failure to recognize the ill-structured nature of instructional design projects can result in poorly conceived or inadequate solutions; inability to meet stakeholders' expectations and program goals; and frustration for both the instructional designers and the project sponsors. While I do what I can to mentor my colleagues to avoid such failures, I believe that instructional designers are thwarted in their design expertise trajectories by academic and industry educational programs that put the emphasis on instructional design models and processes, rather than on problem solving. In other words, I believe that the education of instructional designers needs to first emphasize the thought processes involved in design in general before tackling the specific nature of instructional design problems.

Silber (2007) suggests that instructional design is not the systematic procedure described in leading textbooks and taught in universities but rather the moderately to ill-structured problem solving that makes use of principles and design thinking. Silber advocated for a cognitivist approach that involved presenting learners with principles and their relationships, use of "heuristics for defining the problem space and solving the problem" (p. 12), scaffolded practice, and opportunities for reflection on outcomes. While this approach more closely approximates the ways in which instructional designers operate in workplace settings than the procedural approaches found in many instructional design textbooks (see, for example, Smith & Ragan, 2004, or Dick, Carey & Carey, 2005), it fails to address some fundamental issues. One danger is that novice instructional designers will attempt to design instruction by slavishly applying rules, a practice that is painfully apparent in the one-size-fits-all approaches one sees in many corporate training departments. The other problem is that even skillful application of the principles is no guarantee that the end result will be an effective instructional product. As Rowland (1994) describes with regard to a music composition course, rules do little to help one create or transform bad ideas into good.

How, then, can we develop instructional designers in a way that helps them create new ideas or solve the problems that they encounter in the workplace?

Cross (2001) describes various types of knowledge that designers possess as deriving from participating in, and reflecting upon, design activities as well as the creation of artifacts, as well as knowledge that is embodied in artifacts and gained from the use of those artifacts, and reflecting on the use of the artifacts. Cross builds upon Schön's description (1992) of design as a reflective activity where "design knowledge is knowing in action, revealed in and by actual designing" (p. 3). While instructional design courses typically engage students in the design and creation of instructional products, and thus begin the process of acquiring the knowledge that comes through action, reflection not only upon those processes but artifacts that embody good design is a critical factor in developing the ability to think like a designer. More importantly, such reflection needs to include some way to trigger an appreciation for what distinguishes good designs from bad.

Norman (2004) presents three levels of design that govern the way that we perceive products that we encounter: the *visceral* level, which concerns our involuntary, subconscious responses to sensory aspects of objects; the *behavioral* level, which involves function and usability; and the *reflective* level, which provides enduring aspects of meaning to product consumers. Norman refers to the consideration of these levels during the design process as *emotional design*—that is, design that appeals to both our rational, cognitive selves and our emotional selves.

In the field of instructional design, failure to incorporate the emotional elements that enhance learner engagement, foster motivation, and encourage persistence can result in mind-numbing courses that on the surface follow the rules but ultimately fail to serve the purpose for which they were intended. Dirksen (2012) stresses the need to appeal to emotions through stories, surprise, collaboration, and appropriate use of graphics to create effective designs. In instructional design education, making learners aware of the need to address both the cognitive and the emotional needs of learners, and examination of well-designed instructional products coupled with reflective activities, is an approach that can enhance learners' abilities to think like designers.

Yet another way we can prepare instructional designers is to introduce them to the realities of design activities. First and foremost is fostering recognition that problems are not always what they seem to be; that is, restructuring the problem may be necessary to find creative solutions (Akin, 1994). Ertmer et al. (2008) found that shaping of the problem space is one element that distinguishes expert instructional designers from novices, and they suggest ways to develop this ability in students, such as use of case studies and guidelines that encourage students to consider broader aspects of the problem. When I used case studies with graduate students in an advanced instructional design course, several students expressed surprise and even dismay at the layered complexity and problems described, but the experienced instructional designers confirmed the authenticity of the situations. I believe that the collaborative engagement that occurred during these discussions helped the less-experienced students start to develop some designerly ways of looking at problems.

Yet another area where we can do a better job of preparing novice instructional designers is to introduce them to the constraints and ambiguity that are inherent in real-world design problems. Lawson (2006) describes design problems as being "full of uncertainties" (p. 120) and notes that the goals and the importance of design parameters often change during the design process. These issues are not visible in academic design projects, where the objectives and priorities are typically well within the students' control. In the workplace, though, designers must contend with constraints and judgments imposed by interaction with clients, users, and a host of other stakeholders. As Lawson points out, "Designers, unlike artists, cannot devote themselves exclusively to problems which are of interest to themselves personally" (p. 88). Organizing academic projects in a way that introduces students to constraints and shifting priorities—for example, by introducing a client other than the instructor to the mix—may develop a greater tolerance for ambiguity and appreciation of the difficulties inherent in designing within externally imposed parameters.

Given that design knowledge is developed through experiencing the design process and reflecting on the experience and the artifacts of those processes, academic programs are unlikely to develop high levels of expertise in instructional design students. Such programs can, however, start students on the trajectory to expertise by arming them with the tools and concepts of designer thinking in addition to the instructional models and principles that have formed the mainstay of instructional design education.

References

Akin, O. (1994). Creativity in design. *Performance Improvement Quarterly, 7*(3), 9–21.

Cross, N. (2001). Designerly ways of knowing: Design discipline versus design science. *Design Issues, 17*(3), 49–55.

Dick, W., Carey, L., & Carey, J. (2005). *The systematic design of instruction* (6th ed.). New York: Pearson/Allyn & Bacon.

Dirksen, J. (2012). *Design for how people learn.* Berkeley, CA: New Riders.

Ertmer, P. A., Stepich, D. A., York, C. S., Stickman, A., Wu, L., Zurek, S., & Goktas, Y. (2008). How instructional design experts use knowledge and experience to solve ill-structured problems. *Performance Improvement Quarterly, 21*(1), 17–42.

Jonassen, D. H. (2000). Toward a design theory of problem solving. *Educational Technology Research & Development, 48*, 63–85.

Lawson, B. (2006). *How designers think* (4th ed.). Oxford, UK: Architectural Press.

Norman, D. A. (2004). *Emotional design: Why we love (or hate) everyday things.* New York: Basic Books.

Rowland, G. (1994). It's the sound! *Performance Improvement Quarterly, 7*(3), 3–6.

Schön, D. A. (1992). Designing as reflective conversation with the materials of a design situation. *Knowledge-based Systems Journal, 5*(1), 3–14.

Silber, K. H. (2007). A principle-based model of instructional design: A new way of thinking about and teaching ID. *Educational Technology, 47*(5), 5–19.

Smith, P. L., & Ragan, T. L. (2004). *Instructional design* (3rd ed.). New York: John Wiley & Sons.

RESPONSE BY ELIZABETH BOLING

I spent a decade as a practitioner managing development teams working with instructional designers before joining the university. I observed in the field that the animators, illustrators, graphic designers, and interface designers on my teams were *designing*, whereas most of the instructional designers were following process models, believing that these would yield design solutions—leading to all the difficulties detailed by Kathleen Fortney in her thoughtful statement. As Fortney has done, I diagnosed the primary cause of these problems to be the academic and industry preparation of most instructional designers. I am in fundamental agreement with Fortney's position in this. I will note, however, some discrepancies between Fortney's view of the academic position on instructional design (ID) and what is actually happening, and I call for practitioners to join the effort to improve the academic preparation of instructional designers.

Views of design and pedagogy among academics in the field *are* expanding. Patrick Parrish's study of Dewey's aesthetics (2009) and of literature (2014) have yielded rich views of the experiential qualities of learning. Gibbons (2013) has drawn on engineering design and architecture to propose a large-scale conception of design not based in a process model, and affording scope for designers to work outside boundaries of prescriptive theories. Some scholars have focused on designers themselves, filling a gap in the traditional conception of ID identified in 2009 (Smith & Boling)—the contribution to, or role of, designers within the systematic process models representing scientific design. Yanchar and Gabbitas (2011) apply the constructs of philosophy to conclude that designers' choices are not model-driven but actually adhere to a "conceptual design sense" (p. 385), similar to what Nelson and Stolterman (2012) term *core judgment*. Campbell, Schwier and Kenny (2009) have investigated change agency as a core identity issue for instructional designers, and they discuss the ways in which the practice of instructional design exceeds the boundaries of traditional process models.

Practitioners have a major role to play in revising and improving the way that instructional design is taught. Two forms of involvement are critical: documentation and dissemination of precedent, and engagement with ID programs in colleges and universities. Precedent—direct observations or vicarious observations via representations of designs that convey their literal and experiential qualities to other designers—is the raw material from which any designer takes action in a new design situation (Boling, 2010). In most fields where design is practiced, such representations are produced for conferences, contests, curated collections, magazines, books, and catalogs, but these are almost entirely lacking in instructional design. We have almost no precedent available beyond closed collections of projects and postmortem reports maintained inside some organizations and a few public venues (the Association for Educational Communications and Technology Design & Development showcase, the peer-reviewed online journal *International Journal of Designs for Learning* [*IJDL*]). Much of the precedent available in these venues is produced by academics who engage in instructional design—valuable enough, but a narrow subset of the instructional design carried out in the field, practitioners whose primary professional activity is instructional design. Our preparation for ID practice does not stress, or even include, the expectation that our graduates should engage in disseminating precedent, and we do not teach them how to do so. It is not surprising, therefore, that professionals in the field, while recognizing that precedent can be useful for themselves, do not engage in preparing or disseminating precedent outside their own organizations on any discernable scale. This is a gap in practice created by a gap in preparation; the gap perpetuates itself because without a robust and renewing course of precedent to use in the classroom, it is difficult to demonstrate the value of this form of design knowledge to our students.

Practitioners in our field also need to participate in improving design education for IDs through direct engagement with programs. In addition to occasional appearances as speakers in colloquia, frequent and substantive interaction on the part of practitioners with students would establish the expectation for graduates that they should engage in such interactions themselves. In traditional fields of design such interactions include widespread, employer-supported, formal internship programs with well-established expectations for the kinds of experiences those programs will include. Client relationships associated with service learning or project-based learning need to be augmented with practitioner relationships between students and instructional designers. These might be as targeted and short term as the guest critiques routinely scheduled for design students in other fields, or as substantive and prolonged as visiting scholar and professor of practice appointments to our faculties.

References

Boling, E. (2010). The need for design cases: Disseminating design knowledge. *International Journal of Designs for Learning, 1*(1), 1–8.

Campbell, K., Schwier, R. A., & Kenny, R. F. (2009). Agency of the instructional designer: Moral coherence and transformative social practice. In J. W. Willis (Ed.), *Constructivist Instructional Design (C-ID): Foundations, models and examples* (pp. 243–264). Charlotte, NC: Information Age Publishing, Inc.

Gibbons, A. (2013). *An architectural approach to instructional design*. New York: Routledge.

Nelson, H., & Stolterman, E. (2012). *The design way: Intentional change in an unpredictable world*. Boston, MA: The MIT Press.

Parrish, P. (2009). Aesthetic principles of instructional design. *Educational Technology Research and Development, 57*(4), 511–528.

Parrish, P. (2014). Designing for the half-known world: Lessons for instructional designers from the craft of narrative fiction. In B. Hokanson & A. Gibbons (Eds.), *Design in educational technology* (pp. 261–270). Cham, Switzerland: Springer.

Smith, K. M., & Boling, E. (2009). What do we make of design? Design as a concept in educational technology. *Educational Technology*, July/August, 2009.

Yanchar, S., & Gabbitas, B. (2011). Between eclecticism and orthodoxy in instructional design. *Educational Technology Research and Development, 59*(3), 383–398.

REJOINDER BY KATHLEEN FORTNEY

I am encouraged by Dr. Boling's report that academic institutions are expanding their view of instructional design beyond the traditional process model approach to foster core judgment and introduce change agency to instructional design students. A more comprehensive view of instructional design will better prepare students for the challenges that they may face in practice, easing their transition into the workplace. I also agree that exposure to a variety of design representations is a key element in development of design thinking and judgment.

I do disagree, however, with Boling's contention that opportunities to view designs are "almost entirely lacking in instructional design." Boling (2010) states, "the design case is a description of a real artifact or experience that has been intentionally designed" (p. 2), and goes on to say, "A case may be as minimal as an individual image." While it is true that issues of confidentiality and competitive advantage prevent instructional designers in some organizations from sharing all the details of their projects, a plethora of design cases can be found on learning blogs, such as the Rapid eLearning Blog and Cathy Moore's popular site; in online communities of practice, such as LinkedIn groups; at industry award presentations, such as the Brandon Hall awards; and in the journals and conference presentations of industry organizations, such as the Association for Talent Development (ATD), the International Society for Performance Improvement (ISPI), and the eLearning Guild. Design examples can also be found in a number of excellent books aimed at practitioners (see, for example, Dirksen, 2012 and Kapp, 2012). Many of these design cases include descriptions of the target audiences, objectives, challenges, and constraints that the instructional designer faced during the design process, as well as the outcomes achieved through implementation of the learning design.

Many of my most effective learning program designs have elements of design cases that I have seen in publications or heard about at professional conferences. Conversations with other instructional designers about design cases, either online or during face-to-face meetings, have provided valuable information that I have used to adapt design ideas to my projects. The amount of attention that Boling (2010) expends to distinguish design cases from design research, though, leads me to believe that our different opinions about the availability of design cases arises from the differences in the publications that we read and the professional gatherings that we attend. It may be the case that those instructional design students who are headed to industry would be better served by practitioner organizations and resources than by research-oriented academic organizations like Association for Educational Communications and Technology (AECT).

Which is not to say that those of us in industry do not value academic research; evidence provided by research provides the foundation for effective design. Engagement of practitioners in the academic process, as suggested by Boling, can keep practitioners in touch with research trends upon which to base their designs and also provide researchers insights into industry trends that warrant investigation. In a similar vein, researchers and academic instructors might benefit from venturing out of the university to engage directly with practitioners in organizational settings or professional conferences, as well as by familiarizing themselves with the publications used by practitioners. I believe that doing so would bring more design cases into the classroom.

Industry partnerships with academic institutions might help bridge some of these gaps. I agree that formal internship programs can provide valuable experience for instructional design students. One challenge in organizing such internships is that the capricious nature of many instructional design projects, coupled with the constraints presented by academic calendars, makes it difficult to engage students in meaningful design that they can follow from beginning to end. An extended internship or practicum that engaged students throughout their academic program in activities with an industry instruction design team might traverse these limitations to provide students with a deeper understanding of their chosen field. Key requirements for a successful program would be an organization with a proven commitment to employee development that could sustain an extended partnership, and an academic institution that recognizes the need to prepare instructional design students to work in nonacademic settings. Such a partnership could serve as a model for developing successful instructional design practitioners.

References

Boling, E. (2010). The need for design cases: Disseminating design knowledge. *International Journal of Designs for Learning, 1*(1), 1–8.

Dirksen, J. (2012). *Design for how people learn.* Berkeley, CA: New Riders.

Kapp, K. (2012). *The gamification of learning and instruction: Game-based methods and strategies for training and education.* San Francisco, CA: Pfeiffer.

Chapter 8

Design Education as a Site for Educating Disciplines

Kennon M. Smith

The immediate, visible purpose of most design education activities is to assist individuals in developing greater levels of design expertise. While this end-goal is a sufficient rationale for engaging in the considerable effort of design education enterprises, it need not be their only tangible return. Design education, even while it fosters current design expertise in an individual, is an invaluable site for reshaping what will constitute future design expertise in a discipline.

If design education is concerned with fostering the individual development of design expertise, the endeavor begs the question of what constitutes the qualities of expertise toward which the student should be working. Indeed, considerable effort has been expended across disciplines to study differences between novice and expert designers. Typically this is done with a view toward identifying gaps in the skill, knowledge, or attitudes possessed by individuals in these respective groups and then developing educational experiences that will help the novice bridge those gaps. In other words, when these studies are considered through the lens of design education, they are often interpreted with a view toward changing novices. While of significant value, when presented through such a lens these studies often do not acknowledge a basic underlying assumption—that current manifestations of expert practice are the most desirable end goal for the novice, that current practice and current framing of the profession should be the target to which novices aspire. While many novices do eventually modify their thinking and behavior to bring them more in line with that permeating the field they join, educator-scholars should not assume this is always desirable or that the conflicts surfaced as novices first encounter an area of study cannot influence and challenge disciplinary positions.

Design Education as a Site for Surfacing and Challenging Disciplinary Definitions

There are alternate ways of viewing differences between novices and experts—differences that often become visible when novices intersect with their chosen design field upon entering a formal design education program. As disciplinary beliefs are communicated (intentionally or unintentionally) to students through the traditions embodied in the language and practices of their design education experiences, some portion of these traditions is likely to seem foreign upon first exposure. This very foreignness, and its accompanying tensions, may help draw the attention of both students and educator-scholars to areas of particular concern in evaluating current disciplinary conceptions of design, and shaping future dimensions of the discipline.

The initial intersection between novices and design education settings is conducive to surfacing disciplinary attributes in at least two ways. First, these settings encourage, and often necessitate, the explicit communication of foundational ideas that may remain implicit among professionals already fully assimilated into a given field's traditions. Second, conflicts that inevitably arise as novices begin to function within the cultural traditions of a discipline (as translated into a design education setting) may point to areas that legitimately deserve greater scrutiny within the discipline. Student difficulties present an opportunity to expose ways of thinking and acting in disciplinary practice that are counterproductive, contradictory, or incomplete, but that may be repeated because they are so engrained. Novices, in their interactions with what appears to be strange or foreign in a new discipline, can challenge assumptions and practices that are no longer visible to individuals fully assimilated into the culture of the profession and can encourage innovations that might otherwise not be considered.

Assumptions

In making these assertions, I am grounding my argument in underlying assumptions. First, influenced by the work of Simon (2001), I take the position that the activities and outcomes of design are artificial constructions in the sense that they do not exist *a priori*. I operate from the supposition that design disciplines (in ways that parallel the products of their creation) are constructions that can be intentionally shaped if they are systematically studied. Second, I take the position that design disciplines, while not equivalent to one another, can usefully inform one another's debates. As a designer and educator, my most recent work has been conducted in the fields of architecture and interior design, and examples below will be drawn from these traditions. In borrowing across disciplinary boundaries, I do not assume that one design profession or another has the prerogative to settle questions regarding what is good in design, or that the histories of one design field can be uncritically adopted as "lessons learned" for another design field. In spite of these potential limits on generalizability, I do assert that allied design fields share a kind of family resemblance that may make concerns or findings that have surfaced in one field potentially instructive in matters of self-reflection in other fields, and thus worthy of consideration.

Design Education as a Site for Explicating Hidden Assumptions (Language)

While incoming novices may hold naïve conceptions of design, the inevitable conflict between their initial conceptions and the ideas embedded in projects and dialogue with peers and instructors affords opportunities to make visible the ideas and beliefs they have, as well as those of the more experienced designers with whom they interact. As novices attempt to come to terms with new conceptions of design, students, teachers, and professionals must often operationalize and communicate their own beliefs and convictions regarding design—thus forcing into the open through dialogue and conflict many of the foundational ideas and traditions that remain implicit in dialogue with other professionals.

There is a significant tradition in design pedagogy literature of examining dialogue between students and instructors (e.g., Schon, 1987; Goldschmidt, 2010). More recently, the 2014 Design Thinking Research Symposium was based entirely on recorded examples of student-teacher interactions across a variety of design studios. Such literature can and should be used to inform dialogue regarding the foundational assumptions within the various design fields they represent.

Design Education as a Site for Revealing Potentially Counterproductive Practices (Behaviors)

While many struggles faced by students are inevitable byproducts of the very hard but worthwhile work necessitated in acquiring disciplinary knowledge and skills, there may be instances in which novices' difficulties are indicators of something amiss in disciplinary traditions. In such cases, instead of dismissing them as deficiencies to be overcome, it is more useful to reframe student difficulties as potential indicators of those areas in which it may be as productive to challenge the status quo.

An example of this can be seen in traditional architectural education. It has been common practice in such a setting that students be inducted into a culture that practices public, adversarial critiques of student work. It has been acknowledged that such experiences can be harrowing for students and potentially harmful to the long-term development of expertise (Anthony, 1991). In response, the emphasis has usually been on teaching the student to cope with the system (e.g., Parnell & Sara, 2007), while little has typically been done to reexamine whether the system is really most effective. More recently there has been a growing backlash against these practices, with increasing recognition that they may be damaging to the profession as well as to individual students. For example, there is some thought that the adversarial culture fostered by these critique traditions may limit the number of people from traditionally underrepresented populations who decide to enter the profession after graduation. Additionally, there is growing concern that the exaggerated sense of competition fostered by such public exercises in humiliation may contribute to some of the cut-throat tactics that leave architectural firms willing to invest small fortunes in competitions from which they are unlikely to win contracts. While it is overstating circumstances to suggest that adversarial critique traditions are the sole cause of these larger difficulties, it is instructive to recognize that novice reactions to particularly adversarial critiques have hinted for generations that something was broken in the system—something that is now more generally recognized within the profession and educational systems at large.

Implications

If studies conducted within design education settings can be recast not only as opportunities for improving pedagogical practices but also as contexts for surfacing points of unnecessary friction for fruitful reconsideration, at least two implications follow. First, students may begin to be seen as partners in the disciplines they seek to enter, valued not only because they may make future contributions as disciplinary experts but also because they can make current contributions as disciplinary novices who can see conditions that are no longer visible to individuals fully inducted into the field. This capability to see conditions as strange, as *other*, may be short-lived and should be leveraged to its fullest extent before novices forget their discomfort.

Second, when design education is seen as a site concerned with both educating the student and evaluating the discipline, existing research efforts can be leveraged more fully to help disciplines shape current classroom practices and predict future conceptions of design likely to permeate disciplines populated in coming years by today's students. Systematic study of student and instructor behaviors—in terms of both language and practices—may elucidate intentional and unintentional messages being communicated in this environment, facilitate changes where needed, and help shape future directions for the classroom and the profession.

Conclusion

Conceptions of design have evolved over time, many such conceptions co-exist at any time, and in time design can be changed through purposive interventions. It is not necessary for the activities of design or for the outcomes of such activities to remain as they are. We make design. Indeed, we are in the very process of making it. If we so choose, we can remake it. The voices of design novices, as well as design experts, can and should contribute to the ongoing dialogues that make and remake our conceptions of design. Design education can inform such dialogue by forcing implicit assumptions into the open and by exposing tensions that arise when individuals not fully initiated into disciplinary culture are confronted with traditional assumptions and practices. Design education can become a site not only of educating novices but also of educating disciplines.

References

Anthony, K. H. (1991). *Design juries on trial: The Renaissance of the design studio*. New York: Van Nostrand Reinhold.

Goldschmidt, G., Hochman, H., & Dafni, I. (2010). The design studio "crit": Teacher-student communication. *Artificial Intelligence for Engineering Design, Analysis and Manufacturing, 24*(3), 285–302.

Parnell, R., & Sara, R. (2007). *The crit: An architecture student's handbook*. Amsterdam: Elsevier.

Schon, D. A. (1987). Educating the reflective practitioner: Toward a new design for teaching and learning in the professions. San Francisco, CA: Jossey-Bass.

Simon, H. A. (2001). *The sciences of the artificial* (3rd ed.). Cambridge, MA: The MIT Press.

RESPONSE BY ATSUSI HIRUMI

Revealing foundational ideas about design expertise and conflicts with creativity, Smith posits that design education offers invaluable opportunities to reshape the field. She suggests that initial discourse between novices and experts may reveal foundational ideas and hidden assumptions about the field that may otherwise remain implicit, and that conflicts that arise during such interactions may expose counterproductive practices that may necessitate change to improve the field. She also believes that insights gained for related disciplines of interest may prove useful for advancing the field of instructional design. I would agree. Recent discussions with students in my introductory graduate instructional design (ID) course about the differences between novices and experts, and fostering creativity, illustrate these three points.

In my intro design course, students often ask, "What's the difference between novice and expert instructional designers?" Students want to know what constitutes "expertise" in design, and what they can or should do to gain such expertise to enhance their chances for employment. Job announcements frequently use years of experience to discriminate novice and expert designers but do not always elaborate on the skills, knowledge, attitudes, and abilities that distinguish such expertise. Systematic design skills, interpersonal communications, and teamwork are essential, but concrete measures of how such skills differ among novice and expert designers remain somewhat elusive.

My standard response to the students questions regarding expert vs. novice designers use to be based on a review of expert-novice research across disciplines. In short, experts notice more details and patterns that are more readily retrieved within strategically organized content knowledge, and experts apply an adaptive set of skills and knowledge to formulate unique solutions to given problems based on context (Bransford, Brown & Cocking, 1999). Then, I used to refer students to more recent studies within the ID and performance improvement fields by Ertmer et al. (2009), Hardre, Ge and Thomas (2006), and Fortney and Yamagata-Lynch (2013) among others (e.g., Perez & Emery, 1995) for further details.

Recent collaboration with physicians and software engineers on the design, development, and testing of a virtual patient simulation (Hirumi et al., 2016a; Hirumi et al., 2016b; Hirumi, Johnson & Reyes, 2015; Hirumi, 2014) made the distinctions between novices and experts more explicit. Specifically, I learned that expert and novice healthcare professionals may use fundamentally different problem-solving skills. Novice clinicians may rely on algorithms grounded in basic science, whereas experts may use heuristics based on experience and pattern recognition to diagnose and treat patients. In other words, experts may formulate better solutions to more varied and complex problems faster and with less apparent effort than novices because they use automated, analogical thinking skills, rather than deliberate, analytical design skills (Jonassen, 2011). By making the notion that professionals may use either or both analytical and analogical reasoning to solve problems explicit during conversations between novices and experts, we may better delineate what constitutes design expertise and create experiences that help novices automate basic design tasks that, in turn, may allow them to be more creative and spend more time innovating ways to advance research, theory, and practice.

My work with physicians and software engineers, and related medical education research and literature on the development of clinical reasoning skills (e.g., Higgs, Jones, Loftus & Christensen, 2008), revealed a number of ideas about the differences between experts and novices and gave me insights from related disciplines that may prove useful for advancing the ID field as Smith suggests. Conflicts with students in my basic ID course also revealed counterproductive practices that may necessitate change in my course and potentially other basic ID courses to improve the field.

For decades, creativity has driven the upward mobility, health, and prosperity of individuals in both industrialized and developing nations. In today's global economy, creativity is essential to remain competitive. In a 2010 survey, over two thousand business managers and executives identified creativity as one of four essential Cs (in addition to collaboration, communications, and critical thinking) for twenty-first-century business growth and success. However, conflicts occur when I push students to be creative in their designs in my intro ID course. When given the option, the majority choose to apply teacher-directed instructional strategies because they are more familiar and comfortable with such traditional methods. When asked to use more modern, learner-centered approaches, students often struggle and have difficulties communicating their designs.

The fundamental conflict appears to lie between current conceptions of operational excellence and creativity. In business and industry, excellence is often associated with compliance, reducing variance, and eliminating errors—all practices that are contrary to creativity. In my case, I prepare graduate students to follow a well-defined systematic process, to ensure their designs are grounded in research and theory, and to meet high-quality design standards. I train students to use data to inform analysis, design, and evaluation in an effective, efficient, and systematic manner. Based on input received from graduates and their employers, I feel confident that my courses help prepare good instructional designers with strong ID skills. However, I now see how explicit standards coupled with high expectations may inhibit, rather than foster, students' creativity.

Table 8.1 compares psychological conditions that have been found to inhibit and catalyze creativity. When I first compiled this list (Hirumi, 2013), I was shocked to see how many different ways I was inhibiting, rather than fostering creativity.

What makes such insights even more surprising is that when I ask students how I could better catalyze creativity, most recommend focusing on the design of more innovative, student-centered learning environments in other advanced classes. Evidently, learning how to follow a systematic design process in an intro design course is challenging enough. But at this point, I still wonder what is more counterproductive: asking novices to formulate innovative design solutions, or pushing them meet high quality design standards in a manner that inhibits creativity. While I may not have the answer, I do hope exposing such tensions—along with the notion that experts may use automated, analogical thinking skills based on pattern recognition to solve problems—may help inform the design field.

Table 8.1 Psychological Conditions That Have Been Found to Impede and Promote Creativity

Inhibitors	Catalysts
concentration	unfocused attention
seriousness	playfulness
decisiveness/certainty	contemplative/flexible
stress/demand/pressure	calm/unpressured/relaxed
efficiency/productivity	exploratory/experimental
compliance/error free	open/constructive failure

References

Bransford, J. D., Brown, A. L., & Cocking, R. R. (1999). *How people learn: Brain, mind, experience and school*. Washington, DC: National Academy Press.

Ertmer, P. A., Stepich, D. A., Flanagan, S., Kocaman-Karoglu, A., Reiner, C., Reyes, L., & Ushigusa, S. (2009). Impact of guidance on the problem-solving efforts of instructional design novices. *Performance Improvement Quarterly, 21*(4), 117–132.

Fortney, K. S., & Yamagata-Lynch, L. C. (2013). How instructional designers solve workspace problems. *Performance Improvement Quarterly, 25*(4), 91–109.

Hardre, P. L., Ge, X., & Thomas, M. K. (2006). An investigation of development toward instructional design expertise. *Performance Improvement Quarterly, 19*(4), 63–90.

Higgs, J., Jones, M. A., Loftus, S., & Christensen, N. (2008). *Clinical reasoning in the health professions* (3rd ed.). Philadelphia, PA: Elsevier Limited.

Hirumi, A. (2013). *Fostering innovation and creativity through e-learning, e-teaching and InterPLAY: Essential skills for the 21st century*. Invited keynote presentation at the 7th International Conference on e-Learning and e-Teaching, Shiraz, Iran, Feb. 13–14.

Hirumi, A. (2014). *Advancing virtual patient simulations with InterPLAY: Examining the role of ID principles and practices*. Concurrent Session presented the annual Association for Educational Communication and Technology conference, Jacksonville, FL. Nov. 5–9.

Hirumi, A., Johnson, T., & Reyes, R. J. (2015). *Field-testing strategies to improve the integration of virtual patient simulations into medical school curriculum*. Concurrent session presented the annual Association for Educational Communication and Technology conference, Indianapolis, IN. Nov. 4–6.

Hirumi, A., Johnson, T., Reyes, R., Johnson, K., Rivera-Gutierrez, D., Kleinsmith, A., Kubovec, S., Eakins, M., Bogert, K., Lok, B., & Cendan, J. (2016a). Advancing virtual patient simulations through design research and interPLAY: Part II: Testing and integration. *Educational Technology, Research & Development*. doi:10.1007/s11423-016-9461-6

Hirumi, A., Kleinsmith, A., Johnson, K., Kubovec, S., Eakins, M., Bogert, K., Rivera-Gutierrez, D., Reyes, R. J., Lok, B., & Cendan, J. (2016b). Advancing virtual patient simulations through design research and interPLAY: Part I: Design and development. *Educational Technology, Research & Development, 64*(4), 763–785.

Jonassen, D. (2011). *Learning to solve problems: A handbook for designing problem-solving learning environments*. New York: Routledge.

Perez, R. S., & Emery, C. D. (1995). Designer thinking: How novices and experts think about instructional design. *Performance Improvement Quarterly, 8*(3), 80–95.

REJOINDER BY KENNON M. SMITH

The following will be more an extension of, than rejoinder to, the ideas presented by Atsusi Hirumi in his response to my statements regarding the role of design education as a site for surfacing insights to the dispositions and values of design disciplines. The example raised by Atsusi Hirumi, the tensions that may arise as teachers encourage creativity and students seek tried and tested pathways for realizing effective instructional designs, presents significant opportunities for discussion within the field's educational and professional settings. While there have been some discussions about creativity in the discipline's literature and the topic may be raised by individuals, the field's foundational literature (as embodied in disciplinary definitions, professional standards, and introductory textbooks) has tended to emphasize other considerations in service of replicability, reliability, and efficiency (Smith & Boling, 2009), while giving little if any attention to dialogue about the benefits and/or pitfalls of creativity as a goal or concern for instructional design.

The dialogue ensuing from Atsusi Hirumi's example of tensions surfaced through interactions with students could be taken in many different directions. Below I will briefly explore some of the questions that might ensue. Because my most recent work has been in the areas of architecture and interior design, I will use these disciplines (which have long traditions of emphasizing creativity) as points of contrast.

What Would Be the Benefits, if Any, in Pursuing Creativity in Instructional Design? To Whom Would These Benefits Devolve?

In disciplines like architecture, it has often been designers and clients that enjoy the most visible, immediate benefits of design solutions recognized as being exceptionally creative. Designers win awards, and clients often have profiles raised through the publicity attached to a particularly creative building. Traditionally, the actual occupants of exceptionally creative buildings have sometimes benefitted from these designs, but prestige buildings have actually all-too-often sacrificed comfort and functionality for the sake of novelty (see Brand, 1994). More recently, disciplines concerned with the built environment have developed greater awareness of sustainable-building strategies. These pressures have raised awareness of the occupant experience and the long-term functioning of the building, in some cases leading to creative solutions that prioritize user experiences. If instructional designers are to increasingly value creativity in design, it will be important to do so with a clear-eyed view of how and for whom such creative solutions are pursued.

What Value-Added Could Be Provided by Creative Instructional Design?

As pointed out above, other disciplines have developed a history of recognizing benefits associated with particularly novel solutions. While it is easy to imagine that the intention behind a particularly creative architectural solution might be to communicate characteristics such as wealth, power, or sophistication, a creative instructional design endeavor might not be pursued for the same intentions. What, then, could be the advantages of creative instructional design? Perhaps creativity could be pursued for the sake of creating particularly motivating or engaging designs—motivating and engaging in part because the experiences they provide are in some way distinct or unexpected when compared to other instructional or educational experiences.

Who Would Assume the Risks, if Any, Associated with Creative Design?

In the built environment, it is widely recognized and accepted that there are risks associated with the creation of particularly novel design solutions. Legend has it that Frank Lloyd Wright, one of the most recognized and creative architects of the twentieth century, dismissed complaints that his unconventional building solutions led to leaky roofs by responding something along the lines of, "Of course it leaks. That's how you know it's a roof." Whether this story is true or merely one of the myths that has developed around this eccentric and undeniably creative designer, it foregrounds the acknowledgment that, in architecture, creative design solutions have potentially difficult consequences—precisely because they are innovative and often unproven. I do not imagine anyone in the instructional design discipline would endorse a similarly cavalier dismissal of legitimate concerns (nor am I suggesting they should), but this anecdote raises the question of risk-tolerance in the pursuit of novel, sometimes even untested, solutions and foregrounds the dilemma of who should bear liability burdens should failure ensue.

Is There a Safe Place for Exploring Exceptionally Creative Design While Mitigating Risks?

Within architecture, there is a centuries-old tradition of designers creating proposals that will never be built in their lifetimes. These buildings exceed technological constraints, budgetary limits, and other resources, and yet they are often the recipients of considerable time and attention. Architects have demonstrated a willingness to propose and publicize these ideas as a means of moving the discipline forward, even in the absence of compensation or a client. Is there a way to establish a tradition of designing and publicizing exceptionally creative instructional design work within educational settings, within the safety of the academy? In response to this tension that surfaces in the classroom—this struggle between the seemingly competing interests of creativity and reliability—could the classroom (and the larger academy within which it is situated) provide a safe place for exploring exceptionally creative instructional design, while also exposing students to more traditional, tried-and-true approaches to design problem-solving? Indeed, if the classroom became a laboratory for more creative exploration, it may reshape the kinds of risks professionals are willing to take, while doing so with a clear-eyed view of the potential downsides of such risks—being able to evaluate when it is or is not appropriate to do so and identifying resources to mitigate unexpected negative outcomes should they arise.

These are just a few of the questions that come to mind when considering the tension identified by Atsusi Hirumi, raised in an educational setting, but of importance for the discipline beyond the classroom walls. By continuing to recognize opportunities to surface unseen, forgotten, marginalized, or unconventional viewpoints, by paying attention to how they manifest themselves as novices encounter instructional design, we may be able to constantly reinvigorate disciplinary discourse, even as the professional discipline informs and shapes expectations for the expertise to which novices aspire.

References

Brand, S. (1994). *How buildings learn: What happens after they're built*. New York: Viking.

Smith, K. M., & Boling, E. (2009). What do we make of design? Design as a concept in educational technology. *Educational Technology, 49*(3), 3–17.

Chapter 9

Necessary Ingredients for the Education of Designers

Irene Visscher-Voerman

We all know that the world is changing rapidly and fundamentally. Current graduates will come to work in jobs that do not even exist today and will work on problems we are not able to predict now. They will need specific skills, often referred to as twenty-first-century skills, such as teamwork, problem solving, interpersonal skills, oral communication, learning to learn.[1] Educational programs need to be redesigned in such a way that students are enabled, stimulated, or even required to acquire those skills—also, or maybe it is better to say definitely, the educational programs for designers. Below are some ingredients for the programs of the future.

Educating T-Shaped Professionals

Deep knowledge in a small number of disciplines is, and will stay, very important—not just because expert knowledge in itself is valuable, but also because obtaining and functionally using knowledge on an abstract level is a crucial skill. Programs should also help students to develop a wider range of skills that enable them to transpose expert knowledge to different domains and to communicate and interact with people from other disciplines. Design programs should thus focus both on discipline (deep) and on the boundary-crossing competences (broad), thus creating so-called *T-shaped professionals*.

Project-Led Education as the Educational Model: Learning by Doing and Reflecting

It is essential that students get *involved in the process* of becoming designers, rather than studying what it is to design. Therefore, from day one, they should work on design projects in practice, preferably for real clients. The learning is threefold. First, through projects, students learn how to apply relevant design steps (*technical part*), such as analysis, design, evaluation, and implementation. Second, they learn how to communicate and deal with stakeholders (*sociopolitical part*) who might have different views of the process or the design to be made. In case of multidisciplinary projects, students thus also gather an understanding of different disciplines and learn how to create a "common language." Third, through project work, students learn about the design content and materials (*substantive part*), such as the function of different materials in industrial design, the role of technology in the design of production processes, or the content of a learning program in educational design.

Projects can be designed in such a way that they invite students to *search* for relevant theories, to *study* those individually or with peers (instead of having lectures where they are taught theories selected by the teacher), and to *apply* those theories while designing;

through projects, students can also *deepen* and *develop* new knowledge, by experimenting and by reflecting on existing knowledge (the vertical part of the T).

Moreover, projects provide ample opportunities for students to learn how to work together, to prioritize, to apply time management, to communicate across disciplines, etc. (the horizontal part of the T).

The projects, as well as their assessment, should be as authentic as possible from the beginning of the program.

Students as Partners in the Learning Process

From the beginning of their programs, students should be expected to take responsibility for their own learning process, in similar ways as professionals would take responsibility for their work process. This holds consequences on several levels.

On a *program* level, programs should be flexible enough to provide opportunities for students to choose their own learning route, related to their personal interests and goals. In this way, learning routes become more personalized, enabling learners to make unique profiles.

With respect to the *course* level, students (individually or in their design team) should take responsibility for, e.g., formulating the project proposal or design question, choosing relevant theories for the specific context, conducting the design steps to follow, or applying the right activities to evaluate the quality of the design, both theoretically and in the eyes of the users. As such, they shape their learning in terms of content as well as skills.

On an *individual* level, students should set their own learning goals and act to achieve them—for example, by choosing specific program elements to study or by conducting specific projects or by undertaking specific roles in the project.

Seeing the student as a partner in learning also changes the role of the teacher. Student peers are good sources for learning. As partners in the learning process, students can help each other by providing feedback on assessing the quality of (parts of) their work, or on their professional attitude. The teacher nonetheless has a responsibility—e.g., in ensuring that the level of mastery of knowledge and skills (on both the program and the individual level) is enough to meet the standards of the degree, as well as that the amount of knowledge and skills mastered is sufficient for the degree.

Also, teachers need to design the programs in such a way that they can maximize the learning of students, taking into account different learning preferences, rather than that they hold responsibility for their own instruction. Already, in the mid-nineties, the needed paradigm shift from teaching to learning has been valuably summarized by Tagg and Barr (1995).

Scaffolded Supervising

I have increasingly come to realize that the way teachers operate, in the context of project work, is essential to the learning process of students. A lot of teachers are inclined to prestructure students' work and provide them with solutions on how to progress when students encounter a problem. Since they are experts in their field and are inspired to transfer their knowledge to students, teachers might become too overenthusiastic in helping students, with the effect that they actually decrease the learning opportunity for the students. Think of swimming as a metaphor: it is tempting to help children learn how to swim in a shallow pool. The likely effect is they will take each opportunity to put their feet on the ground and thus hinder the development of their swimming skills. Instead, it is better to have them learn to swim in a deep pool with the swimming teacher next to them in the water to encourage them and to support them should they sink. Floating aids help when acquiring basic skills but have to be taken out of the game as soon as possible. Also, in design education, teachers should set high expectations from day one and have students work on complex problems but provide just enough support so that they will not drown—thus providing challenging assignments that are (far) outside the zones of proximal development, while at the same time establishing a safety net through supervision. This requires a lot of courage and guts of teachers.

The Stage of the Project Should Determine the Scheduling of Formal Curriculum Moments

For their content and resources, students can rely on resources inside and outside their universities, such as literature, experts, peers, and teachers and their lectures, which are increasingly found through the Internet. Traditional programs tend to schedule parallel courses in rigid, weekly structures. For example, students would learn the ins and outs of qualitative interviewing in a six-week course, with weekly lectures and practice sessions. For a design project, however, students will need these skills in the beginning, in the analysis phase. It would be much better to plan one or two full days around the start of the project in which students can practice the basic skills, just in time when they need it in their project. Application and further practice of the skills can then be incorporated in the project. This asks for a far more open and flexible way of scheduling formal contact moments and lessons than we are inclined or used to do. Here, again, the criterion is how the formal curriculum moments foster learning.

And, again, it should be stressed that the most powerful motor for learning is the project itself and all the challenging questions that come forth out of it—rather than the traditional lectures we intend to give.

Research Skills Are as Important as Design Skills

Both in professional and in academic settings, students should learn that research is the key to good designs. Research delivers knowledge on which new designs can be built (theory and situational analysis data), and research provides information on the quality and functionality of the designed products (evaluation data). In an academic setting, a design research approach will provide designers with the opportunity to build upon theory by themselves. Rather than us teachers constantly providing them with new theory, students are better off when we help them develop skills to critically question and test existing theories, and to develop these further.

Assessment

We are used to assessing learning after each course, through standardized tests or paperwork. When projects become the motor for learning, and when students set their own learning goals, this asks for a greater variety in assessment methods, as well as more personalized forms of assessment. Students should develop a portfolio in which they can include proof of their competences, through grades, but also through feedback from peers and through products, and they can add their own reflections. Teachers should design assessments that focus on both the quality of the final design, the amount of theoretical knowledge, the amount of design and research skills, and the progression of learning—related to the learning goals the student attempted to achieve.

Since many projects are conducted in small groups, teachers need to develop group exams, with enough opportunities to demonstrate individual learning—both to prevent free-riding and to safeguard overall quality.

A lot of exciting challenges lay ahead of us. The most exciting is that—although for now we think that we are on the right track in educating designers—in a few years, the rapid changes may have made us realize that we need to change our programs again. . . .

Note: My position paper comes forth out of my experience in three- to five-year programs at the University of Twente as a context. But, in fact, I believe that these principles also hold for smaller programs on other educational levels.

Note

1. (TED-x: Marc Chun, March 24th, 2013).

Reference

Barr, R. B., & Tagg, J. (1995). From teaching to learning: A new paradigm for undergraduate education. *Change: The Magazine of Higher Learning*, 27(6), 12–26.

RESPONSE BY MONICA W. TRACEY

Visscher-Voerman eloquently describes insights into the future of the design field and the need to attempt to prepare designers for the jobs they will be performing. She explains the importance of students possessing specific twenty-first-century skills: teamwork, problem solving, interpersonal skills, oral communication, and learning how to learn while being equipped to communicate and interact with people from other disciplines, and to be partners in their learning process. Teachers, serving as guides, must provide supervision rather than prestructure students' work and offer feedback on process rather than supply concrete answers to problems. Few will disagree with Visscher-Voerman's description of what is needed for the twenty-first-century education of design students. What is missing in this description is the *how*. This is the necessary ingredient needed to educate designers to be arbiters of the design space. How do we prepare design students to possess skills including teamwork, problem solving, etc.? These skills cannot be generic, but rather must be specific, for the development of designer professional identity. In other words, preparing a mathematics students to problem solve requires a different skill set than those needed in order for an instructional designer to problem solve. Here is my point of departure.

Preparing designers to become design thinkers continues to be a gap in the field. While other fields including medicine and psychology focus on developing professional identity simultaneously while teaching field specific content, we tend to assume that design students know how to work in teams, communicate, and problem solve in general. We agree that it is our responsibility to provide opportunities for design students to practice these skills in instructional design situations. However, as designers move through a design space between problem and solution, they must rely on their experience (precedents), intuition, and creativity in order to arrive at meaningful design outcomes. Our design students must think like designers first with instructional interventions being the product they design. Here are some suggestions on how this can be integrated in the necessary ingredients for educating designers.

Educating T-Shaped Professionals

Developing a "wider range of skills that enable them to transpose expert knowledge to different domains." While this is critical for the twenty-first-century designer, these actions require designers to operate in a design-thinking framework. This places the designer as the arbiter of the design space, needing skills to manage uncertainty, leverage failures, and gain insights to deliver meaningful design outcomes building on their designer precedents that allow them to possess the wide range of skills needed for different domains.

Project-Led Education as the Educational Model: Learning by Doing and Reflecting

Getting students involved from "day one" in the process of becoming a designer, according to Visscher-Voerman, includes students working on design projects in practice, for "real clients." Might it be possible that this occurs on day two, after design students have a deeper understanding of the design-thinking framework and a sense of their designer identity? Reflection in general and the strategy of reflective writing can help students explore and interpret their design beliefs, experiences, and self-awareness. This is a productive place to begin the learning and reflecting process with design students—in the studio providing structured opportunities to gain experience, develop identify, explore their beliefs, and become aware of who they are as designers before being introduced to a "real client."

Students as Partners in the Learning Process

Having students "take responsibility for their own learning process" requires students having a foundational understanding of who they currently are as designers in order for them to design their "own learning route." This addresses the *you don't know what you don't know*. Simultaneously, students can provide feedback on assessing the quality of their work and other students' work once they have a sense of what quality looks like through the development and awareness of their design experience (precedents), intuition, and creativity. While these will continually evolve, students need a clear understanding of their starting point in their designer professional identity development in order to design their learning routes.

Scaffolding Supervising

Having students "swim in a deep pool with the swimming teacher next to them in the water" is an important scaffolding technique, although, since the level of swimming ability is different with each person, the teacher must provide different support for each person. Providing scaffolding for students, forcing them to look at design as a holistic activity, and to look at themselves as the mediators of design, is how teachers must operate while developing student designer professional identity. This requires ongoing individual engagement with each student to meet them where they are, while guiding and supporting them in where they are going.

The Stage of the Project Should Determine the Scheduling of Formal Curriculum Moments

As drivers of the project, the "most powerful motor for learning" is not the project itself but the designers of the project. While immersed in the design projects, design students' development, as designers, should determine the scheduling of the curriculum moments.

Research Skills Are as Important as Design Skills

While a design research approach may "provide designers with the opportunity to build upon theory by themselves," designers who lack professional identity will not know how to integrate research and practice.

Assessment

Assessing the "quality of the final design, . . . theoretical knowledge, . . . design and research skills, and the progression of learning" is only possible when design students have the foundational knowledge of who they are as designers. Instructional designers must constantly reconceptualize their own identities and what it means to be a designer. Within instructional design, professional identity development is intimately linked to the concept of design precedents, creativity, and intuition. Focusing on designer professional identity development while providing Visscher-Voerman's necessary ingredients to educate designers provides the *how* in developing designers.

REJOINDER BY IRENE VISSCHER-VOERMAN

Monica Tracey's response starts from an important comment that the "how" is missing in my initial statement. *How* do we prepare students to possess all the skills and knowledge a good designer needs? She argues, at several places, that insight in the professional identity and a solid design base lies at the heart of the design repertoire. Her answer to the *how question* lies in reflection: "Reflection in general and the strategy of reflective writing can help students explore and interpret their design beliefs, experiences, and self-awareness."

In my response, I would like to elaborate on this important addition while addressing several of Tracey's questions and suggestions.

I heartily agree that reflection is a powerful means toward improving one's skills and the development of one's own identity. For a powerful reflection, two elements are essential: experience and concepts. First, starting with a reflection on one's own identity without any experience will lead to a weak reflection. The theories can be learned by heart, but they will not make sense to the student. As such, the reflection stays empty. Second, in many situations, students' reflection activities are no more than a self-reflection—generating apologies ("I did not do well") and good plans and intentions ("I will need to contact my client sooner, next time") or just superficial explanations ("My client was so high-demanding that I forgot to think about the target group of my design"). By not connecting their experience to clear concepts and theory, the students are not likely to derive new or deep insights. As Procee (2006, p. 250)[1] states, following Kant: "Concepts without experience are empty, experiences without concepts are blind."

Therefore, I reasoned that students should start gathering experiences in design as soon as possible, preferably day one. Tracey's suggestion not to start with project work for real clients on the first day seems to reflect a more often promoted belief that students first need theory before they can apply them in projects. Yes, of course, having knowledge would help students make better decisions when being the arbiter of the design space. But in this perspective, projects are primarily "reduced" to situations in which knowledge is being *applied*. From my point of view, projects can also serve as leverage for *collecting* knowledge and *developing* skills. Let me give an example: in a traditional design program for educational designers, it would seem logical to have a course in which a teacher provides several lectures on, let us say, six different learning theories. Given the fact that, in this situation, learning might be very passive, the best outcome could be that students know each of the learning theories and are able to describe the differences between them. In the context of project-led education, we could aim at a more varied and probably also deeper learning outcome: students could be asked to design, in a project, learning materials for a specific target group that are consistent with a learning theory. Because they need to account for their design, the students will start searching for several learning theories. If they plan their activities well (and are rightly supervised by their teachers), they will learn how to search for important theories, about the theories themselves, and how to evaluate them on several criteria, stemming from their projects. They also learn how to design consistent materials according to a specific learning theory. While doing, they learn how to become the arbiter of the design space.

In this type of education, the role of the teacher lies much more in guiding students through a process of deciding "what it is they don't know yet but need to know" and how they can find answers through empirical or theoretical research rather than in explaining them the content.

That is why the teacher or supervisor plays such an important role in the learning process of the student. I think I underexposed the importance of the teacher role in my first statement.

In our university, there are many teachers who think that they can leave the supervision role to less experienced teachers, such as PhD students or even students themselves. I do strongly believe, however, that performing a good supervision role is far more difficult and requires many more skills than regular teaching or instruction tasks. In this respect I would like to refer to an article of Barr and Tagg (1995, p. 21).[2] Instead of fixing the means—such as lectures and courses—teachers who act according to the Learning Paradigm "fix the ends, the learning results, allowing the means to vary in its constant search for the most effective and efficient paths to student learning." For teachers, it requires not only a solid knowledge base in the domain of design and in the design skills in that domain. But they also need to have the authority to address difficulties in students' group work, as well as insights in the processes that come along with designing learning paths and supporting student learning. Yes, that requires teachers to be constantly engaged on the level of the individual student. That is much more challenging but also much more fun than providing a standard lecture to a large group of students.

Having argued that the theoretical foundation for design could be gathered and developed not before, but during, the course of a project, I would like to come back to the notion of reflection. I do agree with Tracey's comment that in order to develop a good sense of their professional identity, student designers also need theoretical concepts. Studying such concepts should be part of the reflection process: after describing the design experience, a second step in the reflection process could be to analyze a specific (new) theory, according to which the design experience can be measured and judged, or that can be contrasted to a designer's own values and beliefs—stimulating students to come up with good suggestions for next time (e.g., improving insufficient skills, or enhancing well-developed skills).[3]

In this respect, a good design curriculum needs to be designed in such a way that students can gain design experiences from the start, are stimulated to study and develop theories, and are guided through deep processes of reflection.

Notes

1. Procee, H. (2006). Reflection in education: A Kantian epistemology. *Educational Theory*, 56(3), 237–253.
2. Barr, R. B., & Tagg, J. (1995). From teaching to learning—A new paradigm for undergraduate education, *Change: The Magazine of Higher Learning*, 27(6), 12–26.
3. Procee, H., & Visscher-Voerman, J. I. A. (2004). Reflecteren in het Onderwijs: een kleine systematiek [Reflection in Education: A systematic Approach]. *Velon Tijdschrift voor lerarenopleiders*, 25(3), 37–44; and Visscher-Voerman, J. I. A., & Procee, H. (2007). *Teaching systematic reflection to novice educational designers*. Paper presented at the AECT, 2007.

Chapter 10

Teaching the Complex Performance of Instructional Design

Why We Cannot Use the (Existing) Tools of Instructional Design

Elizabeth Boling

I hear repeatedly from colleagues who teach instruction design (ID) that because designing is complex, and therefore difficult to learn, we should teach our students a simple process for designing, introducing its complexities to them only after they have mastered that simple process. The textbooks covering basic ID take this simple-to-complex approach (Smith & Boling, 2009), one dictated by basic instructional design theory (Van Patten, Chao & Reigeluth, 1986; Reigeluth, 1999; van Merriënboer, Clark & de Crook, 2002). Such theory holds that "a severe risk of . . . [presenting complex problems directly] is that learners have difficulties learning because they are overwhelmed by the task complexity" (van Merriënboer, Kirschner & Kester, 2003, p. 5). This view—that complexity must in some way be reduced—seems to hold even for promising approaches to teaching ID that aim to present authentic design problems to students rather than deconstructed problems (Ertmer & Cennamo, 1995; Bannon-Ritland, 2001).

Embedded within this view is the perspective, deeply ingrained in the field, that instructional design is *primarily* concerned with systematic process, models, theory, and data (Smith & Boling, 2009) or is a "system or procedures" (Branch & Merrill, 2011, p. 8). Accordingly, it can be reduced to rational components forming what Krippendorf (2006) calls first-order understanding based on causality, objectivity, and consistency, which are not sufficient for effective design where human agency is involved.

The *guarantor of design* (Nelson & Stolterman, 2012), or the "responsibility for outcomes in design decisions" (p. 203), presumably lies within these systems and procedures. However, design theorists reject this view of designing and have done so since shortly after it was introduced (Cross, 1984). Even Archer, who introduced an early and detailed systemic model for engineering design in 1965, took pains to explain that "if the solution to a problem arises automatically and inevitably from the interaction of the data [analysis], then the problem is, by definition, not a design problem" (p. 11).

Many instructional designers view instructional design as a complex task but then use a simple-to-complex approach to teach this process. For example, Merrill states: "At first the learner may only be able to complete simple versions of the task. As skill increases the learner can complete more and more complex versions of the task" (Merrill, 2006, p. 4). The idea seems to be that simple design tasks require simple designing—that they are easier to approach than complex design tasks. However, consideration of design complexity versus scientific, or systems, complexity (Stolterman, 2008) raises serious questions about how legitimate any simplified version of a design task can be and where the guarantor of design must lie. Design theory also holds that designing is not a process, but that design occurs within a changeable space of thought action, shaping and shaped by the designers' thoughts and actions (Schön, 1987; Lawson, 2004). In this view, the complexity in designing lies not in what is to be designed (the design problem) but in the act of designing itself coupled with the designer's specific situation (Stolterman, 2008).

A student approaching a simple design problem must therefore produce as complex a performance as the expert who tackles a problem on a larger scale, a problem with more constraints and requirements. Simply put, it is not possible to present a student with a "simple" design problem and not possible to prescribe a valid, simple process for approaching that problem. This has been acknowledged repeatedly within the field, from Merrill arguing in 1988 (published 1991) that instructional design models require experience and judgment to be used effectively, to Jonassen (in Kemp, Morrison & Ross, 1998) observing that the field has sought—and does not have—empirical principles to offer, leaving designers to rely on judgment. From general design theory, Krippendorf observes that generalized knowledge can tell designers what will *not* work, but cannot tell them what to *do* in the design space (2006).

Initially taught a simple process (or, as they may interpret it, a "pure" process), students never recover (Brooks, 2010). Every subsequent experience of authentic designing is viewed, at some level, as compromised or illegitimate (Boling, Easterling, Hardre, Howard & Roman, 2011). Multiple dimensions of designing (e.g., budget and time constraints, restrictive policies and regulations, stakeholder ignorance and resistance) included squarely, and even generatively, within the design space (Lawson, 2004) are then viewed as the reasons that designers cannot be responsible for their designs (Boling et al., 2011)—meaning, of course, that what they rely on as guarantors of design (their models, principles, and theories) are demonstrably inadequate. In fact, early commitment to what Dunne terms "technical rationality" (1999, p. 708) means commitment to an "ideal [that is] a practitioner-proof mode of practice." This cannot be the result that we want for our students, and it cannot be the most that we expect from them.

While understanding of the studio approach to teaching design differs across and within disciplines (Cennamo et al., 2011), and the approach is not immune to criticism (Boling & Smith, 2014), it is an approach with potential for introducing design as a complex performance from the first moment of learning, without simplifying the task in ways that limit students' understanding of design. Novice designers in studio courses can be viewed as individuals who are capable of behaviors that are "valid precursors to expert behavior" (Boling & Gray, 2015). The support provided to them can begin where they are and respond productively to the discomfort of complexity (Boling & Smith, 2014), resulting in designers who are "prepared-for-action, not guided-to-action" (Stolterman, 2008).

References

Bannon-Ritland, B. (2001). Teaching instructional design: An action learning approach. *Performance Improvement Quarterly, 14*(2), 37–52.

Boling, E., Easterling, W., Hardre, P., Howard, C., & Roman, T. (2011). ADDIE: Perspectives in transition. *Educational Technology, 51*(5), 34–38.

Boling, E., & Gray, C. M. (2015). *Who are these "novices"? Challenging the deficit view of design students*. Submission to American Educational Research Association. Chicago, IL: April 16, 2015.

Boling, E., & Smith, K. M. (2014). Critical issues in studio pedagogy: Beyond the mystique and down to business. In B. Hokanson & A. Gibbons (Eds.), *Design thinking, design processes, and the design studio* (pp. 37–56). New York: Springer.

Branch, R., & Merrill, M. D. (2011). Characteristics of instructional design models. In R. A. Reiser & J. V. Dempsey (Eds.), *Trends and issues in instructional design and technology* (3rd ed.) (pp. 8–16). Upper Saddle River, NJ: Merrill-Prentice Hall.

Brooks, F. P. (2010). *The design of design: Essays from a computer scientists*. Upper Saddle River, NJ: Addison-Wesley.

Cennamo, K., Brandt, C., Scott, B., Douglas, S., McGrath, M., Reimer, Y., & Vernon, M. (2011). Managing the complexity of design problems through studio-based learning. *Interdisciplinary Journal of Problem-based Learning, 5*(2), 11–36.

Cross, N. (1984). *Developments in design methodology*. Chichester, England: Wiley.

Dunne, J. (1999). Professional judgment and the predicaments of practice. *European Journal of Marketing, 33*(87/8), 707–720.

Ertmer, P., & Cennamo, K. (1995). Teaching instructional design: An apprenticeship model. *Performance Improvement Quarterly, 8*(4), 43–58.

Kemp, J., Morrison, G., & Ross, S. M. (1998). *Designing effective instruction* (2nd ed.). Upper Saddle River, NJ: Merrill.

Krippendorff, K. (2006). *The semantic turn; A new foundation for design*. Boca Raton, London, New York: Taylor & Francis, CRC Press.

Lawson, B. (2004). *What designers know*. New York: Routledge.

Merrill, M. D. (2006). Levels of instructional strategy. *Educational Technology, 46*(4), 5–10.

Merrill, D., Li, Z., & Jones, M. (1991). Second generation instructional design (ID2). *Educational Technology, 30*(1), 7–11 and *30*(2), 7–14.

Nelson, H., & Stolterman, E. (2012). *The design way: Intentional change in an unpredictable world*. Boston, MA: MIT Press.

Reigeluth, C. M. (1999). The elaboration theory: Guidance for scope and sequences decisions. In R. M. Reigeluth (Ed.), *Instructional-design theories and models: An new paradigm of instructional theory* (Vol. II, pp. 425–454). Mahwah, NJ: Lawrence Erlbaum Associates.

Schön, D. (1987). *Educating the reflective practitioner*. San Francisco, CA: Jossey-Bass.

Smith, K. M., & Boling, E. (2009). What do we make of design? Design as a concept in educational technology. *Educational Technology, July/August*, 2009.

Stolterman, E. (2008). The nature of design practice and implications for interaction design research. *International Journal of Design, 2*(1), 55–65.

van Merriënboer, J., Clark, R. E., & de Crook, M. (2002). Blueprints for complex learning: The 4C/ID-model. *Educational Technology Research and Development, 50*(2), 39–61.

van Merriënboer, J., Kirschner, P., & Kester, L. (2003). Taking the load off a learner's mind: Instructional design for complex learning. *Educational Psychologist, 38*(1), 5–13.

van Patten, J., Chao, C. I., & Reigeluth, C. M. (1986). A review of strategies for sequencing and synthesizing instruction. *Review of Educational Research, 56*(4), 437–471.

RESPONSE BY M. DAVID MERRILL

Boling makes a strong argument for a studio approach to instructional design that is consistent with recent models of instructional design—i.e., SAM and Pebble-in-the-Pond (Allen, 2012; Merrill, 2013). To better understand her argument, it is also important to distinguish between a progression of increasingly complex tasks and simplified instructional design.

SAM (Successive Approximation Model) advocates a model that works directly with the content to be taught and the instructional strategies to be implemented rather than with specifications for the content and strategies. SAM creates a succession of design-develop-evaluate cycles each resulting in a functional prototype of the instructional product. It is anticipated that early prototypes will be discarded as stakeholders and designers find ways to make each successive prototype more meaningful, memorable, motivating, and measureable. These successive approximation cycles continue until the resulting product is sufficient to meet the goals of the stake holders in the project.

Pebble-in-the-Pond also advocates a model that works directly with the content to be taught and the instructional strategies to be implemented rather than with specifications for the content and strategies. This model also advocates directly designing functional prototypes rather than writing design specifications. It also advocates continual evaluation and redesign to make each successive prototype more efficient, effective, and engaging.

SAM is the more complete model designed for large teams of developers and includes dealing with the many constraints of a large project such as multiple stake holders, budgets, time lines, and other situational constraints. It emphasizes the procedures for instructional development with considerable flexibility rather than a fixed linear process typical of more traditional ISD models. Pebble, on the other hand, emphasizes the design of effective, efficient, and engaging instructional strategies based on First Principles of Instruction and, other than advocating a successive approximation approach, does not include detailed procedures for managing the many constraints of a large project. Allen and Merrill have suggested that these two models are complementary (Allen & Merrill, in press). These models provide existing tools that can inform and guide a studio approach to instructional design as advocated by Boling.

Pebble is aimed at guiding the design of a problem-centered instructional design. A problem-centered approach suggests that learners acquire problem-solving skills best when these skills are acquired in the context of solving a progression of increasingly complex problems. The instances of most complex problems almost always vary in complexity. This complexity is multidimensional and includes the constraints and limitations surrounding a given instance of the problem. Some problem instances require only a low level of the component skills required to solve the problem, whereas other instances require the most advanced application of a given skill. Some problem instances require only a subset of the complete set of component skills required to solve all instances of a given problem class. The Pebble model recommends that each instance should represent a whole instance of the problem, not merely one of the component skills required for the problem solution. By arranging these instances in a progression based on complexity, it then reduces the level and number of skills required to solve the early instances of the problem with the additional increased skill level and additional skills as the progression continues. This facilitates the learning for the student without compromising the integrity of the problem instances involved.

It is not the case that instances early in a progression of problem instances require simplified component skills. All of the skills necessary for a given problem instance must be applied to arrive at a solution to the problem. It is also the case that the instructional events used to teach a given problem instance can also facilitate the learning process. Early instances in the sequence can be used to demonstrate given component skills, whereas learners may be required to apply these component skills to later instances in the progression. Thus, the level of problem-solving skill for a given class of problems increases as learners interact with the problem instances in the progression, hopefully arriving at a more complete set of problem-solving skills by the end of the progression.

This same approach for learning instructional design via learning to solve a progression of successively complex instructional design problems is an appropriate model for instructional design training. This does not imply teaching novice designers a "simplified" approach, but only that less complex design problems require fewer component design skills and a lower of level of skill for some of these component design skills, thus allowing instructional designers in training to acquire these skills a little at a time while still engaging in a complete design process for each of the ID problem instances in the progression.

References

Allen, M. (2012). *Leaving ADDIE for SAM: An agile model for developing the best learning experiences*. Alexandria, VA: ASTD Press.

Allen, M., & Merrill, M. D. (in press). ADDIE, Pebble, and SAM. In R. A. Reiser & John V. Dempsey (Eds.), *Trends and issues in instructional design and technology* (4th ed.). Boston, MA: Pearson.

Merrill, M. D. (2013). *First principles of instruction: Identifying and designing effective, efficient, and engaging instruction*. San Francisco, CA: Pfieffer.

REJOINDER BY ELIZABETH BOLING

I understand the heart of Merrill's comments to be built on two premises: (1) designing can be described and taught as a set of component skills; and (2) newer models of instructional design (specifically SAM and Pebble-in-the-Pond) built on this view of designing are therefore not only compatible with the studio approach to design education but "provide tools that can inform and guide a studio approach." I can accept neither premise as stated but do accept that my previous statement probably did not communicate sufficiently the extent of the differences between our views of design and of studio.

There are, of course, many skills (including many cognitive skills) required for designing. Those skills may be described explicitly outside the context of any individual designer and exercised at varying levels of competence (Lawson, 2007; Lawson & Dorst, 2009) as assumed in the Pebble model. They do not, however, comprise the full requirements for designing, critical among which are the individual store of *precedent* each designer amasses and draws upon during ideation (Oxman, 1994), and professional *design character* from which each designer acts and within which the multiple sensibilities and forms of judgment required for design are integrated into design performance (Nelson & Stolterman, 2012). The first of these is established through continuous immersion in immediate and vicarious experiences of designs (Lawson, 2004) and the second through immersion in a functioning design culture—what Nelson and Stolterman (2012) describe as an "interconnected temporal whole," not reducible to components exercised in response to a structured sequence of increasingly complex problems. Furthermore, designing is not equivalent to problem-solving (Nelson & Stolterman, 2012), even though problem-solving is involved in design, and even though design situations are often referred to as problems, or as "wicked problems" (Rittell & Webber, 1973).

Both models discussed by Merrill are, essentially, models that prescribe processes. In high-level conceptual terms, this makes them little different than traditional ADDIE-type ID models except that they are, in the case of SAM, more consistent with descriptive design theory (Lawson & Dorst, 2009) and, in the case of Pebble, integrated more explicitly with instructional principles (Merrill First Principles). Even if they were used, as suggested, in concert, the fundamental problem would remain. They would provide a structured, rapid, and efficient means to teach instructional designers from a perspective that does not actually address essential dimensions of learning required to be a fully prepared designer. More appropriately, these models might be offered as *methods* in a learning environment that introduces many design methods, reflecting the way designers use multiple, and not always consistent, methods generatively within design situations (Harrison, Back & Tatar, 2006).

Implied but not stated in Merrill's (2002) second premise is the assumption that a studio approach to teaching and learning design requires guidance from one or more explicit models of design. This assumption may be built on the misconception that studio design education, in which an explicit model of design is not necessarily used, lacks *any* structure for designing. The surface structures of the design studio, the dedicated space, and the availability of tools, together with pedagogical structures like reflection, critique, and authentic problems (Cennamo, 2016), may give this impression, particularly in a field mainly familiar with instructional strategies focused on the component skills of problem-solving. However, the epistemological structures of the studio that bound the studio experience by norms in the design discipline also provide an underlying structure—so effectively, in fact, that criticisms of studio education point to the difficulty of dismantling problematic elements of design cultures (Gray & Smith, 2016). This structure is aimed at preparing designers who will take a disciplined approach to design situations they have not encountered before, and for which *no* individual model may be appropriate.

Considering the idea that a studio environment—dedicated spaces, long class hours, critique, and authentic problems—could be implemented in which the Pebble model would be used to sequence design problems addressing component skills of design, and in which SAM would be taught as the process by which to address those problems, I do see a potential step forward in preparing instructional designers. They would likely avoid the problems associated with ADDIE-type models outlined by Allen (2012), but they would still be constrained to design situations susceptible to a single process model and to the types of learning that are decomposable into component skills. Our field promises more than this, and I hope we will continue to investigate paths that may allow us to make good on those promises.

References

Allen, M. (2012). *Leaving ADDIE for SAM: An agile model for developing the best learning experiences*. Alexandria, VA: ASTD Press.

Cennamo, K. (2016). What is studio? In E. Boling, R. Schwier, C. M. Gray, K. M. Smith & K. Campbell (Eds.), *Studio teaching in higher education: Selected design cases* (pp. 248–259). New York: Routledge.

Gray, C. M., & Smith, K. M. (2016). Critical views of studio. In E. Boling, R. Schwier, C. M. Gray, K. M. Smith, & K. Campbell (Eds.). *Studio teaching in higher education: Selected design cases* (pp. 260–270). New York: Routledge.

Harrison, S., Back, M., & Tatar, D. (2006). "It's just a method!": A pedagogical experiment in interdisciplinary design. *DIS 2006*, June 26–28, Penn State University.

Lawson, B. (2004). Schemata, gambits and precedent: Some factors in design expertise. *Design Studies, 25*(5), 443–457.

Lawson, B. (2007). *How designers think* (4th ed.). New York: Routledge.

Lawson, B., & Dorst, K. (2009). *Design expertise*. New York: Taylor & Francis.

Merrill, D. (2002). First principles of instruction. *Educational Technology Research and Development, 50*(3), 43–59.

Nelson, H., & Stolterman, E. (2012). *The design way: Intentional change in an unpredictable world*. Boston, MA: The MIT Press.

Oxman, R. (1994). Precedents in design: A computational model for the organization of precedent knowledge. *Design Studies, 15*(2), 141–157.

Rittell, H., & Webber, M. (1973). Dilemmas in a general theory of planning. *Policy Sciences, 4*(1973), 155–169.

Chapter 11

My Hope for the Future of Instructional Technology[1]

M. David Merrill

Undergraduate Programs

With the widespread interest in exploring the use of technology in so many creative ways and with the fundamental principles of instructional design reasonably well understood, has research on essential instructional design and its teaching in graduate school run its course? Is teaching essential instructional design of little or no interest to most of our university research professors?

Perhaps essential instructional design is sufficiently well understood that further research into this area is seen as uninteresting by university scholars. Dick, Carey, and Carey's classic book *The Systematic Design of Instruction* is in its eighth edition (Dick, Carey & Carey, 2014) and has provided a fundamental model of instructional design for almost thirty years. Perhaps, like measurement theory, it is reasonable to expect learners to come to graduate school with a fundamental understanding of these basic principles of instructional design. I believe it is time that the training of instructional designers moves from graduate programs to undergraduate programs. The curriculum for such an undergraduate program should include an essential course in instructional design such as Dick, Carey, and Carey's book *The Systematic Design of Instruction*, enhanced with a more advanced problem-centered instructional design such as van Merriënboer and Kirschner's (2014) book *Ten Steps to Complex Learning* or Merrill's (2013) book *First Principles of Instruction*. In additional to instructional design an undergraduate curriculum in this area should include courses in the psychology of learning, basic measurement and test construction, use of multimedia and screen design, and the use of computer applications for delivering instruction synchronously and asynchronously.

My first hope for the future is really in the form of a recommendation:

> It is time to move the training of instructional designers to the undergraduate level.

The Science of Instruction and the Technology of Instructional Design

In 1980 I wrote an important paper for the twentieth anniversary of *Educational Technology Magazine* titled "Can the Adjective Instructional Modify the Noun Science?" (Merrill, 1980). In this paper I argued that science has as its primary output principles, models, and theories, whereas technology has as its primary output cost-effective products that teach. I advocated a science-based approach to instructional design in which the "development of actual instructional materials should be done by the use of principle-based procedures" that have been derived from theory that has been empirically verified via experimental research. The paper elaborated and illustrated each of several components for both science and technology. The relationship among the components of instructional science and technology is illustrated in Table 11.1. I suggested that students of instructional technology should acquire skills in both instructional science and instructional technology.

In 1996, in reaction to the overzealous adoption of constructionist philosophy, my colleagues and I published a plea titled "Reclaiming Instructional Design" (Merrill, Drake, Lacey, Pratt & ID2 Research Group, 1996). We felt that the philosophical extremism associated with this movement was obscuring the importance of fundamental instructional design principles. We reiterated the importance of science with the following claims, which are abbreviated here:

- There is a scientific discipline of instruction and a technology of instructional design founded on this science.
- The technology of instructional design is founded on scientific principles verified by empirical data.
- Like other sciences, instruction is verified by discovery and instructional design is extended by invention.
- Instructional design is a technology that incorporates known and verified learning strategies into instructional experiences that make the acquisition of knowledge and skill more efficient, effective, and appealing.
- There are known instructional strategies. If an instructional experience or environment does not include the instructional strategies required for the acquisition of the desired knowledge or skill, then effective, efficient, and appealing learning of the desired outcome will not occur.
- These instructional strategies can be verified by empirical test.
- Appropriate instructional strategies can be discovered; they are not arrived at by collaborative agreement among instructional designers or learners. They are natural principles that do exist and that nature will reveal as a result of careful scientific inquiry.

My second hope for the future is a plea:

> I hope that graduate programs in instructional technology will emphasize both the science of instruction (including theory development and research) and the technology of instruction (including using principles, models, and theories derived from research

Table 11.1 Components of Instructional Science and Technology

Science		Technology		
Research	Theory	Tools	Development	Evaluation
	Outcomes ↓ Concepts ↓	Technology-Based Tools	Instructional Products	Field Research
Experimental Research ←	Propositions, models, theories			

as a foundation for designing instructional design tools that can be used to design instruction that is more effective, efficient, and engaging).

Master's Programs

Companies perceive instructional technology as those who know how to use the technology. As the technology becomes easier to use and as the number of experienced computer users increase, companies are seeing less need to hire professional instructional technologists. Computer science as a field soon realized that almost everyone would soon be able to acquire the skills necessary to use application programs. They realized that their focus needed to change from training computer users to studying computing. Computer scientists began to create tools that would allow everyone to be more effective computer users. Computer literacy as an issue went away. The focus shifted to more and more to user-friendly computer applications.

Is instructional technology facing a similar situation? Do we need to acknowledge that instructional design is and will continue to be done by designers-by-assignment? Do we need to shift our activities from the training of instructional designers to the creation of instructional design tools that allow everyone, designers-by-assignment, to be more effective designers of instruction? Do we need to shift our focus from training instructional designers to the study of instruction?

If you obtain a master's degree in instructional technology and go to work in the training department or business university of a large company, what is your role most likely to be? It most likely will not be developing instruction. It is far more likely, because of your education, that you will be a training manager. What does a training manager do? You are likely to hire designers-by-assignment to actually develop the training products your company will use. Is learning how to develop courses sufficient to be a training manager? Will you be equipped with the management skills you will need? Will you have had experience in helping subject matter experts develop instruction themselves? Will you have tools and materials designed to assist you in training your designers-by-assignment to create the necessary training materials for your company? The answer to all of these questions, if you graduated from one of the many instructional technology master's or PhD programs in the United States, is most likely no. Your time in school concentrated on learning to design instruction. Your time on the job will most likely be spent in management and training others to design instruction.

Unfortunately, many instructional products currently designed for corporate America fall far short of their potential. They are inefficient and often ineffective. Many of these products just plain do not teach. Of what use is a training course that fails to help the learners acquire the desired knowledge and skills? Many of our students suffer significant frustration when they realize that the products produced by their training department, especially if they are in charge, fall far short of the quality instruction they learned to design in school. How can you be better equipped to assist lay designers to create more effective and efficient training products?

What is needed are tools that have built-in instructional strategies that are based on scientifically verified principles of instruction. Tools that enable designers-by-assignment to not only easily use the technology but that provide them with extensive guidance in effective instructional design or provide them with verified, effective, predesigned instructional strategies. These tools should provide guidance, templates, and pre-built strategies that would allow comparison of existing products, data assessing usability, and, most important, data assessing student learning and performance.

What should be the curriculum for our master's students in instructional technology? If essential instructional design is moved to the undergraduate level, then students entering our graduate programs would have a head start toward this new curriculum. For starters, we should significantly increase the amount of project management provided to our master's degree students in instructional technology. In addition, they should still learn to use theory and research to design instruction. But the emphasis should shift from our students-as-instructional designers to our students-as-instructional-design-tool-builders for designers-by-assignment and as trainers of designers-by-assignment. As learning-oriented instructional design tools are developed, they should have experience first in using these tools to design instruction but more importantly in helping novice designers to use these tools.

My third hope for the future of instructional technology is also a recommendation:

> It is time to restructure our master's programs to prepare our students to manage designers-by-assignment (DBA) and to prepare them in designing instructional design tools that would enable DBA to produce more effective, efficient, and engaging instructional materials.

Note

1. This paper contains excerpts from: Merrill, M.D. (2014). My hopes for the future of instructional technology. *Educational Technology*, 4, 22–26.

References

Dick, W., Carey, L., & Carey, J. O. (2014). *The systematic design of instruction* (8th ed.). Upper Saddle River, NJ: Pearson.
Merrill, M. D. (1980). Can the adjective instructional modify the noun science? *Educational Technology*, 20(2), 37–44.
Merrill, M. D. (2013). *First principles of instruction*. New York: Pfeiffer.
Merrill, M. D., Drake, L., Lacy, M. J., Pratt, J., & ID2 Research Group. (1996). Reclaiming instructional design. *Educational Technology*, 36(5), 5–7.
van Merriënboer, J. G., & Kirschner, P. A. (2014). *Ten steps to complex learning* (2nd ed.). New York: Routledge.

RESPONSE BY TONIA A. DOUSAY

1. Undergraduate Programs

The call to move instructional design (ID) to the undergraduate level has fallen on deaf ears for decades. Programs such as those at Ithaca College, Western Illinois, Cal State–Chico, and others actively graduate undergraduate instructional designers, some for more than thirty years, while programs like Penn State are launching new undergraduate degrees, emphasizing ID. Even the for-profit educational arena, including Walden and Ashford, offer undergraduate degrees in ID. These programs offer targeted curriculum in communication, media design, evaluation, and pedagogy. Why are we not looking to these programs for inspiration, lessons learned, and best practices? Missing from the conversation, too, is a call for faculty with professional, nonacademic instructional design experience. Just as we often want former teachers and technology integration specialists teaching K12-focused technology integration coursework, we should also attract former instructional designers into higher educational faculty positions.

More colleges of education should diversify their student base and meet rising employment concerns by offering ID for undergraduate study. We can only expect learners to come to graduate school with prior ID knowledge if they received this in undergraduate study or as professional development, and not enough undergraduate ID programs exist. Most current undergraduate instruction in instructional design focuses on one ID model over the countless others. In some cases, a program other than ID manages this coursework. By inserting ourselves into the conversation as leaders of education and industry, we empower our field and our students. This conversation must include the existing programs as we tread carefully into the future. Programs that coexist with curriculum theory or other related fields would do well to serve as a bridge, bringing together educational psychology, measurement and assessment, and interface design. Just as instructional designers are often the project manager in the field, our programs should manage this project in academia.

Looking to the future, we must consider professional organizations—e.g., eLearning Guild, ATD, and Online Learning Consortium. Stronger connections to industry help us evaluate the effectiveness existing coursework at all levels. A recent ATD Research (2015) report detailed the top-five tasks for instructional designers and what models and processes these practitioners commonly employ. Our programs need to both prepare students for these expectations and predict future trends through graduate-level research.

2. Science of Instruction and Technology of Instructional Design

The science of instruction certainly informs the practice of instructional design. Within the notion of instructional design lies the processes, recommendations, and practices used to employ instructional technology. Now is the time to conduct meta-analyses of prior studies, investigate reproducibility, and further explore the connections inherent to our work. Pathways to new research are open with neuroscience, artificial intelligence, and other breakthroughs happening every day. These advancements in technology and measurement give us cause to reevaluate past studies and shape future studies. Underlying any research could be Merrill, Drake, Lacey and Pratt's (1996) foundational tenets, a practical framework through which research results are evaluated for implications and practice.

3. Master's Programs

If undergraduate degrees in ID become mainstream, a gap will develop in the workforce, and ultimately our students. This example of curriculum compression becomes more apparent as more students holding bachelor's degrees are capable of filling the jobs currently sought after by our graduate students. We need to put the design into the hands of the undergraduates and the science in the hands of the graduate students, allowing room for flexibility and movement between the levels.

Master's programs could expand to develop professional skillsets, including managerial roles and the many facets of design. From hybrid programs offering a dual master's degree—in education, science, or art and a master's of business administration—to opening the conversation to public sector and inclusive design, we need master's degrees that put forth individuals who can fill an increasing demand for interdisciplinary leaders, serving both private and public educational organizations. These leaders take with them the science behind their instructional decisions and broadened definitions of design and create a framework upon which ID can move into the twenty-first century. Doctoral programs must also adapt to take full advantage of these changes, designing and developing tools/applications and extending previous research in the science and emphasizing the different paths doctoral students take: tenure-track faculty, educational consultant, and/or learning technology entrepreneur.

References

ATD Research. (2015). *Skills, challenges, and trends in instructional design*. Alexandria, VA.

Merrill, M. D., Drake, L., Lacey, M. J., & Pratt, J. (1996). Reclaiming instructional design. *Educational Technology*, 36(5), 5–7.

REJOINDER BY M. DAVID MERRILL

I endorse the suggestions added to this discussion by Dr. Dousay. I hope that this discussion inspires one or more graduate students to undertake an extensive review of the current undergraduate programs in instructional design. What is being offered? How do these programs compare with one another? How good are these programs at helping these undergraduate students acquire the skills that have been identified by professional organizations? Another possibility is for AECT or ATD to sponsor a working committee to undertake such a study and make recommendations for undergraduate instructional design programs. Such a study would be valuable to existing programs and may inspire other institutions to offer similar undergraduate instructional design programs.

Many of the most creative instructional designers with whom it has been my opportunity to interact have come from other disciplines, bringing new insights and ideas to enhance the instructional design process. I could not agree more that universities that include programs in instructional design should be flexible in inviting these experienced practitioners to be part of their faculty to bring this additional professional experience and outside ideas to their curriculum.

The science of instruction should take a more prominent position in the research conducted by students pursuing advanced degrees in instructional technology. It has long been my belief that instructional design is an interdisciplinary area and that our students should be encouraged to pursue interlocking degrees that cut across traditional curriculum borders. Years ago, when we were planning the PhD program at Brigham Young University, we created an interdisciplinary program consisting of psychology of learning from the psychology department, computer science from the computer science department, and statistics from the statistics department. Our students found that these courses within the disciplines were more rigorous and valuable than similar content reviewed in courses offered by instructional technology faculty. If I were planning a master's program today, I would pursue cooperation with schools of business to include management training along with instruction in training and instructional design.

We live in the most exciting period of time in the history of education and training. Never before have there been so many technology options to the delivery of instruction, to the enhancing of problem solving, to increasing the accessibility to information. The fields of neuroscience, biology, and many other areas continue to advance our understanding of mental functioning, learning, and the capabilities of human beings in acquiring skill. Perhaps our greatest need not only for our students but also for all scholars in the field of instructional technology is to cross disciplinary lines, to investigate the many new ideas from different fields, and to find ways to incorporate these ideas with the fantastic array of technology available to find new ways to help our students acquire problem solving skills.

If I could have one professional wish, it would be to be to begin my career again now with a lifetime ahead to explore and engage in what promises to include the most exciting advances in the promotion of human learning in the history of the world.

Chapter 12

Preparing Instructional Designers

Monica W. Tracey

A transformation in current academic preparation of instructional designers is occurring. There is a growing trend in instructional design to shift from traditional, process-oriented conceptions of the field toward a view that aligns instructional design (ID) with the broader design community of practice and cross-discipline design thinking. As the design thinking approach becomes more established in the ID discourse, the field will have to reconsider the professional identity of instructional designers (Tracey, Hutchinson & Gryzbyk, 2014). Rather than passively following models or processes, a professional identity rooted in design thinking calls for instructional designers to be dynamic agents of change who use reflective thinking to navigate the design space and develop solutions to ill-structured problems (Tracey & Hutchinson, 2013). In this view, design is complex and iterative (Visscher-Voerman & Gustafson, 2004), requiring designers to embrace uncertainty as a motivating force; balance abstract principles against concrete details; alternate periods of intense work with relaxation in order to nurture inspiration; use models and prototypes to refine concepts and solutions; and leverage failure as a way to gain information and insight into the design problem (Cross, 2011). Those who view design from this lens, and who study how it occurs in practice, present design not as a smooth systematic process but instead as that designer's values, belief structures, prior experiences, knowledge and skills, and approach to design affect the final outcome (Nelson & Stolterman, 2003).

As such, design thinking highlights the central role that designers play in developing novel, functional solutions to ill-defined problems (Siegel & Stolterman, 2008). Designers recognize that problems and solutions are entwined concepts but that the relationship between the two is complex, evolving, and often oblique. And as designers move through the design space between problem and solution, they must rely on their design intelligence and intuition, derived from large pools of experience and lessons learned from prior successes and mistakes, in order to arrive at meaningful and inventive outcomes. These experiences are also known as design precedents, or episodic memories of design experiences both experienced and observed, that designers store, refine, and continually access as they make design decisions (Tracey & Boling, 2013).

Thus, as the identity of instructional design evolves, instructional designers must also begin to reconceptualize their own identities and what it means to be a designer. Developing a professional identity that is aligned with design thinking will exert an ongoing influence on designers' professional actions, values, beliefs, decisions, and commitments. They must position themselves as active drivers of the instructional design activity, whose judgment, experience, and intuition guide the efforts and resources needed to move between problem and solution.

This raises questions related to how professional identity is developed and what experiences support that process for established and emerging designers. Graduate programs in

ID must prepare students to manage the complexities they will encounter in their professional practice, including the establishment of design precedents, reflective thinking skills, and the foundations of professional identity. In other design fields, instructors focus on teaching designers to be "ethical, to define their own talents, to understand the world, have passion for design, acquire their own voices" (Bichelmeyer, Boling & Gibbons, 2006, p. 42). It is within this framework that the goal becomes creating designers rather than teaching a process of design.

Educating instructional designers by focusing on teaching a systematic process of design results in professionals in the field with little experience in dealing with the uncertainty and constraints inherent in every design project. The preparation of instructional designers must begin with the designers themselves. In addition to teaching the *what* of design and design thinking, academic programs must develop the *who*—not to replace the *what* of design, but rather to enhance it, focusing on developing designer identity includes a plethora of cognitive skills. Innovation is an essential requirement for designers. Designers must employ methods to arrive at innovative design solutions (Brown, 2009). Understanding information combined with the context in which that information resides is also crucial. This requires a level of intuition combined with experience (Dreyfus, 2004). Proficiency in design thinking is critical for instructional designers. Design thinking takes a holistic view, characterizing the design space as not only requiring iterations as is discussed in traditional instructional design education but also exploration and chaos (Braha & Reich, 2003). How designers see and how designers think are at the core of design thinking (Razzouk & Shute, 2012).

Developing professional identity includes maturity in intrapersonal skills including responsiveness to uncertainty, identifying and managing constraints, and the ability to collaborate. Uncertainty involves cultivating the ability to move between the abstract and the concrete throughout the design. Designers enter the design space with the initial step of gathering information. It is in this gathering that uncertainty and initial constraints are often discovered and solution generation begins. Because the design problem and constraints are not clearly defined, the deeper the designer delves into the design, constraints can provide an opportunity to redefine the problem and the solution, alternating between the concrete and the abstract. Collaboration during design assists designers in embracing uncertainty and constraints. Designers working in collaborative teams actually used collaboration to manage constraints (Tracey, in press). The ability to collaborate includes expressing ideas, listening, and negotiating (Brereton, Cannon, Mabogunje & Leifer, 1996), all requisite skills in developing designer identity answering the need to develop the *who* in design.

It is essential that ID curriculum include the development of the *who*—the designers' professional identities and their ability to solve complex design problems. Students need opportunities to explore their concepts, experiences, and beliefs related to design, which serve as the foundation for their emerging professional identities as instructional designers. ID programs must construct an educational environment that molds students while supporting them in developing a sophisticated professional identity to become dynamic agents of change (Tracey et al., 2014).

References

Bichelmeyer, B., Boling, E., & Gibbons, A. S. (2006). Instructional design and technology models: Their impact on research and teaching in instructional design and technology. In M. Orey, V. J. McClendon, & R. M. Branch (Eds.), *Educational media and technology yearbook* (Vol. 31, pp. 33–73). Westport, CT: Libraries Unlimited.

Braha, D., & Reich, Y. (2003). Topological structures for modeling engineering design processes. *Research in Engineering Design, 14*, 185–199.

Brereton, M. F., Cannon, D. M., Mabogunje, A., & Leifer, L. J. (1996). Collaboration in design teams: How social interaction shapes the product. In N. Cross, H. Christiaans, & K. Dorst (Eds.), *Analysing design activity* (pp. 319–341). Chichester: John Wiley and Sons.

Brown, T. (2009). *Change by design*. New York: Harper Collins.

Cross, D. (2011). *Design thinking*. New York: Berg.

Dreyfus, S. E. (2004). The five-stage model of adult skill acquisition. *Bulletin of Science, Technology & Society, 24*(3), 177–181.

Nelson, H. G., & Stolterman, E. (2003). *The design way: Intentional change in an unpredictable world: Foundations and fundamentals of design competence*. Englewood Cliffs, NJ: Educational Technology Publications.

Razzouk, R., & Shute, V. (2012). What is design thinking and why is it important? *Review of Educational Research, 82*(3), 330–348.

Siegel, M., & Stolterman, E. (2008). Metamorphosis: Transforming non-designers into designers. In D. Durling, C. Rust, P. Ashton, & K. Friedman (Eds.), *Undisciplined! Proceedings of the Design Research Society Conference*. Sheffield, UK: Sheffield Hallam University.

Tracey, M. W. (in press). Design team collaboration with a complex design problem. In B. Hokanson, G. Clinton, & M. Tracey (Eds.), *Design in educational technology*. Association for Educational Communications and Technology 2014, Research Symposium.

Tracey, M. W., & Boling, E. (2013). Preparing instructional designers and educational technologists: Traditional and emerging perspectives. In M. Spector, D. Merrill, J. Elen, & M. J. Bishop (Eds.), *Handbook of research on educational communications and technology*.

Tracey, M. W., & Hutchinson, A. (2013). Developing designer identity through reflection. *Educational Technology, 53*(3), 28–32.

Tracey, M. W., Hutchinson, A., & Quinn Gryzbyk, T. (2014). Instructional designers as reflective practitioners: Developing professional identity through reflection. *Educational Technology Research & Development, 62*(3), 315–334.

Visscher-Voerman, I., & Gustafson, K. L. (2004). Paradigms in the theory and practice education and training design. *Educational Technology Research and Development, 52*(2), 69–89.

RESPONSE BY BRAD HOKANSON

Monica Tracey, in her writing, "Preparing Instructional Designers," presents instructional design education as shifting away from a mechanistic procedural approach for instructional design education to one of "design thinking." In other words, it is moving away from teaching a codified process to a more valuable and explorational set of qualities. It is a shift that is occurring throughout instructional design education, and it may raise existential questions for the field.

Shifting the education of instructional designers to this form and concentration would be a substantial change in the shared goals of instructional design education and would encourage a focus on developing the capabilities of the learner. This change moves ID from an algorithm-based approach for developing educational materials to a heuristic approach that relies on internal skills and experience, one that is informed by research. This is seen through changes in curricular structure, and also results in changes in the nature of the professional identity of instructional designers.

Central to these observations is a need to develop skills and character traits of the new instructional designer; "knowing-how," gaining the capability for problem seeking and definition; for creative directions and conceptualization; for collaboration and engagement—all without falling back in to a rote, procedural mode of teaching.

However, for instructional design, merely directing the field to "design thinking" may be of limited value, particularly if design thinking is used solely as another set of techniques, replacing current procedural models of instructional design education. Design thinking should not be substituted for a more complete developmental process. The qualities needed by instructional designers extend beyond any narrow definition of design thinking and certainly require a dedication of additional time. Design thinking should not be the new "ADDIE," another packaged "lite" definition of what is needed to know.

While this may be a semantic argument, one of the challenges with describing proposed changes with instructional design curriculum as "design thinking" is that it diminishes the value and potential acceptance of Tracey's argument. Some writers have questioned if "design thinking" had failed, preferring instead to focus on the aspects or traits to be learned (Nussbaum, 2011). Designers themselves have viewed the short-term gain in attention positively but have also questioned the possibility of developing true design skills through a shortened process. New instructional designers need a richer learning experience than is implied with the term "design thinking." They are *becoming* designers, as that better captures the professional responsibilities and their professional identity, as they are not focused exclusively on learning *about* instructional design.

Currently, the learning process of designers is different than most efforts in education, which often rely on declarative knowledge: "knowing-what." Up until recently, in the field of instructional design, understanding the information, methods, and theories—i.e., propositional knowledge—has been seen as essential, while the skills that could be described as "designerly" (per Cross, 2006), practice-based, or "knowing how" have been a side show. This is a shortfall for the learner: "To *know how* to do something suggests an ability to do it, whereas to *know that* something is the case does not immediately suggest a corresponding ability" (Fantl, 2008, italics added).

Tracey is correct in identifying a subsequent change in professional identity; her comment that "those who view design from this lens and how it occurs in practice" illustrates the shift in the field. But the shortfall of the writing may be in missing the larger epistemological change we should be witnessing within the field of instructional design. It is one that begins to identify the two broader aspects of the field of educational technology: one of which is focused on practice, or knowing-how, and the other focused on research, or knowing-what. It may be a division between instructional design and what could be described as "instructional science." Instructional science can provide many of the solutions, but it is instructional design's role to provide many more questions and directions, as design is what happens past done.

Design itself is broader than a single field, and, similarly, the value of the learning must extend past designers alone. The professional values implicit in design should be recognized as a broader set of skills and values needed for education as a whole. We seek to educate more for the larger role than the completion of a simple task. W.E.B. Dubois (1989) pressed for education beyond simple training as well, building the qualities of the individual. Here, too, semantics may affect our present day understanding of his words regarding the larger role of all in advancing society: "We are training not isolated men but a living group of men, nay, a group within a group. And the final product of our training must be neither a psychologist nor a brick mason, but a man. And to make men, we must have ideals, broad, pure, and inspiring ends of living, not sordid money-getting, not apples of gold" (86).

References

Cross, N. (2006). *Designerly ways of knowing* (pp. 1–13). London: Springer.
DuBois, W.E.B. (1989). *Souls of black folk. 1903.* New York: Bantam.
Fantl, J. (2008). Knowing-how and knowing-that. *Philosophy Compass*, 3(3), 451–470.
Nussbaum, B. (2011). Design thinking is a failed experiment. So what's next. *Co. Design, April*, 6.

REJOINDER BY MONICA W. TRACEY

Brad Hokanson, in his response to "Preparing Instructional Designers," acknowledges the shift of moving away from teaching a codified process to a more valuable and explorational set of qualities. He correctly defines this shift as one that is moving to a heuristic approach relying on internal skills and experience, which is informed by research. Developing designers in this heuristic approach must include developing instructional designers in the "knowing-how."

Hokanson is accurate in his observation that this may be semantics, as embracing this heuristic approach to preparing instructional designers does not require a replacement of one set of techniques for another. Rather, it is an evolution, a moving from the sole focus of the step-by-step process, and content and ultimate product, to now recognize the complex, iterative nature of design and include the designer as the arbiter of the design space.

It is therefore not a shortened process as Hokanson indicates may occur but a deeper, richer, holistic process employing the experiences, beliefs, and self-awareness a designer brings to the design space. The responsibility of those preparing designers is to create a design space that includes educational experiences engaging designers in the process and thus developing their "know-how," removing it from the sidelines where Hokanson indicates it currently resides.

The original position statements focus on practice and not the broader aspects of educational technology; research or "knowing-what" aligns with the historical "driven by practice" development of the field. As such, if we choose to transform our preparation of practice to include this holistic, complex, iterative approach, aligned with the broader design community, it will expand the questions and directions ultimately providing a platform to broaden our research.

Part 3

Contexts of Learning, Design, and Technology

INTRODUCTION TO PART 3

With a clearer vision of what design practice entails and how design professionals can be prepared, we now look at some important issues that emerge when design is considered in specific contexts—from dramatic changes in K-12 schools, to shifts in thinking about performance in corporate contexts, to the space for gender politics in Learning, Design, and Technology as a field. The positions here are perhaps most illuminating with respect to their intended contexts, but many of the concerns around change, innovation, and equity apply to other contexts as well.

Schank argues that our entire education system is broken and needs to be completely replaced. Highlighting all of the ways that traditional schooling is failing our youth, he asks us to start anew. Peck, in a slightly less pessimistic stance, agrees with Schank that schools are flawed, but points out that schools work for some well enough to keep our levels of dissatisfaction in check. Peck adds that a fix is already emerging from an intersection of competency-based models of learning and commercialized technology.

Reigeluth argues that both means and ends of K-12 education need to be reconsidered in the same vein as the Schank/Peck dialogue. He points out that systemic/paradigmatic rather than piecemeal change is essential. Schank then rounds out this dialogue around K-12 contexts by illustrating the point with examples of what we teach and how we teach it as a response to Reigeluth.

Marker shifts the conversation to a corporate context but continues the questioning of means and ends begun in the prior dialogue. He suggests that neuroscience may yield insights that help those seeking to improve performance—for example, by balancing a short-term focus on profit with long-term social and environmental factors. Foshay counters that, while neuroscience may yield insights about such things as management decision-making, the type of balance that Marker is seeking is more a matter of ethics.

Finally, we have a timely and important dialogue around gender politics in technology and learning. Audrey Watters starts this dialogue with an ethical position statement on the mistreatment of women in technology-related fields. Marra then offers examples of women taking action—channeling anger and righteous indignation into the type of generative design solutions for which Watters calls.

Chapter 13

Education Is Completely Broken

Roger C. Schank

Education is completely broken. While I am sure this is not a popular sentiment, it is nevertheless important to take what I say here seriously. Here are the main issues:

1. the subject matter is wrong
2. the teaching methods are wrong
3. the certification methods are broken
4. the types of schools we have are wrong
5. classrooms are a bad idea
6. professors are in control and there is no stopping them

What do I mean by this? Who needs to study literature, algebra, chemistry, history, economics, and any other subject that high school and college students must take? No one. Nearly every functioning adult in the world knows next to nothing about these subjects, but we force them down the throats of students for historical reasons that make no sense. These subjects are required for reasons long since forgotten, and no one can change it. After all, we have all those tests that students must pass. Why? No one remembers.

Teaching is not a matter of information transmission. Professors like to lecture, but no one can retain anything that someone says for an hour. So there are tests that students cram for, and then they forget all that they learned in order to pass those tests. When I asked my students year after year if they could pass last year's exams now, no one ever said they could. They asked if they could study for them. And now we have MOOCs. Terrific.

Good teaching looks a lot like good parenting. A child wants to do something, and the parent steps in if needed. Schools need to have teachers who can mentor students. The students need to be allowed to pursue anything they want and then show results. Mentors can criticize and help them get better at what they are trying to achieve. This is entirely possible in the online age. If you want to design an airplane, someone from Boeing can mentor you.

We need to stop issuing certifications that are about nothing. If you want to be a project manager, you have to pass a test run by the PMI. One can study for that test, pass it, and have no idea how to manage a project. Similarly, one can graduate from Harvard and not know how to do anything worthwhile (except maybe write a paper about Chaucer or quote Kant or be able to discuss transformational grammar). But employers will hire that person because that person graduated from Harvard.

High school is a terrible idea. It was originally meant to be the end of one's educational experience. This is why Charles Eliot made the high school curriculum be a simpler copy of the Harvard curriculum (in 1892). He figured very few were going to college so college could come to them. He assumed that the subjects Harvard taught at the time were very important. Harvard has changed its curriculum since 1892. The high schools have not.

Now high school is about preparing for college. Unfortunately, both high school and college are useless. By and large, neither prepares anybody to do anything. Even in computer science, professors refuse to teach programming even though the students want to become programmers. Instead they teach their pet theories that are of no use to anyone. Colleges have a dirty secret. They are in the professor training business. They really want to produce more people like them. You are considered a successful student at Harvard if you go on to the PhD (at least in eyes of the faculty.) Even in business courses, they do not teach you how to start or run a business (possibly because most professors have never done that.)

Professional schools do teach people to do useful things. But the price of entrance (finishing boring high school and paying for four years of usually irrelevant college) is way too high. I once asked a chemistry professor at Columbia if what he taught in college chemistry would be useful in the future life of a doctor (all his students were premeds). He said no. What he taught was mandated by the AMA and test makers. I asked if there was chemistry a doctor should know. He said, "Of course, but they can't teach it because it's not part of the mandated curriculum."

We need to create professional schools that can be attended by anyone interested in attending them—no college degree or high school diploma required. We are starting to see this in computer programming in the form of "hacker academies." If you can do the work, you get to stay in the program. We used to train doctors and lawyers that way too. It was called apprenticeship.

Classrooms need to be torn down. Who ever thought it was a good idea to put forty eight-year-olds in the same room and tell them to sit still and be quiet while we teach them something they do not want to learn? Every time I see my eight-year-old grandson, I ask him how school is. Every time he says, "Boring. The only good part is recess."

We do not tear down schools, because parents need the day care. The state *should* provide day care for kids. It should provide safe environments where anything a child wants to learn is available. Teachers can turn into advisors who encourage students to try new things and help kids work together on projects and create things that they are proud of. We have the technology to build simulations of anything and everything, all of which would allow students who want to be doctors to try that out for as long as they were interested, and those who want to design buildings to do that for a while, and those who want to open a business to do that. Why do we not do this? Not because we cannot. There is money and technology available to build hundreds if not thousands of such simulations and plenty of people who could be trained to mentor them.

We do not do this because of all the vested interests from teachers' unions, book publishers, politicians, and colleges, all of whom have a stake in a broken system remaining the same. There is a lot of money to be made in keeping things the same. Test makers are making money hand over fist in test preparation, test grading, and book publishing. The goal is having every kid on the same page every day. That makes it so much better for everyone (except the kids). What if a kid wants to go in his or her own direction? Not allowed. I once asked teachers at the Santa Fe Indian School what curriculum they would have me build if money could be found. They replied: "casino management." Good idea. Were we allowed to do it? Of course not. Then they added that "land use" would be good too. Were we allowed to do that? Of course not. Every kid in every state has to be studying the same things so that there can be more math teachers and math tests and a general obsession about how we rank against other countries on international tests.

Does anyone care about the kids or the local economy? Not really. It is more important to have them pass algebra and then go to work at Starbucks than it is to help them make good career decisions in high school. It is more important to have them read Dickens and learn lies about George Washington than it is to teach them how to raise a child or how to relate to other people, or how to plan, or how to speak well, or how to form a reasoned judgment based on evidence. No, we must teach solid trigonometry and the names of phyla even if there are not jobs that actually require any of that stuff.

Can we fix this? Probably not. Professors at every university are against what I am saying here, and universities are in control. How do I know that? For most of my life, I was one of them. My career was about research. I raised money for my research, wrote papers and books about my research, and believed, like every other professor, that I was doing the right thing. If I was asked to teach more, I refused. I had more important things to do. I noticed that students were not being well served. I changed my teaching style to a Socratic one. I gave everyone an A so I could stop students from obsessing about grades. I refused to lecture. I encouraged students to argue with each other. I told them there was no truth that I could teach them. I could only tell them what I thought, and I was not sure they really needed to know what I thought.

The administration was not amused. At a research university, research is King. And it is the research universities that effectively run the school system by enabling the general obsession about getting into a top college and then making up the rules and requirements for that.

Should we eliminate school, as we know it? Yes. Will we? I doubt it.

RESPONSE BY KYLE PECK

Thanks, Dr. Schank for a well-deserved critique of a system run amok, but I do not see the educational system as "broken."

Far from broken, the system you describe continues to rage on, gobbling up learners, educators, money, time, and other precious resources and consuming opportunities to do things differently. It is a runaway train to a destination to which nobody wants or needs to go, but one people are compelled to ride, day after day (for over fifteen thousand hours). Most riders accept their fate, learning to be compliant, and earning the one-size-fits-all credential that labels them as such and qualifies them to board yet another inefficient, tradition-bound train, and to pay dearly for the opportunity. Others reject their assigned role in this misguided system, are blamed for their own lack of success, and are labeled as failures. Far from being broken, the system is in great shape. Like all systems, mechanisms and literally millions of people are employed to maintain the system. Unfortunately, the system is not broken and does not show signs of breaking any time soon, and the prevailing attitude seems to be, "If it ain't broke, don't fix it."

Having said that, I do strongly agree with you that the subject matter, teaching methods, certification methods, and types of schools are "wrong," and also with your contention that "classrooms are a bad idea" and that the people in charge have no incentive (other than conscience) to correct these problems. I also like your vision of students pursuing interests with well-informed mentors providing guidance and resources, and agree that it *is* increasingly possible in the online age.

Education is the last one-size fits all enterprise in an emerging era of "mass customization." Think of the diversity in cars, beers, coffees, and teas. In a "have it your way" culture, why is there only one approach to education—the MOST IMPORTANT product/service? It does not make sense, and it will not last. We need a variety of new, competing models that are far more compelling and that will attract the resources currently devoted to the current system, causing it to slowly grind to a halt.

In the 1990s, I talked with education reform leader Dr. Philip Schlechty, who described his vision of a local school board's role as managing a series of educational options—a portfolio of alternative approaches to education that parents could select based on factors such as each child's interests, background, attributes, and predicted future path. Instead of maintaining the existing system and selling it to all, the board would understand the needs of the community and support the development of a series of options that fit community needs. The popular models would grow, and the unpopular ones would shrink and perhaps disappear. All educational models would be expected to accomplish a rather small shared set of expected educational outcomes (like arithmetic and basic reading and writing), but each would be free to add to that set and to achieve its outcomes in ways that made sense. The model you begin to describe could be one such option, and it would appeal to a segment of the population and would work for many learners.

Toward the end of your remarks, you write, "Can we fix this? Probably not." I understand your skepticism, and history is on your side. There have been few, if any, meaningful changes in the "what" or "how" of education, and it does seem that nobody has the power to stop or redirect this monolithic juggernaut.

But I would like to amend your conclusion to . . . "Can we fix this? Probably not, but it will fix itself, and probably soon." I say this because the educational system is part of a larger system that is undergoing changes of a tectonic nature. A "perfect storm" is forming, and that storm will alter the coastline causing the system to be rebuilt. The factors in this perfect storm include the following:

- Increasingly powerful and intelligent computers (thanks for your contributions in the domain of artificial intelligence that fuel this)
- Research (primarily with adult learners) that has demonstrated that online learning is as effective as face-to-face instruction
- Proof from massive open online courses (MOOCs) that learners can learn (some) college-level content on their own and with peer support
- Digital badges and other forms of "micro-certification" that render traditional transcripts and diplomas obsolete
- A resurgence of interest in competency-based approaches to learning, in which outcomes are clearly stated and measured well
- Open educational resources (that provide free ways to learn just about anything online)
- The inefficiency of traditional approaches in comparison with emerging adaptive learning systems that base next steps on expanding profiles about each learner
- Growing dissatisfaction among employers of traditionally educated graduates
- The ever increasing cost of traditional approaches to education
- Online shopping, which is elevating expectations for the type of information available before making a buying decision and for the ability to get what you need, when you need it.

I believe that these factors will be creatively combined by a new generation of learning providers, and it is inevitable that their creations will increasingly divert resources that have been devoted to the care and feeding of the runaway system. I see many of the same issues you do, but I predict good times ahead.

Thank you, Dr. Schank, for the work you have done and the careers you have inspired, both in the development of tools that will improve education and in the development of the awareness that it is past time to replace our antique educational system with a series of alternatives that are in much better alignment with modern goals for learning and what we know about how meaningful, useful, long-lasting, transferrable learning happens.

REJOINDER BY ROGER C. SCHANK

I enjoyed reading Peck's response on the word "broken." Unfortunately, I tend to agree with him. Teachers, principals, colleges, parents, and students: none of these think the system is broken. They accept it all. Students like getting good grades. Teachers like being in charge and teaching the "truth." Parents like having a place to drop their children so they do not have to take care of them.

But really the problem is the colleges and the politicians and the testing/publishing companies. The system works really well for them. There is a lot of money to be made. Pearson is very happy. More testing. More money. Politicians like "accountability." They like being able to say when a school is doing well or badly. They use test scores to make these determinations so they are "objective." The fact that no politician could pass these tests means nothing to them. No one knows the quadratic formula except those memorizing it for the tests. Making kids do this makes no sense except to the vested interests, and there are many of those.

The biggest vested interests are the colleges. They have sold the idea that "everyone must go to college" so well that we consider people to be very dumb indeed if they did not go to college. Colleges require lists of courses that must be taken in high school and tests that must be passed, and therefore you cannot change a thing in high school without parents saying, "But how will my kid get into college (if we don't teach algebra)?"

High school is of no value.

We need to replace high school with something more useful (e.g., every kid works for two years in an actual job supervised by teachers who make sure the kid is thinking and learning on the job and not being abused). Or we need to let kids go from middle school into professional programs of their choice. ("You want to be a doctor? OK, go to medical school; skip college.") Make medical school more engaging and more tolerant of the fact that the students will be quite young. If the kids do not like it, after a bit, they could do something else. They would have lost nothing, as they would have lots of time to make a decision as to what they do want to do.

Colleges need to stop being primarily research institutions. It is all well and good for Harvard and Yale to behave that way, but how about Elon College and Florida Atlantic? Actually, it is unfortunate that Harvard and Yale behave that way too. I have no objection to the faculty there doing research or even being primarily committed to research. But when they teach, they act as if the students all want to become researchers. So kids who sign up for Psych 101 learn about experimental methods and statistics instead of learning why their boyfriends or girlfriends are screwed up, which is really what they were interested in. Students in developmental psychology classes learn about research being done and not about how to raise a child, which is why they signed up. Students in computer science learn about the mathematics underlying programming instead of how to get a job at Google, which is why they signed up. Economics students learn about economic theories and not about how to start a business, which is what they wanted to know.

Professors at research institutions feel they have the absolute right to tell students about their own research interests and the theories that underlie them independent of the fact that that is not why students are taking those classes. The ignoring of students' needs and interests starts at college and trickles down, so there are always more important things to teach than getting a kid to actually be able to do something.

Can we fix all this? Of course. Stop caring about what Harvard demands of its applicants and start caring what Google wants potential employees to be able to do. Stop caring about arbitrary biology courses required for medical school and start asking students what questions interest them and help them find out the answers.

And most of all stop listening to people like Bill Gates, who only seems to want to focus kids on more tests and less flexibility, and stop listening to Pearson, who, like any other business, has as its first priority its shareholders, not your kids.

Chapter 14

Paradigm Change

Its Time Is Now

Charles M. Reigeluth

Introduction

Think of our schools[1] as a horse and buggy. It worked well in a different time, but the times have changed. Educational needs have changed as much as transportation needs. Reforms to a horse and buggy will never give us an airplane. Yet we seem to expect that reforms to our schools will meet our new educational needs. And why should we not?

We have never experienced a paradigm change in education. All we know is piecemeal reforms. But there *has* been a paradigm change. In the mid-1800s, as our communities transformed from agrarian to industrial societies, the one-room schoolhouse no longer met our educational needs and was gradually replaced by the current factory model of schools. This was a *paradigm change* because the fundamental structure of the one-room schoolhouse was different—it had no grade levels, no courses, and no standardized norm-referenced tests.

Could it be that once again our educational needs have changed so dramatically that only paradigm change will work? To answer this question, we should first determine whether our current educational systems are no longer meeting our needs. Consider the following:

- More than half of America's high school seniors are not proficient in reading, and 75 percent cannot do math, according to the recently released National Assessment of Educational Progress.
- The PISA test administered by the Organisation for Economic Co-operation and Development in 2012 found that the United States ranked seventeenth in reading, twenty-seventh in math, and twentieth in science among the thirty-four OECD countries
- The hidden curriculum—compliance and tolerance for boring, repetitive tasks—was very important for manual labor during the Industrial Age but is counterproductive for the initiative and problem-solving skills needed for knowledge work in the Information Age.
- Our communities are increasingly segregated by socioeconomic status, resulting in greater disadvantages for many students.

Clearly, our schools are not performing as well as we would like and need them to perform in an increasingly competitive global economy.

This poor performance is not due to lack of effort. Since "A Nation at Risk" was published in 1987, billions of dollars have been spent on educational reforms. So why have educational reforms failed, and are they destined to continue to fail, no matter how much money we spend on them?

Position Statement

The primary reasons for this poor performance have to do with fundamental changes in society—its educational needs and tools. To understand this, it is helpful to consider a fundamental truth about learning—that students learn at different rates. Yet our current paradigm of education tries to teach a fixed amount of content in a fixed amount of time. So the current structure, by basing student progress on time rather than learning ...

- forces slower students on before they have mastered the material (so they accumulate gaps in knowledge that make future learning of related material more difficult and virtually condemn those students to flunking out), and
- holds faster learners back, demotivating them and squandering their sorely needed talents.

As described in the recent book *Reinventing Schools: It's Time to Break the Mold*, a system designed to *not* leave children behind would have each student move on *only* when s/he has learned the current material, and *as soon as* s/he has learned the current material. **Until schools make this fundamental structural change, they will continue to leave children behind, no matter what educational reforms we make—more high-stakes testing, more teacher professional development, smaller class sizes, more focus on basic skills, longer school day or year, or whatever the latest fad.**

So what does this have to do with changes in society? Alvin Toffler has convincingly described how societies undergo massive waves of change, from the Hunting-and-Gathering Age, to the Agrarian Age, the Industrial Age, and the Information Age. Each wave has brought about paradigm change in all of society's systems:

- the family (extended family in the Agrarian Age, followed by the nuclear family, and now the working-parent family—dual-income and single-parent);
- transportation (horse and sailboat in the Agrarian Age, followed by a combination of the railroad and steamboat, and now the automobile and airplane);
- lighting systems (flame, incandescent bulb, and LED);
- healthcare systems;
- legal systems;
- communication systems; and
- of course, education systems.

The one-room schoolhouse was the predominant paradigm of education in the Agrarian Age, the current "factory model of schools" in the Industrial Age, and the learner-centered paradigm (which only exists in about 1 percent of schools in the United States so far) in the Information Age.

The reason for these paradigm changes is that each wave of change creates different ends and means – different purposes for education and different tools for education. Regarding purposes, during the Industrial Age, manual labor was the predominant form of work. We did not need to educate many people to high levels; rather, we needed to separate the future laborers from the future managers and professionals by flunking them out. We needed a system that could sort the students—that would leave the slower students behind. So we invented time-based student progress, norm-referenced testing, and letter (or number) grades.

But in the Information Age, knowledge work is becoming predominant, so we need a system that is focused on maximizing every student's learning, which is evidenced by our talk about no child left behind. This requires a system in which student progress is based on learning, not time. Furthermore, the hidden curriculum in the Industrial Age paradigm was compliance and tolerance for boring tasks, which were important preparation for the assembly line, but they are counterproductive for knowledge work. Now we need a hidden curriculum of initiative, problem solving, collaboration, and lifelong learning, which can perhaps best be achieved through self-directed, project-based learning.

Regarding different tools for education, information technologies make it much easier and less expensive to customize student progress and other aspects of instruction, enhance intrinsic motivation, integrate criterion-referenced testing with teaching (as is done in the Khan Academy), and keep track of what each individual student has learned.

There are many schools in which paradigm change has already been happening—over 140 are listed in *Reinventing Schools*. But in contrast to piecemeal reforms, paradigm change entails fundamental changes throughout the entire system:

- the instructional subsystem (from teacher-centered to learner-centered and self-directed, from standardized to customized, from extrinsic to intrinsic motivation),
- the assessment subsystem (from norm-referenced to criterion-referenced, from separate from instruction to integrated with instruction, from artificial to performance-based),
- the record-keeping subsystem (from comparative grades to an inventory of attainments),
- the roles of teachers (from "sage on the stage" to "guide on the side"),
- the roles of students (from passive, teacher-directed to active, self-directed),
- the roles of parents (from cookie bakers to partners in their children's learning),
- the roles of technology (from tool for the teacher to tool for the learner), and
- much more.

Where piecemeal educational reforms are destined to fail, paradigm change will inevitably eventually succeed. This is a point that policy-makers fatally overlook, with devastating consequences for our children and consequently our communities and economy.

The recognition that students learn at different rates also requires rethinking the definition of "achievement gap." It is traditionally defined as the gap in achievement between groups of students of the same age—typically by racial or socioeconomic groups. This definition arose out of Industrial Age thinking (expecting all students to be the same) and results in a misplaced emphasis for improving education.

The achievement gap that we should be most concerned about is the gap between what an individual student has learned and what that student could have learned. The goal should be for all children to reach their potential, not for all to have learned the same things by the same age. The only way for all to learn the same things by the same age would be to hold back the faster learners.

The United States espouses the goal of leaving no child behind, but it is clear that our Industrial Age system with time-based student progress is *designed* to leave children behind, and no educational reforms within that paradigm can change that dismal fact. Toffler's insights show us why paradigm change is needed at this point in history—indeed, why it is *inevitable*, just as the transformation from the one-room schoolhouse to the factory model was inevitable. The major concern is how long this paradigm change will take, and how much damage will be done to our children, their communities, and our economy before it happens.

Toffler's insights also help us to see what the new paradigm should be like and how it will greatly improve student learning, equity, and cost-effectiveness while simultaneously professionalizing the teaching occupation. The book *Reinventing Schools* elaborates on that vision, describes three school systems that fit the new paradigm (along with evidence of their effectiveness), and offers guidance for what school systems and policymakers can do to engage in this transformation.

Until educators, policymakers, and the public understand that **the paradigm must change** from one in which student progress is based on time to one in which it is based on learning, we will continue to leave children behind, regardless of what piecemeal reforms we make.

Note

1. Everything in this article applies equally to training systems.

RESPONSE BY ROGER C. SCHANK

Any article that mentions that "the United States ranked seventeenth in reading, twenty-seventh in math, and twentieth in science among the thirty-four OECD countries" on the PISA test makes me very upset. How can tests like those possibly matter in any way? Why are the results of a multiple-choice test a measure of how our schools are doing?

Our schools are terrible places. Reigeluth is correct about every single thing he says about what is wrong with them. He gives a good history of how they got that way and rightly complains about so-called educational reform. But he leaves out the only thing that really matters. As I have been saying for years, "There are only two things wrong with school: what we teach and how we teach." He ignores one and barely just touches on the other.

Who cares how the United States is ranked in reading? Is there a reading contest I do not know about? I care how we are ranked in the ability to make rational decisions as a nation. Spending billions on invading Iraq or fighting Ebola without any debate whatsoever and without a whole lot of rational discussion speaks volumes about how well we are educated. It is too bad we cannot read Dick and Jane stories and answer questions about what the main theme is. Our problem is not that we cannot recall the quadratic formula; it is that we teach the quadratic formula at all and somehow imagine that learning it will help us to reason better. We, as a people, have trouble having coherent conversations. In fact, conversation, which is, in my view, the only way we really learn without actually doing something, is disappearing. When everyone texts all the time (in the middle of lecture is a very good time) and people communicate by emojis, we have a problem. Can the schools help? They could, in principle, if we made school something that excited kids and gave them things they really wanted to talk about. But instead we bore them to death by teaching them the name of phyla or balance chemical equations that will help them do well on a PISA test or an SAT or will satisfy the ancient requirements set down by Harvard about what subjects they must master, independent of whether they will ever have any use for the stuff they had to memorize.

"Clearly, our schools are not performing as well as we would like." Really? Is that the issue? Schools are not supposed to perform at all. They are supposed to provide daycare and bore kids to death and make them do a lot of test prep. They are performing very well at that. Who cares if kids "learn at different rates"? What is important is that kids are actually different one from the other. One is fascinated by animals and another by road construction. Can we just let them follow their own interests? I understand why that would be difficult in the era of the one-room school house that Reigeluth discusses. But it is quite possible in the age of the Internet where software can be built to simulate any environment and teachers can become mentors in any area of learning augmented by people who are experts who might be located anywhere.

You want to try building airplanes? Why can we not build an aerospace engineering course relying on industry experts to help design and mentor it? We have to stop thinking that what we teach has to stay the same forever. We have been teaching useless subjects ever since Charles Eliot had his meeting in 1892. Actually, Petronius complained about the useless curriculum in the schools in ancient Rome. Let us stop talking about an "achievement gap" and start allowing kids to determine for themselves what they would like to achieve. They will do that anyway.

A "good teacher"—and I have that in quotes because I do not really believe in teaching—is a good guide. A good mentor is someone who listens to what a student cares about and then makes that student think harder and expands his or her horizons. You do not like algebra? Then do not study it. You will not remember it anyhow. As Peggy Sue says in *Peggy Sue Got Married*: "I happen to know that in the future I will not have the slightest use for algebra, and I speak from experience." I was a math major. I never used algebra after my schooling was finished either.

REJOINDER BY CHARLES M. REIGELUTH

Roger Schank seems to have missed my major point, that piecemeal change cannot meet our current educational needs in the Information Age—that only paradigm change can meet our new educational needs. I agree completely with his comments about tests. My intent there was to show that, even by arcane measures valued by many policymakers, our schools are not doing well, and I indicated several other measures that reflect truly important criteria.

I also strongly agree with Schank's comment about the need to change both what we teach and how we teach. I have written extensively about the need to change *how* we teach (Reigeluth, 1987; 1999; 2006; 2011; 2012; 2014; Reigeluth & Garfinkle, 1994; Reigeluth & Karnopp, 2013) and more recently about the need to change *what* we teach (Reigeluth, 1999, 2012; Reigeluth & Karnopp, 2013; Reigeluth, Myers & Lee, in press), especially regarding social and emotional development and other aspects of the full, well-rounded development of each student; but I did not address either to any significant extent in this piece, because my focus here is on the *need* for paradigm change. Nevertheless, I do address *how* to teach extensively in my other piece in this book, and in more recent work I strongly support Marc Prensky's thinking about a new paradigm of curriculum that is no longer organized around the four major pillars of math, English, science, and social studies (MESS) but instead organized around the four pillars of thinking effectively, acting effectively, relating effectively, and accomplishing effectively (Prensky, 2014, in press).

Furthermore, regarding what to teach, I have expressed support for Schank's admonition that we should let students "follow their own interests" and cultivate their individual talents (though I also think some basics should be required of all students in public education). And I agree with Schank's concern about our ability to make rational decisions as a nation. The fact that our schools are failing miserably at this today reinforces my main point that paradigm change is sorely needed in our educational systems. Similarly, Schank's contention "What is important is that kids are actually different one from the other" is part of my main point. It is the need to address those differences that requires paradigm change at this point in human history.

I found it disappointing that Schank led off with a criticism of my citing PISA test scores as one of several indicators of the failings of our current paradigm of education, but I was heartened by his affirmation: "Our schools are terrible places. Reigeluth is correct about every single thing he says about what is wrong with them. He gives a good history of how they got that way and rightly complains about so-called educational reform." If there is one thing I hope the reader takes away from this piece, it is that piecemeal reforms are futile—that only paradigm change can solve our educational woes.

References

Prensky, M. (2014). The world needs a new curriculum. *Educational Technology, 54*(4), 3–15.
Prensky, M. (in press). A new paradigm of curriculum. In C. Reigeluth, R. Myers, & B. Beatty (Eds.), *Instructional-design theories and models: The learner-centered paradigm of education* (Vol. IV) (pp. 121–140). New York: Routledge.
Reigeluth, C. M. (1987). The search for meaningful reform: A third-wave educational system. *Journal of Instructional Development, 10*(4), 3–14.
Reigeluth, C. M. (Ed.) (1999). *Instructional-design theories and models: A new paradigm of instructional theory* (Vol. II). Mahwah, NJ: Lawrence Erlbaum Associates.
Reigeluth, C. M. (2006). A vision of an information-age educational system. *TechTrends, 50*(2), 53–54.

Reigeluth, C. M. (2011). An instructional theory for the post-industrial age. *Educational Technology, 51*(5), 25–29.

Reigeluth, C. M. (2012). Instructional theory and technology for the new paradigm of education. *RED, Revista de Educación a Distancia, 32*. Retrieved from RED, Revista de Educación a Distancia website.

Reigeluth, C. M. (2014). The learner-centered paradigm of education: Roles for technology. *Educational Technology, 54*(3), 18–21.

Reigeluth, C. M., & Garfinkle, R. J. (1994). Envisioning a new system of education. In C. M. Reigeluth & R. J. Garfinkle (Eds.), *Systemic change in education* (pp. 59–70). Englewood Cliffs, NJ: Educational Technology Publications.

Reigeluth, C. M., & Karnopp, J. R. (2013). *Reinventing schools: It's time to break the mold*. Lanham, MD: Rowman & Littlefield.

Reigeluth, C. M., Myers, R. D., & Beatty, B. J. (2017). *Instructional-design theories and models: The learner-centered paradigm of education* (Vol. IV). New York: Routledge.

Reigeluth, C. M., Myers, R. D., & Lee, D. (in press). The learner-centered paradigm of education. In C. Reigeluth, R. Myers, & B. Beatty (Eds.), *Instructional-design theories and models: The learner-centered paradigm of education* (Vol. IV). New York: Routledge.

Chapter 15

The Unbalancing of Corporate Systems

The Neuroscience of Intellect vs. Wisdom

Anthony Marker

By enabling businesses to pursue maximum profit to the near exclusion of other factors, Human Performance Improvement (HPI) practitioners have perhaps inadvertently helped to perpetuate a seriously unbalanced system. Businesses are arguably the dominant institution of our time: large, multinational corporations have more influence than most governments. The majority focus narrowly on profit and, in so doing, contribute to adverse social and environmental outcomes that outstrip our biological, psychological, and even spiritual abilities. Current neuroscience and psychology researchers—Richard Davidson at the University of Wisconsin, Paul Glimcher at NYU, and Jonathan Cohen at Princeton, among many others—offer insight into how the world we have created seems mismatched to the long-term health of its inhabitants.

Perhaps understandably in recent decades corporate systems have put a premium on intellect at the expense of wisdom. Intellect—characterized by analytical problem solving, knowledge and skill in a particular domain, and the application of technology—is useful for solving short-term symptomatic problems in more isolated, or siloed, domains. Intellect helps us identify "how," but frequently neglects "why": how to do things the right way, but not necessarily the wisdom to do the right things. Wisdom is characterized by patience, moral reasoning, emotional regulation, fairness, compassion, altruism, knowing what is important, humility, and the ability to deal with uncertainty.

To better appreciate how deepening our understanding of neuroscience might help researchers and practitioners in our field, we can look to one of many examples,[1] that of how our brains deal with delayed gratification. For decades, George Ainslie—an American psychiatrist, psychologist, and behavioral economist—has worked to understand the tug of war that ensues in our brains as we try to balance the pros and cons of immediate and delayed rewards. In the 1980s, David Laibson, then a Harvard student, heard Ainslie lecture and as a result created a way to predict not how we *should* act but how we *do* act when we have to decide between short-term or longer-term rewards. His model—*hyperbolic discounting*—shows us that the value of a delayed reward decreases over time but not in a constant way. In this model, also known as "temporal discounting," the value we place on something falls rapidly for a short time, but then falls more slowly as the delay increases. Stephen Hall gives us a clearer example of this. Hall says, "An experience you can have a year from now—a day at the races, a night with your lover—will feel about as valuable as the same experience a year and a day from now. But an experience you can have tomorrow will feel twice as valuable as the same experience the day after tomorrow."

An analogy may make it even easier to understand this principle. Imagine that, in the distance, there are two trees—one closer to you and one farther away. The closer one is fifty feet tall and the distant one is one hundred feet tall. Yet, as you approach the shorter tree, it begins to look taller and taller until, finally, it fills your vision and dwarfs the still distant but taller tree. Perceptual warps of this kind are similar to those that occur when you face a choice between immediate gratification and future rewards. What is close to us, more immediate in time, takes on greater value than it might otherwise have, and consequently what is farther off may appear of less value when competing with immediate sources of gratification. Knowing this neurological tendency may help HPI practitioners to devise strategies for creating counter balances to tendencies that favor short-term thinking. This is arguably a useful tool in a world that is constantly tempting us with rewards for immediate action and short-term gains such as quarterly profits.

Developments in neuroscience similarly shed similar light on issues from Dr. Barry Schwartz's (2004) research on how we deal with the plethora of choices we face in our business and personal lives, to the cognitive costs and drop off in productivity experienced when people try to multitask, and even to Nobel Prize winner Dr. Daniel Kahneman's (2011) work on knowing when to rely on intuition versus analytical thinking when faced with different types of problems.

From our own field, Peter Senge (Senge et al., 2008) tells us that maximizing around any single input or output is by definition nonsystemic, and Brethower (2006) reminds us that maximizing one part of *any* system suboptimizes the other parts. Instead of optimizing outputs to achieve a long-term sustainable balance, our current approach spins us ever faster out of control like an unbalanced child's top—one with which our brains cannot easily cope. From a global perspective, making profit the ultimate measure of success has prompted everything from conflating consumption with patriotism, to grievous government power struggles or population upheavals resulting from shrinking water reserves or temperature changes.

To see this principle of maximizing around a single input, profit, in action, let us start with the prototypical Kafkaesque example from the 1946 movie *It's a Wonderful Life*, a movie that was ostensibly about the power of doing the right thing for the right reasons. In it, George Bailey, played by Jimmy Stewart, runs the Bailey Building and Loan, a financial institution that serves as a community resource allowing the hardworking average folk of the fictional town of Bedford Falls to borrow money from one another to finance their homes. The Bailey Building and Loan provides a public service while making a modest profit for the owners. It seems clear in watching the movie that profit earned by the Building and Loan was a byproduct of pursuing the company's mission. George Bailey clearly saw the larger picture, the system if you will, and the role that his organization played in the health of the community. This is a far cry from the profit-driven motive of Mr. Potter's bank with its single-minded and at times heartless pursuit of profit.

Before we discount such Hollywood examples as removed from our current circumstances, let us fast forward to today and take a look at a couple of less prosaic examples. While we do still have corporations that seem determined to maximize their systems around the single input of profit (i.e., Enron manipulating markets while hurting low-income families needing electricity to heat or cool their homes, or Apple moving its headquarters overseas to avoid taxes),[2] we have also recently seen the rise of a new kind of corporate structure, the "B Corporation." While there are several alternative configurations for the B Corporation, the goal is generally the same: to create corporations that can earn a profit but whose primary reason for existence is to provide some needed service to the community or to pursue a larger mission. Often, profits for B Corporations, and the payments to their shareholders, are capped, the excess going back into the organization's efforts to achieve its community-centered goals. Patagonia, a manufacturer of high-quality outdoor sporting and recreation gear is an excellent example. It has spent several years trying to find a viable substitute for its petroleum-based neoprene wetsuits. The company has finally succeeded. Their newest high-performance suit is from a natural rubber, Yulex, derived from a desert shrub. Patagonia executives are convinced that this material will eventually be used in other products like sneakers and yoga mats (Cardwell, 2014). In other words, because they have developed the process and sponsored the growth of a new agricultural structure to support this innovation, they stand to gain considerable competitive advantage, and of course profit. However, rather than milk the innovation for the last available penny, as some might, Patagonia has shared the technology with competitors, hoping to see greater adoption lead to an increase in its use and drive down prices. The move is, obviously, not entirely altruistic. The company will still make a profit, but will earn that profit from doing something beneficial rather than something that ultimately harms the environment or society. Peter Drucker, a well-known and respected management consultant, captured this ethos rather succinctly when he said, "Profit for a company is like oxygen for a person. If you don't have enough of it, you're out of the game. But if you think your life is about breathing, you're really missing something."

HPI practitioners learn the importance of aligning solutions to organizational goals; this is both necessary and laudable. However, if we want a world that sustainably balances people, planet, and profit, we must also engage in building corporate systems that truly leverage systemic approaches to create a healthier world, not a merely profitable one. Therefore, HPI practitioners *must* expand their focus and capabilities to help organizations apply good long-term and systemic judgment to the challenges of a complex and dynamic world; they must help organizations act with intellect *and* wisdom.

While one necessary step in this process is to understand how our brains cope with these unbalanced environments we have created and then to work to manage those environments accordingly, we should, in fact, be taking this much farther. The principles of wise decision making and the long-term balancing of organizational systems must be included in the curricula from elementary schools to graduate schools not only in this country but abroad. It must be done now. Typically, our species tends to wait until there is a universally felt threat or crisis before actively addressing a common societal-level problem. If we delay for the sake of sure signs this time (indeed, many would argue that those signs are already there), we will find that we are the frog in the proverbial boiling pot, cooked before we recognize the problem is life threatening. We may not be able to force others to be wise, but we can, and should, create contexts in which it is easier to act with greater wisdom. Not doing so will being inviting disaster for, and justifiable recrimination from, our children's children.

Notes

1. This example, hyperbolic discounting, was originally summarized from Hall in Marker, 2013.
2. I am commenting on the business ethos used, not the quality of the company's products or services.

References

Brethower, D. M. (2006). Systemic issues. In J. A. Pershing (Ed.), *Handbook of human performance technology* (3rd ed., pp. 111–137). San Francisco, CA: Pfeiffer.

Cardwell, D. (2014, July 30). At Patagonia, the bottom line includes the Earth, business. *The New York Times*.

Hall, S. (2010). *Wisdom: From philosophy to neuroscience*. New York: Alfred Knopf.

Kahneman, D. (2011). *Thinking, fast and slow*. New York: Farrar, Straus and Giroux.

Marker, A. (2013). The development of practical wisdom: Its critical role in sustainable performance. *Performance Improvement, 52*(4), 11–21.

Schwartz, B. (2004). *The paradox of choice: Why more is less—How the culture of abundance robs us of satisfaction*. New York: Harper Perennial.

Senge, P., Smith, B., Kruschwitz, N., Laur, J., & Schley, S. (2008). *The necessary revolution: How individuals and organizations are working together to create a sustainable world*. New York: Doubleday.

RESPONSE BY ROB FOSHAY

Marker's call for a humane workplace, aligned with the long-term interests of the global society, is in the tradition of those who have challenged the perceived imbalance of narrow economic interests against true fulfillment of human nature. This tradition goes back at least to the dawn of the industrial revolution.[1] The call for managers to value "doing the right thing" was issued by Peter Drucker a half century ago (Drucker, 1966).

For HPI practitioners, Marker's warning is essentially a question of professional ethics: to what extent are we obliged to accept our client's or host organization's definition of value? The HPI code of ethics begins with this statement: "[I will] strive to conduct myself and manage my projects and their results in ways that add value to my clients, customers, and communities they serve and the global environment."[2] This statement clearly calls upon the HPI practitioner to define the value of performance improvement in terms beyond a narrow definition of economic value, whether at the level of work, the workplace, the organization, or the organization's environment. When this code of ethics was developed, there was considerable debate over how HPI practitioners should handle conflicts of interest between the clients, their customers, and the community as a whole. For example, are HPI practitioners always obliged to accept the client's definition of what adds value, even if it exploits workers, customers, or the community? Should HPI practitioners complete a project that the client wants, but that is likely to be ineffective and add no value? Is there ever a time when HPI practitioners should fire their clients? The meaning of the wording of this ethical principle is that the ethics of our profession require practitioners to seek goals that add value at *all three levels*: the clients *and* their customers *and* the larger community. Projects inconsistent with this three-level alignment should not be accepted by ethical HPI practitioners.

On this issue, Kaufman's work on strategic alignment and definition of value at the highest level of the organization's fit with its environment is perhaps the most influential within the HPI community (Kaufman, 1992; Kaufman & Keller, 1994). Kaufman argues persuasively that ultimately the goals of the organization and the larger long-term goals of global society must be aligned, and only when this alignment is successful—and carried through to the levels of the workplace, the worker, and the work—will the organization's value be fully defined and maximized in the long term.

As fascinating and important as the cognitive neuroscience work on emotion and mechanisms of decision making is (see, for example, Kahneman, 2011, for a good overview), it is difficult to attribute an assertion of ethics and values to a model of how the brain makes decisions. It would be more useful, perhaps, to examine this important body of research for guidance on how HPI practitioners can more effectively intervene in management decision-making practices. The ultimate goal of the intervention, however, is essentially a question of values, not of neuroscience.

Reframing Marker's argument as more ethical than scientific does not diminish its importance. He would do better to remind practitioners to pursue the practice of HPI with attention to the field's professional ethics, and thus lead clients to understand their value added in the largest and longest-term of frames. It is worthwhile to remind HPI practitioners in each new generation of this obligation.

Notes

1. As an example, see William Wordsworth's poem "The World Is Too Much with Us," published in 1807.
2. International Society for Performance Improvement, n.d., *Code of Ethics*.

References

Drucker, P. F. (1966). *The effective executive: The definitive guide to getting the right things done.* New York: Harper.

Kahneman, D. (2011). *Thinking, fast and slow.* New York: Macmillan.

Kaufman, R. (1992). *Strategic planning plus: An organizational guide.* Thousand Oaks, CA: Sage.

Kaufman, R., & Keller, J. M. (1994). Levels of evaluation: beyond Kirkpatrick. *Human Resource Development Quarterly, 5*(4), 371–380.

REJOINDER BY ANTHONY MARKER

I find little to object to in Foshay's response, which as usual is well thought out and professionally presented. That said, I would like to clarify where I feel our stances are out of sync. As I understand, he agrees that HPI practitioners should use ethics and values to guide professional practice and intervene as needed with the client's or host organization's definition of value. However, he questions whether neuroscience convincingly demonstrates a biological basis for our ethics, one that can shape decision making.

We may be communicating at cross purposes on this point since I would counter that current neuroscience research encourages a wider acceptance among HPI practitioners to see that science and ethics do not stand apart as separate influences but are in fact *intertwined*. For instance, research outcomes from Jonathon Haidt, a University of Virginia psychologist (Hall, 2010, p. 102), demonstrate that inherent biological response to environmental factors can influence moral reasoning. He shows that when asked to evaluate another's behavior, a person will judge the seriousness of behavior outside his or her moral norm differently simply when making that judgment in a filthy environment. Such environmental influence appears to influence us almost entirely outside our awareness. In the presence of disgusting environments, we make harsher judgments of morally questionable behavior such as cheating on an exam. The environment, and our invisible biological response to it, influences our moral judgment, something we have traditionally held up as the very apotheosis of what it means to be human, our independent exercise of morality.

As mentioned in my original argument, Paul Glimcher (Hall, 2010, p. 82–83), who heads the Center for Neuroeconomics at New York University, has shown that test subjects tend to make short-term economic decisions that demonstrably conflict with their long-term economic interests. However, he also showed that he could interrupt and change their poor decision making. To do so, he inserted timely reminders explaining to subjects that their desire for immediate gratification can influence these short-term decisions. The result was that raising awareness directly influenced decisions.

How does this relate to HPI practice? Anecdotally, there is a long-held belief that clients frequently ask for training in circumstances where training is not warranted. Indeed, Stolovitch and Keeps wrote an entire book about this premise (Stolovitch and Keeps, 2006). Having an awareness of this tendency, we HPI professionals therefore can take steps to maintain our awareness of that inclination in order to counter it, just as being aware of the dangers of "groupthink"[1] may help us avoid that potential decision-making error.

Just as we have trained ourselves to manifest a greater sensitivity to unnecessary training, I believe we can also use a greater understanding of neuroscience to arm ourselves against poor decision making—our own and our clients'. I see these situations in parallel. We often frame avoiding providing unnecessary training as a matter of economic interest; training is expensive, and, if it does not close the performance gap, it wastes resources. However, one could also argue that such a waste, when knowingly committed, is an ethical one. So too, I would argue, are larger decisions that waste a community resource or that harm society's interest for the sake of short-term organizational gain. In both cases we can train ourselves to act with a greater awareness of these tendencies and in so doing avoid these wasteful decisions and their resultant behaviors.

So, to a large extent, the divergence of Foshay's and my thinking might be said to appear in his response title. He appears to suggest that science and ethics are, perhaps, incompatible in this context when he interprets my original argument as a choice between "science, *or* ethics" (emphasis added). I have come to believe that science and ethics are not separated by the academic divide we once thought existed between the two. Previously, we seemed to find the realms of philosophers and scientists to exist at the opposite ends of an academic spectrum. We believed that the moral foundations of human decisions and behavior were almost entirely separate from the dictates of our biology.

However, recent scientific developments such as those I have described lead me to believe that we should no longer consider "science, *or* ethics" but instead "science *in* ethics." Such an apparently minor change can, I believe, have a significant influence on how we approach client relationships, their projects, and our own relationships with one another as HPI professional practitioners and academics.

In the end, I believe Foshay and I point in the same direction, though perhaps for different reasons. I think we probably agree, as he puts it, that we should remind "practitioners to pursue the practice of HPI with attention to the field's professional ethics, and thus lead clients to understand their value added in the largest and longest-term of frames." However, I would go a bit further and say that we would benefit from an explicit understanding of how human biology, and specifically neurobiology, influences our decisions regarding value, fairness, altruism, and other components of wise behavior. I suggest that we stand to benefit from actively using a greater metacognitive understanding of how our neurobiology *influences* our values, and through those values one's decision making so that we can, in fact, make better decisions. I offer this as a specific strategy for Foshay's recommendation that we "examine this important body of research for guidance on how HPI practitioners can more effectively intervene in management decision making practices." Doing so may enable us to more skillfully generate valuable *practical* insights and strategies for dealing with the increasing high levels of uncertainty and conflicting value assignments in our field.

Note

1. According to Janis (1982, p. 9) as cited in Rose (2011), an academic definition of groupthink is "a mode of thinking people engage in when they are deeply involved in a cohesive in-group, when the members striving for unanimity override their motivation to realistically appraise alternative courses of action."

References

Hall, S. (2010). *Wisdom: From philosophy to neuroscience.* New York: Alfred Knopf.
Janis, I. (1982). *Groupthink* (2nd ed.). Boston, MA: Houghton Mifflin.
Rose, J. (2011). Diverse perspectives on the Groupthink Theory—A literary review. *Emerging Leadership Journeys, 4*(1), 37–57.
Stolovitch, H., & Keeps, E. (2006). *Training ain't performance.* Alexandria, VA: ASTD Press.

Chapter 16

Women in Educational Technology

Audrey Watters

Last year, when Walter Isaacson was doing the publicity circuit for his latest book, *The Innovators*, he'd often relate the story of how his teenage daughter had written an essay about Ada Lovelace, a figure that Isaacson admitted that he'd never heard of before. Sure, he'd written biographies of Steve Jobs and Albert Einstein and Benjamin Franklin and other important male figures in science and technology, but the name and the contributions of this woman were entirely unknown to him. Ada Lovelace, the woman whose notes on Charles Babbage's proto-computer the Analytical Engine are now recognized as making her the world's first computer programmer. Ada Lovelace, the author of the world's first computer algorithm. Ada Lovelace, the person at the beginning of the field of computer science.

"Ada Lovelace defined the digital age," Isaacson said in an interview with the *New York Times*. "Yet she, along with all these other women, was ignored or forgotten."[1]

So even a book that purports to reintroduce the contributions of those forgotten "innovators," that says it wants to complicate the story of a few male inventors of technology by looking at collaborators and groups, still tells a story that largely ignores women. It tells a story too that depicts and reflects a culture that doesn't simply forget but systematically alienates women.

I will come right out and say it, because very few people in education technology will: there's a problem with computer technology. Culturally. Ideologically. There's a problem with the Internet. Designed *by* men from the developed world, so the story goes, it is built *for* men of the developed world. Men of science. Men of industry. University men. Military men. Venture capitalists.

Despite all the hype and hope about revolution and access and opportunity that these new technologies will provide us, they affirm hierarchy, history, privilege, and power. They reflect those things. They channel them and concentrate them, in new ways and in old.

Harassment—of women, people of color, and other marginalized groups—is pervasive online. It's a reflection of offline harassment, to be sure. But there are mechanics of the Internet—its architecture, affordances, infrastructure, culture—that can alter, even exacerbate, what that harassment looks like and how it is experienced.

For advocates of education technology, this is a bitter pill to swallow: Internet technologies are not simply generative or supportive; they can be destructive. But this, all of this is an ed-tech issue. It is a technology issue. It is an education issue. It a societal issue. It is a political issue. We cannot ignore it. But that's precisely what most people—or at least the most prominent people—in ed-tech seem to do.

The following sentence sounds so weird, I realize, typed by someone who writes about ed-tech for a living: I have received death threats. I've had people respond to my work by saying they wanted to kill me, they wanted to see me die. I've had death threats, rape threats—subtle and overt. I have no business writing about education technology, these messages tell me. Like Ada Lovelace, I'm some sort of ed-tech interloper. Too loud. Too brash. As an education technology writer, I've been harassed. I've been told to shut up. I've been threatened. Some is sporadic; some serial. In response, I've taken the comments off my blog. The harassment continues via email. It happens on platforms like Twitter and Facebook and Google+. When I tell people that these are my experiences, they often respond, "Are the threats real?" That's a question that is hard to answer. No, nobody has come to my door. But, yes, they are real. I experience them as real. Even if nobody physically hurts me, these threats take a very material toll on me. They affect my work, my mental health, my physical health, my relationship with my partner, my life. The Internet is real. Harassment on the Internet is real.

For a long time, I wondered what it was about *my* work, about me, that was so controversial. And true, my work is critical, sometimes bitingly, angrily so.

But I know that the threats and the harassment are not, at their core, about the content of my writing. They are because I am, quite simply, a woman who works in technology, because I am a woman who expresses an opinion on the Internet.

Because I am a woman.

One of my favorite essays is by the writer Rebecca Solnit: "Men Explain Things to Me" (2014). Since then, the term "mansplaining" has become commonplace, used to describe the Internet version of men explaining things to women.

"Mansplaining" is a micro-aggression, a practice of undermining women's intelligence, their contributions, their voice, their experiences, their knowledge, their expertise; and frankly once these pile up, these mansplaining micro-aggressions, they undermine women's feelings of self-worth. Women then decide not to speak. As Solnit writes, "The battle with Men Who Explain Things has trampled down many women."

And today, men use technology—social media, email, and the like—to explain education technology to me. To explain open source licenses or open data or open education or MOOCs to me. Men explain learning management systems to me. Men explain the history of education technology to me. Men explain privacy and education data to me. Men explain venture capital funding of education startups to me. Men explain online harassment to me. Men explain blogging to me. Men explain, they explain, they explain.

It's exhausting. It's insidious. It doesn't quite elevate to the level of harassment, to be sure; but these micro-aggressions often mean that when harassment or threats do occur, I am already worn down. For many women, myself included, our profession, our work demands we be online. We are writers and artists and journalists and actors and speakers and educators and students. We cannot *not* be online.

It's easy for some people to suggest, I think, that some of us are targeted because of our high(er) profile. And we are, I suppose, easier—or more recognizable at least—targets. But that's also beside the point. Because here's the thing that comes with being "Internet famous": as high(er)-profile Internet users, some of us also have powerful connections to, say, staff at Twitter or Tumblr that elevate and prioritize our complaints, that shut down the accounts of our harassers more rapidly than "regular" users will ever experience. And "regular users" do indeed experience online harassment. According to a recent Pew Research study, one in five Internet users reports being harassed online. Young women—those age eighteen to twenty-four—experience the most severe harassment online: "26% of these young women have been stalked online, and 25% were the target of online sexual harassment."[2]

In fact, I want to argue that online—computer technologies, Internet technologies—actually reinscribe our material bodies, the power and the ideology of gender and race and sexual identity and national identity. Why? In part because of who is making these tools.

Seventy percent of Google's employees are male. Of Google's "technical" employees. Eighty-three percent are male. Seventy percent of Apple's employees are male. Eighty percent of Apple's "technical" employees are male. Sixty-nine percent of Facebook employees are male. Eighty-five percent of Facebook's "technical" employees are male. Seventy percent of Twitter employees are male. Ninety percent of Twitter's "technical" employees are male.

What do these demographics look like for education technology companies? What percentage of those building ed-tech software are men? How does this shape what gets built? How do privileges, ideologies, expectations, values get hard-coded into ed-tech?

We tend to view the education profession as a female one. But it's a mistake to think that education is somehow "female-dominated," that women are well-represented in leadership or decision-making roles, or that women in education do not experience work-related harassment or discriminatory treatment. And once we add technology to the picture, I daresay it gets worse.

Again: how do these bodies—in turn, their privileges, ideologies, expectations, values—influence our education technologies? How does all this get "hard-coded" into ed-tech?

What we can do to resist that hard-coding? What we can do to subvert that hard-coding? What we can do to make technologies that our students—all our students, all of us—can wield?

The answer can't simply be to tell women to not use their real name online. If part of the argument for participating in the open Web is that students and educators are building a digital portfolio, are building a professional network, are contributing to scholarship, then we have to really think about whether or not promoting pseudonyms is a sufficient or an equitable solution.

The answer can't be simply be "don't blog on the open Web." Or "keep everything inside the 'safety' of the walled garden, the learning management system." If nothing else, this presumes that what happens inside siloed, online spaces is necessarily "safe." I know I've seen plenty of horrible behavior on closed forums, for example, from professors and students alike. I've seen heavy-handed moderation, where marginalized voices find their inputs are deleted. I've seen zero-moderation, where marginalized voices are mobbed.

The answer can't simply be "just don't read the comments." I would say that it might be worth rethinking "comments" on student blogs altogether—or rather the expectation that they host them, moderate them, respond to them. See, if we give students the opportunity to "own their own domain," to have their own websites, their own space on the Web, we really shouldn't require them to let anyone that can create a user account into that space. It's perfectly acceptable to say to someone who wants to comment on a blog post, "Respond on your own site. Link to me. But I am under no obligation to host your thoughts in my domain."

This starts to hint at what any sort of "solution" or "alternative" has to look like: it has to be both social *and* technical. It must involve the reconstruction and retelling of the history of technology. If, as I've argued, the current shape of education technologies has been shaped by certain ideologies and certain bodies, we should recognize that we aren't stuck with those. We don't have to "do" tech as it's been done. We can design differently. We can design around. We can use differently. We can use around.

The answer to all of this—to harassment online, to the male domination of the technology industry—is not silence. That is after all, as Rebecca Solnit reminds us, one of the goals of mansplaining: to get us to cower, to hesitate, to doubt ourselves and our stories and our needs, to step back, to shut up. The answer instead, as it so often is in our field, is aggressive, critical, but generative design solutions.

Notes

1. Bilton (2014).
2. Duggan (2014).

References

Bilton, N. (October 1, 2014). The women tech forgot: 'The Innovators' by Walter Isaacson: How women shaped technology. *New York Times*. Web.

Duggan, M. (October 22, 2014). Online harassment: Summary of findings. *Pew Research Center*. Web.

Solnit, R. (2014). *Men explain things to me*. Chicago: Haymarket Books.

RESPONSE BY ROSE MARRA

When I read Watters' piece on women in technology and women using technology to express themselves, my initial reactions were both "Amen" and "OK—but let's DO something about it!"

First, the "Amen" part. As a woman software engineer working for AT&T Bell Laboratories in the mid-1980s and early 1990s, I have lived the women in technology conundrum. I was one of a few women working on coding sophisticated telecommunications computers. Although I remember my years there positively, I do recall the annual feedback from my—always—male supervisors. Year after year I heard that I needed to be careful to not be perceived as being too "aggressive." I was not expressing my opinions on the Internet, but I was speaking up at meetings, offering alternative designs—and generally doing my job without smiling all the time, acting nurturing and apologizing a lot. Hmmm. Aggressive. Sounds like doing my job to me, but the feedback was a clear example of what Virginia Valian calls "accumulation of disadvantage," the small slights that add up to marginalize a person.

The data backs up the underrepresentation of women in tech fields. The Computing Research Association shows that the disparity is firmly established in college; in 2011 about 12 percent of computer science and computer engineering degrees went to women.[1] And as Watters posits via the employment data for companies such as Google and Facebook, a part of the overall scene of how women are perceived in Internet environments does originate in the male-dominated status of tech-oriented firms.

So, yes, the problem is there. But this problem is not unlike many other societal problems that have been around a long time. Various sources attribute the roots of our patriarchal society to 4000 B.C.; and even it if only goes back to records of property ownership (and thus power) being limited to males, we are still talking about hundreds of centuries. I am certainly not defending a paternal society but simply saying that it takes a while to overcome such deeply rooted—if ill-founded—traditions.

And as Watters implies, the advent of the Internet makes such problems more visible, and more commonly experienced by many, and easier to perpetrate. The intense (and needed) focus on racism in this country is a good example as smart phone videos and body cams document the ugliness in our midst.

Having said that, yes, we have to be working on changing this reality. And although I feel her pain, and have participated in a few rants myself over the years—beyond the potential initial attention, it does not get us much of anywhere. That is why I was glad to see Watters' piece ending on the note of recommending "generative" change. And I submit that—indeed—such change has been and continues to go on.

The National Center for Women in Technology is a great example of an organization whose approach is both informational and generative. It provides a one-stop Web site of tools readily usable to help us make the case for women in tech. It helps a lot if you do not have to build it from scratch.

Further, some of the same companies that Watters cites as being offenders—Google—are also leaders in creating family friendly work environments that make it more palatable for women to stay in these workforces.

And here is an example that is making the news as I write this. Isis Wenger, an attractive young female software engineer, made a social media posting about an ad campaign for her software company employer in which she was featured. Her initial post was about the nature and content of the ad; however, a significant number of replies questioned whether "she" could really be an engineer—she did not look like one. Well that did it.

The #ILookLikeAnEngineer grassroots campaign began with over 26,000 tweets in less than twenty-four hours. This tweet, accompanied with a photo, is representative—women declaring their ability to be an engineer and feminine at the same time:

> I'm female, wear pink and I'm pregnant. I'm also a full stack software engineer. #ILookLikeAnEngineer

The movement will soon be sporting its own billboards—showing that the same social media feeds that can be used destructively can also be used for positive societal change.

The initiatives I have mentioned are all focused on promoting women in computing and engineering. But none of this would have prevented the Isaacson book from being published without underrepresenting or entirely leaving out women innovators. That would have required a *publisher, or editor* who said, "Have you researched women and minority accomplishments in this area?"

And that, I believe, gives one a sense of how many areas of our society and education systems have to become aware of and continue to foment awareness of (we are humans, we have to be constantly reminded) . . . of the importance and necessity of equity and diversity in all aspects of our lives.

Anger and righteous indignation, well, yes, that may be an initial part of the equation of change. But if it stops there . . . it is really just self-indulgent. So let us build from the good ideas and activities that have been are going on—and help implement lasting change. Sadly—but realistically—it may take a while.

Note

1. Varn, K. (August 5, 2015). Woman behind #ILookLikeAnEngineer says campaign against gender stereotypes is 'long overdue.' *New York Times*.

Part 4

Technology

INTRODUCTION TO PART 4

This section of the dialogues focuses on the application of technology, very broadly defined, to learning. Countering the common tendency in our field to jump to the potentials of various technologies and media, the positions urge caution and attention to the limits of technology and media in serving the real needs of learners. They range from the enduring need for teachers, to the potentials for online learning, to the implications of big data.

To begin this set of dialogues, Reigeluth calls for a paradigm change to more learner-centered education—for example, progress based on attainment rather than on time, and, consequently, changes in superstructure and technology to support this. Harmon agrees but says we need to go beyond attainments and help learners gain adaptive expertise.

Reeves, in his paper on learning *from* and *with* media and technology, argues that we should define learning more broadly and support it in its full complexity. This, he says, requires that we shift research from one-off studies of the latest technologies by individual scholars, an all-too-common phenomenon in our field, to more open and collaborative efforts by large groups—for example, the "top one hundred" researchers. Savenye concurs and refines Reeves' call to include younger researchers who are bringing fresh views using more complex methods.

Foshay argues that we typically design technologies for the teachers and students we *wish* we had rather than the full range of stakeholders we *actually* have, and this limits their scale of adoption. In thinking about scale, Bishop responds by shifting the focus from individual learners to organizations and writes of the systemic double-loop learning necessary for broad adoption.

Cates and Hammond take the position that in the near term instructional technologies will remain incapable of solving wicked problems, including teaching, and thus will not eliminate the need for human teachers. Mitra responds to Cates and Hammond by giving us just four short but powerful points that narrow the focus to technologies that have already replaced teachers in some ways.

Savery posits that big data is a technology that has the potential to revolutionize human learning. He looks at future trends, including lifelong learning record systems, personalized learning environments, and expanded learner control of time, place, and pace. Quinn responds by adding the integration of meta-learning skills and the breakdown of the barrier between formal and lifelong learning.

In the final dialogue of the technology section, Kennedy and Freidhoff argue that promoting "any time, any place, and any pace" with respect to online learning may actually serve to undermine the importance of time, place, and pace. They describe research and personal experiences for each dimension and compare what the phrase connotes for learning with what is recommended for telework. Raish counters that implications of the phrase are positive and the meaning can be clarified through conversations and engagement with students.

Chapter 17

The Learner-Centered Paradigm of Instruction

Charles M. Reigeluth

Instruction (in both education and training contexts) must change from the Industrial Age paradigm, which was designed to sort students by basing student progress on time rather than on learning, to the Information Age paradigm, which is designed to maximize learning for all by basing student progress on learning rather than on time (Reigeluth & Karnopp, 2013). Instruction must change ...

- from teacher-centered to *learner-centered* (task-based learning with just-in-time instructional support),
- from standardized to *personalized*,
- from time-based to *attainment-based*[1] *student progress*,
- from passive (learning by listening or reading) to *active* (TBL with just-in-time instructional support),
- from teacher-directed to *self-directed learning*, and
- from a content-centered to a *task-centered organization*.

This is a true paradigm change that requires massive changes in ...

- the roles of *teachers* from sage on the stage to guide on the side (including teacher as designer or selector of student work, facilitator of student work, and mentor for the student),
- the roles of *students* from passive to active, self-directed learners,
- the roles of *parents* (in education) or managers (in training) from marginalized to active partners in learning, and
- the roles of *technology* from primarily teacher tools to primarily learner tools (including the functions of recordkeeping for student learning, planning for student learning, instruction for student learning, and assessment for and of student learning).

So what are the implications of this for instructional design? Certainly, instructional theory must offer some different *methods* for learner-centered instruction than for teacher-centered instruction. But the more important, and often overlooked, implication is that instructional theory must address what might be called the *instructional superstructure*—the more comprehensive features that truly learner-centered instruction requires. I start with the latter.

Instructional Superstructure

Attainment-Based System

The most important feature of the instructional superstructure for the learner-centered paradigm is *attainment-based student progress* (Reigeluth & Karnopp, 2013). Rather than students moving on when a certain amount of time has passed, each should move on only when s/he has mastered the current attainments, and as soon as s/he has mastered them (Bloom, 1968). However, for it to work, attainment-based student progress requires *attainment-based student assessment*, often called competency-based or criterion-referenced assessment. Without this, it is impossible to tell when each student is ready to move on. This kind of assessment, in turn, requires *attainment-based student records*. Rather than a report card that lists courses and grades, which only compare students with each other, this requires a report card that lists individual attainments and indicates whether or not each has been mastered yet by the student and which ones are within the student's reach, similar to Vygotsky's (1978) "zone of proximal development." These three aspects of an attainment-based system (Reigeluth & Karnopp, 2013) are seldom thought of as instructional strategies, yet they likely have a larger impact on student learning than any other instructional strategy and need to be an integral part of any instructional design to truly maximize student learning.

Personal Learning Plan

Given that students learn at different rates, in order to allow each student to move on as soon as s/he has mastered the current attainments, the instruction must be personalized (Martinez, 2001; Wolf, 2010; Lee, 2014), or learner-centered (McCombs & Whisler, 1997; McCombs, 2013). This means that each student must have a personal learning plan, which is a tool for identifying and monitoring the attainments on which each student is currently working. It uses information in the attainment-based student records to help the learner and his/her mentor to decide which attainments to pursue next. This, too, is seldom thought of as an instructional strategy yet is essential to maximize each student's learning.

Instructional Methods

If different students are progressing at different rates through different learning plans, the instructional methods must change from teacher-centered to learner-centered or personalized. This requires more reliance on intrinsic motivation and self-directed learning (i.e., cultivating both the desire to learn and skills to learn).

Task-Based Learning

Perhaps the most important way to do this is with task-based learning (or learning by doing), which includes project-based learning, problem-based learning, case-based learning, inquiry learning, and so forth. For brevity, I follow the lead of several others (Merrill, 2007; van Merriënboer & Kirschner, 2007; Francom & Gardner, 2014) by referring to them all as *task-based learning* (TBL). In many cases, TBL should be collaborative (team-based) so that students can help each other learn, based on a social-constructivist approach. To promote intrinsic motivation and self-direction, tasks for a personal learning plan should typically be designed or selected by the student, based on the student's goals, targeted attainments, and prior learning (from the attainment-based student records). Computer-based simulations or virtual worlds can provide powerful immersive task environments.

JIT Instructional Support

However, TBL alone can be inefficient and ineffective, as Kirschner, Sweller and Clark (2006) point out. Therefore, it should usually be accompanied by just-in-time (JIT) instruction (e.g., tutorials, mini-simulations, and/or drill-and-practice, depending on the kind of learning) for the attainments that need to be developed, especially when transfer or automatization is desired (Reigeluth, 2012). This JIT instruction is now typically provided by teammates, other students, and/or the teacher. However, a technology program like the Khan Academy could be designed to provide a virtual pedagogical agent that tutors the student and provides ample opportunities for practice in divergent situations before the student uses the new attainments on the task. Overlaying this instructional support onto TBL provides a powerful integration of constructivist, cognitive, and behavioral pedagogies.

Integrated Student Assessment

Such a technology program would make it easy to certify and record mastery by having the student practice until a mastery criterion is reached of, say, the last ten practice correct unaided (summative assessment), and it could automatically enter the mastery information into the attainment-based student record (Reigeluth & Karnopp, 2013). When the student needs help, feedback could be provided (formative evaluation). Such integration of assessment with instruction saves much teacher time, which can be more productively spent being the student's mentor and guide on the side. So, while attainment-based student assessment is an important part of the instructional superstructure, it should also be integrated into the instruction, and this should be addressed by instructional theory to maximize student learning.

Technology Functions

Technology is seldom addressed by instructional theory. Some believe that instruction can be carried out (equally well?) with any medium (Clark, 1983, 1994). However, there is no doubt that truly personalized, attainment-based instruction for large numbers of learners can benefit greatly from technology to make it more effective while reducing its costs.

As mentioned earlier in this article, there are four important functions that technology can serve to support student learning in this new paradigm of instruction (Reigeluth et al., 2008):

1. Recordkeeping for student learning: to keep track of each student's learning and their personal characteristics that influence instruction.
2. Planning for student learning: to help students choose what attainments to work on next and to help them design or select tasks that require them to learn those attainments.
3. Instruction for student learning: to provide immersive task environments and JIT instructional support.
4. Assessment for and of student learning: to provide formative feedback and summative determination of when a student has mastered a competency.

These four functions should be seamlessly integrated in a single system so that information can be passed automatically from one function to another, but it should also have an open, modular architecture, somewhat like the iPhone so that small developers can develop apps for the system, but apps that are designed to share information with other apps within the system.

We talk a lot about "no child left behind" in public education. Corporations also want their employees to be competent at what they do. It is time we transform our education and training systems from a sorting focus with time-based student progress to a focus on maximizing learning for all with an attainment-based design. To do so, we need instructional-design theories that address not only the learner-centered paradigm of instruction but also the instructional superstructure and the functions of technology to support the new paradigm.

Note

1. I use the term "attainment-based" rather than "competency-based" because there are important kinds of learning besides competencies, including such dispositions as honesty and industry, as well as emotional development and psychological health, among others.

References

Bloom, B. S. (1968). Learning for mastery. *Evaluation Comment, 1*(1), 1–12.
Clark, R. E. (1983). Reconsidering research on learning from media. *Review of Educational Research, 53*(4), 445–459.
Clark, R. E. (1994). Media will never influence learning. *Educational Technology Research and Development, 42*(2), 21–29.
Francom, G. M., & Gardner, J. (2014). What is task-centered learning? *TechTrends, 58*(5), 28–37.
Kirschner, P. A., Sweller, J., & Clark, R. E. (2006). Why minimal guidance during instruction does not work: An analysis of the failure of constructivist, discovery, problem-based, experiential, and inquiry-based teaching. *Educational Psychologist, 41*(2), 75–86.
Lee, D. (2014). How to personalize learning in K-12 schools: Five essential design features. *Educational Technology, 54*(3), 12–17.
Martinez, M. (2001). Key design considerations for personalized learning on the web. *Educational Technology & Society, 4*(1), 26–40.
McCombs, B. L. (2013). The learner-centered model: From the vision to the future. In J. H. D. Cornelius-White, R. Motschnig-Pitrik, & M. Lux (Eds.), *Interdisciplinary handbook of the person centered approach: Connections beyond psychotherapy*. New York: Springer.
McCombs, B. L., & Whisler, J. S. (1997). *The learner-centered classroom and school: Strategies for increasing student motivation and achievement*. San Francisco, CA: Jossey-Bass Publishers.
Merrill, M. D. (2007). A task-centered instructional strategy. *Journal of Research on Technology in Education, 40*(1), 5–22.
Reigeluth, C. M. (2012). Instructional theory and technology for the new paradigm of education. *RED, Revista de Educación a Distancia, 32*.
Reigeluth, C. M., & Karnopp, J. R. (2013). *Reinventing schools: It's time to break the mold*. Lanham, MD: Rowman & Littlefield.
Reigeluth, C. M., Watson, S. L., Watson, W. R., Dutta, P., Chen, Z., & Powell, N. (2008). Roles for technology in the information-age paradigm of education: Learning management systems. *Educational Technology, 48*(6), 32–39.
van Merriënboer, J. J. G., & Kirschner, P. A. (2007). *Ten steps to complex learning: A systematic approach to four-component instructional design*. Mahwah, NJ: Lawrence Erlbaum Associates.
Vygotsky, L. S. (1978). *Mind in society: The development of higher psychological processes* (M. Cole, V. John-Steiner, S. Scribner, & E. Souberman, Eds.). Cambridge, MA: Harvard University Press.
Wolf, M. A. (2010). *Innovate to educate: System [re]design for personalized learning; A report from the 2010 Symposium* (p. 42). Washington, DC: SIIA in collaboration with ASCD and CCSSO.

RESPONSE BY STEPHEN W. HARMON

It is an old aphorism that generals always prepare to fight the previous war. The same might be said of Professor Reigeluth's call for educational reform. One the one hand he is absolutely correct. Our current system, with its basis in the industrial era, was well suited to preparing students for factory or manufacturing jobs. When this system was put into place, there was a pressing need for workers who had routine expertise and could successfully churn out the same product over and over again. The more identical the workers were, the more easily they could be swapped out and moved around as circumstances dictated. As Professor Reigeluth notes (1994), those days have passed. As we have moved from the Industrial Age to the Information Age, education has been among the least affected of society's institutions. But his call does not go far enough.

The pace of change is accelerating at an exponential rate (Kurzweil, 2001). We are already moving from the Information Age into a new, as yet unnamed, era. For purposes of this response, let us call it the Knowledge Age. Instead of the mass production of the industrial era, we are rapidly moving to a time of mass customization. Instead of preparing students for jobs where they spend a lifetime doing the same task over and over, it now seems likely that jobs in the future will be relatively short-lived. Today's students might have many different careers over the course of their lifetimes. Instead of changing our educational system merely to better prepare students to be routine experts, we need also to change the goal to prepare students to have adaptive expertise.

Whereas routine expertise allows performers to be efficient and accurate, adaptive expertise goes beyond this to include innovation and a high degree of transfer (Hatano & Inagaki, 1986). Adaptive experts have a deep conceptual understanding that allows them to develop new solutions to problems, or even to reconceptualize the problems themselves. In the rapidly approaching future where the only constant is change itself, learners must be prepared to continuously reinvent not only themselves but also the environments in which they operate. Professor Reigeluth moves toward this with his calls for self-directed, task-based learning, with an increased emphasis on personalization and intrinsic motivation, but he should include more emphasis on lifelong learning, life-wide learning (Bransford, Slowinski, Vye & Mosborg, 2008), innovation, and the conative domain (Reeves, 2006). In an age of continuous scientific and technological advance, what it means to be educated will always be changing, hence the need for lifelong learning. Given that the amount of content necessary to master even very narrowly focused fields is so vast, and that the amount of time students spend in formal educational settings is so small, there is also a need for students to expand their learning in informal settings throughout their waking hours. (To be fair, Professor Reigeluth does begin to address this with his call for just-in-time instruction.) In the industrial model of education, innovation is not encouraged and is often discouraged. Factories wanted workers to do everything the same way every time. But in an age of mass customization and change, innovation will be essential. The recent rise of the maker movement is a step in the right direction for enhancing innovation as a learned skill. Beyond these recommendations though, there is an overarching need to enhance students' ability in the conative domain. The conative domain deals with willpower and drive. It is different than intrinsic motivation in that it focuses on follow-through more than just desire.

All of the above recommendations are consistent with what Professor Reigeluth has recommended. It is in dealing with technology, however, that his essay falls somewhat short. We are consistently becoming more integrated with, and more reliant, on our technologies. In the developed world we are seldom more than a few button clicks away from the sum total of human knowledge. We are continuously off-loading portions of our cognitive routines and thought processes onto our devices. At the same time, our devices are becoming more and more a part of us. The smartphones of today will become the smart-glasses of tomorrow, and the neural implants of the day after that. While this is happening, our technology is itself becoming smarter. Some argue that machine intelligence is the next step of evolution (Müller & Bostrom, 2014). This is the future for which we must reform our educational system. It is already too late to prepare for the Information Age.

References

Bransford, J., Slowinski, M., Vye, N., & Mosborg, S. (2008). The learning sciences, technology and designs for educational systems: Some thoughts about change. In J. Visser & M. Visser-Valfrey (Eds.), *Learners in a changing learning landscape: Reflections from a dialogue on new roles and expectations* (pp. 37–68). Dordrecht, The Netherlands: Springer.

Hatano, G., & Inagaki, K. (1986). Two courses of expertise. In H. Stevenson, H. Azuma, & K. Hakuta (Eds.), *Child development and education in Japan* (pp. 262–272). New York: Freeman.

Kurzweil, R. (2001). The law of accelerating returns. Retrieved from http://www.kurzweilai.net/the-law-of-accelerating-returns.

Müller, V. C., & Bostrom, N. (2014). Future progress in artificial intelligence: A survey of expert opinion. *AI Matters, 1*(1), 9–11.

Reeves, T. C. (2006). How do you know they are learning?: The importance of alignment in higher education. *International Journal of Learning Technology, 2*(4), 294–309.

Reigeluth, C. M. (1994). The imperative for systemic change. In C. M. Reigeluth & R. J. Garfinkle (Eds.), *Systemic change in education* (pp. 3–11). Englewood Cliffs, NJ: Educational Technology Publications.

REJOINDER BY CHARLES M. REIGELUTH

Steve Harmon addresses an important issue—that what we teach needs to change dramatically—but that was not the topic of this piece. My main point is that instructional theorists need to develop "instructional-design theories that address not only the learner-centered paradigm of instruction, but also the instructional superstructure and the functions of technology to support the new paradigm" of education and training. I agree completely with Harmon that we need "to change the goal to prepare students to have adaptive expertise," and I go considerably beyond this in much of my writing (see e.g., Reigeluth & Karnopp, 2013). The fact that my "call does not go far enough" was because limited space in this piece forced me to focus on instructional theory and omit addressing the need for paradigm change in curriculum theory. Such a curriculum change is a major part of Volume IV of "The Green Book" (Reigeluth, Myers & Beatty, in press), represented primarily by Marc Prensky's work to define a new paradigm of curriculum—one that is based on the four pillars of thinking effectively, acting effectively, relating effectively, and accomplishing effectively—rather than the four pillars of math, English, science, and social studies (MESS) (Prensky, 2014, in press). So I suggest that Harmon's call for adaptive expertise does not go far enough.

My major concern about Harmon's comments have to do with his statement that we are leaving the Information Age and entering the Knowledge Age. I believe a careful read of Toffler's work (1980, 1990) reveals that the key markers of the Information Age still predominate: customization rather than standardization, diversity rather than uniformity, team-based organization rather than bureaucratic organization, shared decision making rather than autocratic decision making, initiative rather than compliance, holism rather than compartmentalism, autonomy with accountability rather than centralized control, and cooperative relationships rather than adversarial ones, among others. Certainly, additional "ages" are likely to come. So, in Toffler's frame of thinking, what might the next one be? Since the Industrial Age was an extension of our physical capabilities and the Information Age an extension of our mental capabilities, it seems likely to me that the next major stage of societal evolution will be the Spiritual Age, an extension of our spiritual awareness and capabilities. But that is pure speculation on my part. The point is that our society is squarely within the Information Age as described by Toffler.

Finally, I am somewhat baffled by Harmon's concern that my suggestions regarding technology "fall somewhat short." I agree that technology is likely to continue to evolve in ways he suggests. My intent was to propose that technology needs to play very different roles in the learner-centered paradigm than in the teacher-centered paradigm and that consequently theorists and designers need to design the features of the technology systems that they will use in instruction, not just the instructional strategies. Certainly, as new affordances arise and costs decline, design principles must evolve. But the four main functions to support student learning—recordkeeping, planning, instruction, and assessment—will still be important. I fail to see how this falls short.

As Harmon points out, all his recommendations except those for technology "are consistent with what Professor Reigeluth has recommended." But they are largely separate issues from the main point in my piece—the need for instructional theorists (and designers) to devote more attention to the instructional superstructure and the functions of technology that support the learner-centered paradigm, in addition to instructional principles for the learner-centered paradigm.

References

Prensky, M. (2014). The world needs a new curriculum. *Educational Technology, 54*(4), 3–15.
Prensky, M. (in press). A new paradigm of curriculum. In C. Reigeluth, R. Myers, & B. Beatty (Eds.), *Instructional-design theories and models: The learner-centered paradigm of education* (Vol. IV). New York: Routledge.
Reigeluth, C. M., & Karnopp, J. R. (2013). *Reinventing schools: It's time to break the mold*. Lanham, MD: Rowman & Littlefield.
Reigeluth, C. M., Myers, R. D., & Beatty, B. J. (in press). *Instructional-design theories and models: The learner-centered paradigm of education* (Vol. IV). New York: Routledge.
Toffler, A. (1980). *The third wave*. New York: Bantam Books.
Toffler, A. (1990). *Powershift*. New York: Bantam.

Chapter 18

Learning From and With Media and Technology

Thomas C. Reeves

There has long been controversy over the value of using media and technology as things to "learn from" or to "learn with" (Jonassen & Reeves, 1996). The use of media and technology in ways that assume people will learn "from" them has always been much more prominent than efforts to use media and technology as cognitive tools "with" which people can learn (Kim & Reeves, 2007). For example, consider the massive open online courses (MOOCs) that have attracted enormous attention in the press and literally millions of enrollees (albeit with extremely high rates of attrition). The most predominant type of MOOCS, xMOOCs, are primarily populated with brief videos that learners are expected to learn from simply viewing them and multiple-choice quizzes to assess "learning" (Daniel, 2012). MOOCs wherein learners use cognitive tools to complete authentic tasks or solve real world problems for actual clients (sometimes called pMOOCs or project-based MOOCs) are quite rare (McAndrew, 2013; Reeves & Hedberg, 2014).

The essence of this controversy about how to most effectively use media and technology in education can be traced back to different views about what it means to learn. Some prominent researchers such as Kirschner, Sweller, and Clark (2006) have emphasized the preeminence of memory as a cognitive function, indicating that they hold a mental model of learning as the process of filling some sort of organic filing cabinet. Kirschner et al. (2006) maintained, "The aim of all instruction is to alter long-term memory. If nothing has changed in long-term memory, nothing has been learned" (p. 77). Contrast this with the perspective of other scholars, who acknowledge the importance of memory functions, but describe a mental model of learning as a complex network in which the solitary human mind is just one node (Downes, 2012). Or consider Jonassen (2011), who regarded the "learning equates to long-term memory change" perspective as doomed to failure in addressing other interpretations of learning, which include (1) biochemical activity in the brain, (2) a relatively permanent change in behavior or behavioral dispositions, (3) conceptual change, (4) problem solving, (5) social negotiation, and (6) creativity, among others.

Resolution of such widely varying interpretations of what it means to learn eludes us, and the debate will continue. However, coming to a better understanding of what it means to learn may have to precede a shift from using media and technology as tools to learn "from" to methods that employ media and technology as tools to learn "with." My own perspective on learning is that it is incredibly complex, and that those of us working in the intersection of "Learning, Design, and Technology" know far too little about it to observe or measure it adequately, much less predict or control it.

I also contend that viewing learning as reducible to changes in the registers of long-term memory ignores the complexity inherent in learning at our peril. The impulse to oversimplify the definition of learning to memory change is obvious. It enables the conduct of experimental studies of learning that can be rapidly turned into refereed journal publications, the currency of success in academe. But the impact of these experimental studies on improving the messy conditions of real world teaching and learning in schools and universities around the world is unacceptably low.

Kirschner et al. (2006) have used their restricted definition of learning as a club to bash constructivist, discovery, problem-based, experiential, and inquiry-based approaches to teaching and learning, arguing instead for the widespread adoption of "direct instruction." Here again the emphasis is on control and the measurement of what can be easily quantified (e.g., recall and the application of simple rules) as opposed to what is arguably much more important to assess (e.g., the ability to question the assumptions underlying a theoretical argument or the conative drive to advance one's learning). Direct instruction, perhaps delivered via an intelligent tutoring system, works in well-structured domains (WSDs) such as algebra, albeit with much lower effectiveness than often claimed the proponents of direct instruction (VanLehn, 2011).

Spiro and DeSchryver (2009) defended constructivist approaches to teaching and learning by providing evidence that "the success of direct instruction in well-structured domains (WSDs) cannot extend to ill-structured domains (ISDs), in principle, because of the very nature of those domains" (p. 106). Proponents of direct instruction such as Kirschner et al. (2006) ignore learner intention and motivation, a failure that is compounded when direct instruction is focused on ill-structured domains "characterized by being indeterminate, inexact, noncodifiable, nonalgorithmic, nonroutinizable, imperfectly predictable, nondecompositional into additive elements, and in various ways, disorderly" (Spiro & DeSchryver, 2009, p. 107).

Learning, design, and technology researchers have focused primarily on questions related to "What works?" in regard to teaching and learning with media and technology with findings that almost always amount to "no significant differences" (Russell, 2001; Hattie, 2009). Mielke (1968), Schramm (1977), Clark (1983), and Reeves (2000), among others, have criticized this sterile trend of research for nearly fifty years, but it persists. Partly, this stems from that fact that our research agendas are overly focused on things (e.g., tablet computers) instead of problems (e.g., the underrepresentation of women and minorities in science, technology, engineering, and mathematics [STEM] careers).

There is a way forward that can make progress on how to effectively use media and technology to support learning in its full complexity. Educational design research fundamentally can shift the focus of our research from "what works?" questions to "what is the problem and how can we solve it?" intentions. Also known by other names such as "design-based research," educational design research (McKenney & Reeves, 2012; Plomp & Nieveen, 2013) addresses significant educational problems in real-world settings and has two primary goals: to develop new knowledge (usually in the form of reusable design principles), and to develop robust treatment interventions (e.g., a multiuser, virtual environment that engages students in inquiry-based science learning [Barab, Thomas, Dodge, Carteaux & Tuzun, 2005]).

Bold actions are needed to shift our research agendas from an emphasis on things to a more socially responsible focus on problems. Fortunately, there are role models in other fields that we can emulate. For example, Professor Randy Schekman from the University of California, Berkeley, won the Nobel Prize for Medicine in 2013. In the same week he won the most prestigious award for scientific achievement, he announced that his Berkeley lab would no longer submit papers to closed-access journals such as *Nature*, *Cell*, and *Science*. He characterized such publication outlets as "luxury journals" that artificially limit the capacity of scientists to share their work. He is now the editor-in-chief of *eLife*, a peer-reviewed open-access scientific journal for the biomedical and life sciences. There has been inevitable criticism of Schekman from defenders of traditional science journals, but also a great deal of support within the biosciences research community for the kinds of radical changes he is promoting (Schekman, 2013).

Imagine if, instead of continuing to pad our CVs with one-off studies of the latest technological innovations, a hundred or more of the top-learning design and technology researchers from around the globe formed a consortium through which they would identify ten significant educational problems on which to focus our collaborative research agendas for the next ten years. This would be a "moon shot" research agenda similar to the one established by neuroscientists three years ago to reveal the fundamental working of the brain (Ledford, 2011). Although all research genres would be supported, special emphasis would be placed on educational design research that requires close collaboration with practitioners and learners. Instead of throwing our research results over the walls of physical or online "classrooms," we would carry out our educational design research studies in the very environments where improvements in efficacy and efficiency are most needed. Members of this consortium would eschew traditional refereed journals with their restrictive word limits and limited circulations to peer-reviewed open-access scholarly online publications. Every such scientific publication would be accompanied by clear implications for practice, and acceptance would require relevance as well as rigor (Reeves, 2011).

When the famous American inventor Thomas Edison was interviewed about the educational potential of the motion picture system that had been developed at his Menlo Park laboratory, he proclaimed, "Books will soon be obsolete in the public schools. Scholars will be instructed through the eye. It is possible to teach every branch of human knowledge with the motion picture. Our school system will be completely changed inside of ten years." More than one hundred years later, the commercial interests behind the latest technological marvels such as tablet computers, 3D printers, wearable technology, clickers, and SmartBoards continue to make similar predictions. Learning, design, and technology researchers must step forward in advancing a bold new design research agenda focused on meaningful problems in teaching and learning. This is the only socially responsible way forward.

References

Barab, S., Thomas, M., Dodge, T., Carteaux, R., & Tuzun, H. (2005). Making learning fun: Quest Atlantis, a game without guns. *Educational Technology Research and Development*, 53(1), 86–107.

Clark, R. E. (1983). Reconsidering research on learning from media. *Review of Educational Research*, 53(4), 445–459.

Daniel, J. (2012). Making sense of MOOCs: Musings in a maze of myth, paradox and possibility. *Journal of Interactive Media in Education*, 3, 1–20.

Downes, S. (2012). *Connectivism and connective knowledge: Essays on meaning and learning networks*. Retrieved from http://www.downes.ca/me/mybooks.htm.

Hattie, J. A. C. (2009). *Visible learning: A synthesis of over 800 meta-analyses related to achievement*. New York: Routledge.

Jonassen, D. H. (2011). *Learning to solve problems: A handbook for designing problem-solving learning environments*. New York: Routledge.

Jonassen, D. H., & Reeves, T. C. (1996). Learning with technology: Using computers as cognitive tools. In D. H. Jonassen (Ed.), *Handbook of research on educational communications and technology* (pp. 693–719). New York: Macmillan.

Kim, B., & Reeves, T. C. (2007). Reframing research on learning with technology: In search of the meaning of cognitive tools. *Instructional Science*, 35(3), 207–256.

Kirschner, P. A., Sweller, J., & Clark, R. E. (2006). Why minimal guidance during instruction does not work: An analysis of the failure of constructivist, discovery, problem-based, experiential, and inquiry-based teaching. *Educational Psychologist*, 41(2), 75–86.

Ledford, H. (2011). Neuroscientists unite for 'moon shot.' *Nature*. doi:10.1038/news.2011.324

McAndrew, P. (2013). Learning from open design: Running a learning design MOOC. *eLearning Papers*, 33.

McKenney, S. E, & Reeves, T. C. (2012). *Conducting educational design research*. New York: Routledge.

Mielke, K. W. (1968). Asking the right ETV research questions. *Educational Broadcasting Review*, 2(2), 54–61.

Plomp, T., & Nieveen, N. (Eds.) (2013). *Educational design research—Part B: Illustrative cases*. Enschede, the Netherlands: SLO. Retrieved from http://international.slo.nl/bestanden/Introduction_Part_B.pdf/.

Reeves, T. C. (2000). Socially responsible educational technology research. *Educational Technology*, 40(6), 19–28.

Reeves, T. C. (2011). Can educational research be both rigorous and relevant? *Educational Designer: Journal of the International Society for Design and Development in Education*, 1(4), http://www.educationaldesigner.org/ed/volume1/issue4/article13/.

Reeves, T. C., & Hedberg, J. G. (2014). MOOCs: Let's get REAL. *Educational Technology*, 54(1), 3–8.

Russell, T. L. (2001). *The no significant difference phenomenon* (5th ed.). Montgomery, AL: International Distance Education Certification Center.

Schekman, R. (2013). How to break free from the stifling grip of luxury journals. *The Conversation*. Retrieved from http://theconversation.com/how-to-break-free-from-the-stifling-grip-of-luxury-journals-21669.

Schramm, W. (1977). *Big media, little media*. Beverly Hills, CA: Sage.

Spiro, R. J., & DeSchryver, M. (2009). Constructivism: When it's the wrong idea and when it's the only idea. In T. M. Duffy & S. Tobias (Eds.), *Constructivist instruction: Success or failure?* (pp. 106–123). New York: Routledge.

VanLehn, K. (2011). The relative effectiveness of human tutoring, intelligent tutoring systems, and other tutoring systems. *Educational Psychologist*, 46(4), 197–221.

RESPONSE BY WILHELMINA C. SAVENYE

The opportunity to respond to Thomas Reeves's chapter has been exhilarating! My own career began many years ago, with my interest in photography and later video production as a youth. My first training was in the age of audio-visual education, then media technology, instructional technology, onward to today. I have been privileged to have been a part of our field of learning design and technologies as the field has evolved.

I commend Reeves's call to action! He is so correct, unfortunately, that often our research is not as impactful and meaningful as it could be, and he challenges us to shake up our research work and views in a great way. In fact, a recent issue of the *Chronicle of Higher Education* also focuses the spotlight on making research matter more (Basken, 2016).

Reeves begins, again, so appropriately, by directing us to consider our definitions of learning and "what it means to learn," and here, too, to challenge us with the view that we still do not necessarily have adequate definitions of learning, that learning is very complex and is not necessarily carried out only in classrooms. As Reeves notes, the broader, deeper definitions of learning espoused by Gagne (1985), Jonassen (2011), Merrill (2013), Spector (2000) and van Merriënboer (1997) with regard to complex learning are those that are more productive, as well as challenging, today. I would extend Reeves reminders that learning design is now carried out often in informal as well as formal environments (National Research Council, 2009) and requires that we design and study learning using more nuanced and richer methods, with perhaps the additional reminder of Falk and Dierking (2002) that we design and study "free-choice" learning.

I would agree with Simonson, Smaldino, Albright, and Zvacek (2003) in their textbook on distance education. These authors conclude their book with the hope that in the future, in my view, that is, now, we would not be discussing "distance education," but would instead just be discussing "education." Let us extend that to "learning."

His piece is also refreshing in that Reeves takes us beyond the older "media comparison" research—that is, he takes us from the notion of learning "from" to learning "with" media (Jonassen & Reeves, 1996). Reeves begins by describing the early generations of MOOCs, which admittedly have not necessarily made the difference once expected. Our own university, for example, was not an early adopter of MOOCs; however, now our president supports the development of several and notes that "massive open online courses (MOOCs) can make higher education more accessible, immersive and comprehensive, if deployed with due caution" (Crow, 2013). Some might argue that the evolution of MOOCs and how our field views them mirrors that recorded historically for any new technology. In the evolution of learning technologies, we often have heard from those outside the field that we "must" use the newest technologies, as they will be the solution, perhaps the panacea, to our learning and educational problems. Perhaps it is the same with MOOCs.

I would extend Reeves's argument about learning with media to suggest that our definitions of media, too, are becoming more nuanced. For instance, our university president, again, rather than simply discussing online learning, defines the university's learning technology offerings as follows:

- Full immersion—on campus, technology enhanced
- Digital immersion—online, technology enhanced
- Digital immersion—massive scale, technology enhanced, and
- Education through exploration—technology enhanced. (Crow, 2016)

One very encouraging trend, as Reeves notes, is the convergence of the fields of learning sciences, learning design, and learning technologies. We have noted that the jobs in our field often are still listed as "training specialist" or "instructional designer"; however, we are also beginning to see job titles in industry such as "learning leader" and "learning designer," "learning experience designer," and, of course, "evangelist."

Turning to our study of learning with media—that is, the research in our field—Reeves very clearly explicates the value of design-based research and its ability to enable us to both conduct research and support the design and development of ever-more effective learning technologies and learning environments.

However, Reeves also proposes a sort of "straw man" proposition—that is, that research is either objectivist or constructivist—citing the work of Kirschner, Sweller, and Clark (2006) and others as only supporting "direct instruction." Instead I would contend that research approaches, too, are becoming more nuanced, complex, and appropriate. What I see in working with younger researchers in our field, as a teacher, colleague, reviewer, and editor, is more reliance on mixed-method research, with the goal of describing and, at times, prescribing applications of learning technologies in a deeper, more useful manner. Smith and Ragan (1999) might call this approach to research, just as with learning design, "pragmatic," or we could call it eclectic, or complex, or nuanced.

The challenge Reeves issues is an important one and one that researchers in our field should rise to—that is, to conduct research that makes a difference and improves student learning. His solution—that is, that the top one hundred researchers in our field accept this challenge and together develop research agendas that span ten years and are more valuable to learning—could indeed greatly improve the impact of research in our field.

However . . . I would like to challenge researchers in our field to accept Reeves's call to action and begin to propose additional solutions to the problem of "meaning" in learning technology research.

One shortcoming in Reeves's recommendation is that there may be a danger of promulgating less-diverse views if those of us who are "senior" in the field only take up the challenge. The "top one hundred" researchers may not be as diverse as we would hope, in terms of gender, race, ethnicity, class, religion, or sexual orientation, for instance. (Current events in our nation and internationally support this challenge.)

Let us take up Reeves's challenge, answering it in many different ways. I contend that the younger members of our field are advancing research in powerful and meaningful ways. We could support them better. We could work to identify and support those whose research is "different" or who themselves have "different" views, and look for high-quality impactful research being conducted by all. We who are more senior could attempt to influence funding agencies to support more high-quality newer work, as well as supporting those whose research is more proven.

Additionally, younger researchers are typically not simply padding their vita, as Reeves mentions, though, of course, that does occur. Our younger colleagues work in academic systems that have their own requirements, with which the young must comply in order to keep their jobs, advance their careers, feed their families, and build lives that are as fortuitous as ours have been. We who are more senior or established could support them better, as many in our field have done, by working to improve the academic incentive systems to reward longer-term research, for example, especially in school systems, or more applied research, or to extend the public benefits from research, which might yield fewer, but more impactful, publications.

I imagine my colleague Reeves and our readers could argue that in a way I am saying let us both challenge and support the next generations of researchers in our wonderful field of learning design and technology . . . and they would be right.

References

Basken, P. (2016, January 29). Is university research missing what matters most? *Chronicle of Higher Education*, A19–A22. Available from http://www.chronicle.com/article/Is-University-Research-Missing/235028.

Crow, M. M. (18 July 2013). Digital learning: Look, then leap. *Nature*, 499, 275–277. Published online 17 July 2013. doi:10.1038/499275a

Crow, M. M. (2016). What is innovation? Community conversation, January 13, 2016. [PowerPoint slides].

Falk, J. H., & Dierking, L. D. (2002). *Lessons without limit: How free-choice learning is transforming education*. Walnut Creek, CA: AltaMira.

Gagne, R. M. (1985). *The conditions of learning and theory of instruction* (4th ed.) Fort Worth, TX: Holt, Rinehart & Winston.

Jonassen, D. H. (2011). *Learning to solve problems: A handbook for designing problem-solving learning environments*. New York: Routledge.

Jonassen, D. H., & Reeves, T. C. (1996). Learning with technology: Using computers as cognitive tools. In D. H. Jonassen (Ed.), *Handbook of research on educational communications and technology* (pp. 693–719). New York: Macmillan.

Kirschner, P. A., Sweller, J., & Clark, R. E. (2006). Why minimal guidance during instruction does not work: An analysis of the failure of constructivist, discovery, problem-based, experiential, and inquiry-based teaching. *Educational Psychologist*, 41(2), 75–86.

Merrill, M. D. (2013). *First principles of instruction*. San Francisco, CA: Pfeiffer.

National Research Council (2009). *Learning science in informal environments: People, places, and pursuits*. Committee on Learning Science and Informal Environments. Phillip Bell, Bruce Lewenstein, Andrew W. Shouse, & Michael A. Feder (Eds.), Board on Science Education, Center for Education, Division of Behavioral and Social Sciences and Education. Washington, DC: The National Academies Press.

Simonson, M., Smaldino, S., Albright, M., & Zvacek, S. (2003). *Teaching and learning at a distance: Foundations of distance education* (2nd ed.). Upper Saddle River, NJ: Merrill.

Smith, P. J., & Ragan, T. J. (1999). *Instructional design* (2nd ed.). Upper Saddle River, NJ: Merrill.

Spector, J. M. (2000). Building theory into practice in learning and instruction. In J. M. Spector & T. M. Anderson (Eds.), *Integrated and holistic perspectives on learning, instruction and technology: Understanding complexity* (pp. 79–90). Dordrecht, Netherlands: Kluwer.

van Merriënboer, J. J. G. (1997). *Training complex cognitive skills*. Englewood Cliffs, NJ: Educational Technology Publications.

REJOINDER BY THOMAS C. REEVES

Please let me begin my response by expressing sincere gratitude to my colleague Professor Willi Savenye of Arizona State University for her thoughtful analysis of my original contribution to the *Issues* book. I especially appreciate her stress on the importance of "learning design" as the future research agendas of our field are refined. Savenye's reminder of the need to engage diverse perspectives in efforts to reform educational technology research is also praiseworthy.

In addition, Savenye wisely counsels that those of us who are senior in the field of educational technology should support our younger colleagues better. I agree. My career in the field of educational technology can be traced back more than fifty years to the early 1960s when I learned to make overhead transparencies for the Redemptorists Fathers at St. Mary's College in North East, Pennsylvania, where I was a young seminarian from 1961–1965. A few years later, when I was serving in the U.S. Army, I completed a one-week audiovisual training school at Fort Hamilton, New York, where among other things, I learned to thread a 16mm projector in seconds while blindfolded. Later, after working as an elementary school teacher, I earned three graduate degrees in our field, one from Georgia State University, and two from Syracuse University. I have spent the bulk of my professional career at the University of Georgia, where I am now a professor emeritus.

As a young assistant professor, I received strong support from most of the senior faculty members in my department, and I was able to successfully jump through the promotion and tenure hoops with their guidance. Today, I think an argument can be made that while support from senior faculty largely continues, the hoops have gotten more difficult to negotiate, especially with respect to publications and grant-funding. The increased pressures to "publish or perish" and "go fund yourself" are arguably increasing the stress levels of young academics more than ever before (Buckholdt & Miller, 2013).

Although our official roles as academics are threefold, research, teaching, and service, most of the evidence used to judge our merit focuses on research activities, especially for those of us working in research-intensive institutions. Complaining about this is unlikely to effect significant change, but perhaps we could modify the rules of the game if unassailable evidence could be found that the research we are doing is making a difference in the lives of teachers, learners, and society at large.

As I noted in my original contribution to this book, the educational technology field has a long history of research that provides insufficient guidance to practitioners. Indeed, this body of research can largely be summed up as a legacy of "no-significant differences" (Russell, 2001). However, the lack of impact on policy and practice is hardly unique to educational technology. Thomas J. Kane, the Walter H. Gale professor of education and faculty director of the Center for Education Policy Research at Harvard University, recently wrote: "If the central purpose of education research is to identify solutions and provide options for policymakers and practitioners, one would have to characterize the past five decades as a near-complete failure" (Kane, 2016, pp. 81–82). This sounds harsh, but I agree with Kane and remain convinced that for the most part educational technology research has a similar lack of impact on practice.

Kane (2016) went on to argue that the federal agencies that provide the majority of the financial support for educational research in the United States, such as the National Science Foundation (NSF) and the Institute of Education Sciences (IES), should "redirect [their] efforts away from funding the interests and priorities of the research community and toward building an evidence-based culture" (p. 86) within state agencies, school districts, and individual schools. He maintained that local stakeholders are much more likely "to act based on findings from their own data than on any third-party report they may find in the What Works Clearinghouse" (p. 87). Kane's recommendations are well-aligned with my proposal that educational technology researchers should more widely engage in educational design research (design-based research), partnering closely with practitioners to fundamentally shift the focus of our research from "what works?" questions to "what is the problem and how can we solve it?" intentions (McKenney & Reeves, 2012). This may not be the only path toward more socially responsible educational technology research agendas, but it is certainly one worth trying.

References

Buckholdt, D. R., & Miller, G. E. (2013). *Faculty stress*. New York: Routledge.

Kane, T. J. (2016). Connecting to practice: How we can put educational research to work. *Education Next, 16*(2), 80–87.

McKenney, S. E, & Reeves, T. C. (2012). *Conducting educational design research*. New York: Routledge.

Russell, T. L. (2001). *The no significant difference phenomenon* (5th ed.), Montgomery, AL: International Distance Education Certification Center.

Chapter 19

Building Educational Technologies to Scale in Schools

Rob Foshay

The most common finding of research on effectiveness of ICT in K-12 schools is "no significant difference." Even RCT studies done under near-perfect "hothouse" conditions rarely show effect sizes greater than 0.3 or so. And even the best applications rarely make it past the early adopters and into wide adoption. The reasons we usually give point to a variety of weak implementations, which we attribute to a variety of causes: the educational system, policy, funding, teacher attitudes and technology competence, and so on (a classic critique is Cuban & Cuban, 2009). We always argue that "more PD is needed." But perhaps, dear Brutus, the fault is not just in our star schools and teachers but in ourselves.

My position is that all too often, we design our ICT applications for K-12 classrooms in ways that unintentionally limit the likelihood of their adoption to the few hardy early adopters who are willing to invest the effort and take the risk of trying out our brain children, in hopes of discovering some value. When we design an application, we do not take into account adequately the needs, values, concerns, and abilities of middle adopter teachers. Instead, we design for the teachers and classrooms we wish we had, rather than the ones we actually have. The net effect is that we unintentionally design our applications to self-limit, rather than to go to scale. This simply will not do.

Grounded theory research done by Ken Ruthven on how algebra teachers adopt technology (Ruthven & Hennessy, 2002; Hennessy, Ruthven & Brindley, 2005) provides an example of the design challenge. He argues that teachers perceive their work environment within this framework:

- **Working environment**: including classroom management, school policies and schedules, and so on
- **Resource system**: all curriculum materials, tools, references, and the like that are available for use in teaching
- **Activity format**: the small number of familiar "teaching routines" with which each teacher is comfortable; usually learned in the first few years of teaching
- **Curriculum script**: the scope and sequence, pacing guides, tests, lesson plans, and so on that the school provides to guide teaching of the content area (supplemented by the teacher's extensive investment in a "teaching file" of activities and resources)
- **Time economy**: the moment-by-moment allocation of classroom time to activities that fit within activity formats and classroom management rules.

An important point here is that middle adopter teachers usually view most of these framework components as externally determined and thus invariable. Thus, any innovation, including ICT, must make sense to the teacher within its perceived framework.

As an example of this model's explanatory utility, I cite paraphrased concerns stated by middle adopter teachers in formative product evaluations[1] I have done:

- The product will waste time in class, as students focus on getting logged in and set up, and then waste time playing with the product. All this is off-task time. [Time economy]
- Giving the product to the class will cause me to lose control of the class, as the buzz of off-task class talk increases, and especially when the technology collapses in the middle of the lesson (as it always seems to). [Working environment, resource system]
- Figuring out how to use this product and integrate it into my curriculum will require an unacceptable amount of my planning and preparation time. [Time economy, resource system, curriculum script]
- If I show I cannot use the product in front of my students, my authority will be damaged. [Working environment]
- My students will not be able to do that. [Activity format]
- I would love to use this product, but I have to give priority to teaching the content specified in the district pacing guide. [Activity format, curriculum script]

The point is that these teachers view use of the product as risky, not only because it is untried, but also because it requires abandonment of a tried-and-true solution that is known to fit within their working environment, time economy (within and outside the classroom), curriculum script, resource system, and the teachers' repertoire of activity formats that they know will work with their students.

Ruthven then goes on to characterize the way teachers perceive the proximal, intermediate, and distal benefits of technology. Figure 19.1 shows his model of how teachers gradually discover the value of an ICT product in teaching. When read from left to right, we see that in the left-hand column are the benefits first perceived. In the middle column are intermediate benefits that are discovered only with continued use of the ICT product. The right-hand column has the major claimed benefits of many ICT products, but these benefits emerge only after sustained use and full mastery of the ICT environment. This process often takes years of experience—and, often enough, teachers who do not see the proximal benefits simply shelve the technology without ever discovering any of the more distal major benefits.

I believe models such as Ruthven's go a long way toward explaining why middle adopters rarely use our products as designed and often abandon them after a tentative first use. Any product that requires a major change in any part of the work environment framework will be seen as unacceptably risky or costly (especially in time, in or outside the classroom). Any product that does not immediately present the benefits in the left column of Figure 19.1, and fit within the framework of the teachers' work environments, will be abandoned before the teachers use them enough to discover the benefits in the middle and right columns. This, I argue, is a common cause of failure to implement.

I believe the cause is a failure of our design philosophy and methodology. I argue that we often misconstrue and mis-apply the theoretical framework of activity theory (Engeström, 2001) and discipline of user-centered design (Georg, 2011). All too often, we follow our own vision, rather than understanding our users. All too often, user-centered design discipline is applied only to the final stage of user interface design, rather than at the very beginning of conceptualization of the product and its purpose. All too often, we fail to understand that ICT for schools has at least these types of users, each with different requirements:

- The students
- The teacher

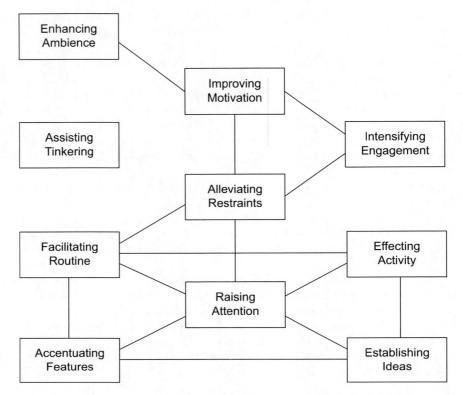

Figure 19.1 A Practitioner Model of the Use of Computer-based Tools and Resources in Secondary-school Mathematics

Source: Ruthven and Hennessy (2002).

- The curriculum administrator(s) and stakeholders
- The technology coordinator
- (And perhaps) the parents

To be adopted at scale, an ICT product must show value to *all* these types of users and must do so on first use. Furthermore, the product must be designed to guide the teacher to more sophisticated uses over time, so that the major benefits can be realized. And all this must be accomplished without unacceptably costly investment in professional development, coaching, and tech support.

As an example, we can return to the way an ICT product for instructional use in a classroom must present itself to middle adopters. If we apply Ruthven's framework and model, then the product must first show to the teacher that:

- Getting from first "program start" to "ready for use in tomorrow's class" takes no more than twenty minutes. No formal professional development required.
- It saves time, both within and outside the class (can be instructional time or other classroom activity time).
- It is an easy, one-for-one substitution for a familiar learning activity.
- Students are always on task, from the moment they open the first screen. No tinkering required or allowed.

- It augments a familiar activity format, rather than requiring abandonment of one and mastering another.
- It solves a familiar "tough to teach/tough to learn" problem within the existing curriculum script.
- It is absolutely dependable, in the hostile user environment of the real-world classroom.

A similar list of requirements could be developed for the other stakeholders, including the administrators and curriculum coordinators, the technology coordinators, and the parents.

To reiterate: only a product that can succeed according to these criteria—on the first try—will ever be used again. If (and only if) it is used again, then these teachers will gradually master the product sufficiently to see the benefits in the middle and right columns of Figure 19.1.[2] The product itself must be designed to promote this kind of teacher growth, organically as a natural consequence of use. Other stakeholders must understand this organic growth process and set their expectations accordingly. In technology product evaluations I have facilitated,[3] it is not unusual for the "real" (right-hand column) benefits to appear only after three years or more of use. The unfortunate reality is that many teachers never grow enough to achieve these benefits—or even to realize that they are possible.

This argument is also cautionary to the venture capitalists and grant officers who invest in ICT for schools. It is rare to see grant programs or venture capitalists who insist on this kind of product design discipline. In my experience, most make naïve assumptions about scalability of ed tech and are unwilling to fund the hard and costly work of true user-centered design, which must start at the initial stages of design. These development methodology lessons should also be built into our professional training programs. Until these lessons are learned by those who develop and disseminate ICT for schools, I believe ICT will not go to scale for instructional use and will not show a substantial return on the investment in improved learning that schools, parents, and policy makers expect.

Notes

1. Since my work has been with commercial companies, these studies unfortunately are unpublished.
2. Another implication of this argument is that technology effectiveness evaluations in schools need to be longitudinal, or they should be done after only three years or more of successful use.
3. Interested readers are referred to the collections of evaluation studies for the PLATO Learning System® and for the Texas Instruments® graphing calculators. Some studies have been published in books and journals, and more are available on the company Web sites or upon request to the companies.

References

Cuban, L., & Cuban, L. (2009). *Oversold and underused: Computers in the classroom*. Cambridge, MA: Harvard University Press.

Engeström, Y. (2001). Expansive learning at work: towards an activity theoretical reconceptualization. *Journal of Education and Work*, 14(1), 133–156.

Georg, G. (2011). *Activity theory and its applications in software engineering and technology literature search results and observations* (C. S. Department, Trans.). Fort Collins, CO: Colorado State University.

Hennessy, S., Ruthven, K., & Brindley, S. (2005). Teacher perspectives on integrating ICT into subject teaching: Commitment, constraints, caution, and change. *Journal of Curriculum Studies, v37 n2 p155–192 Mar-Apr 2005*, 37(2), 155–192.

Ruthven, K., & Hennessy, S. (2002). A practitioner model of the use of computer-based tools and resources to support mathematics teaching and learning. *Educational Studies in Mathematics*, 49(1), 47–88.

RESPONSE BY MJ BISHOP

Dr. Foshay is correct that we have had a hundred-year-long history of technologies bursting onto the scene accompanied by great excitement over their potential to transform education... that then never materializes. And, as Dr. Foshay argues, while this bleak story of technology's impact on education is well known to those of us in the instructional design and development field, we have taken remarkably far too little responsibility for addressing the barriers to widespread adoption of our "brain children." The problem comes in figuring out what, exactly, the barriers are and how to overcome them. Dr. Foshay's framing of teacher adoption concerns within Ruthven's theories provides some excellent guidance in this regard.

However, while addressing what it will take to persuade teachers to adopt innovation is certainly necessary, I doubt it will be sufficient to break the ineffectual educational technology adoption cycle. Dr. Foshay alludes to the fundamental problem when he makes the point that "middle adopter teachers usually view most of these framework components as externally determined and thus invariable." As long as middle-adopter teachers believe that their working environment, resource system, activity format, curriculum script, and time economy cannot be altered, then it may never be possible for us to achieve scale with educational technologies.

Argyris and Schön (1974, 1978) referred to the difference between our intentions to do something and what we actually do as the gap between our *espoused theory* (what we would like others to think we do) and our *theory-in-use* (the theory that actually governs our actions, usually made up of tacit structures). When these two theories do not match, there are two possible responses. *Single-loop learning* involves looking for another strategy that works within the existing governing variables, further operationalizing those variables rather than questioning them. *Double-loop learning* subjects the governing variables themselves to scrutiny, modifying "an organization's underlying norms, policies, and objectives" (p. 3) and shifting the framing of our strategies entirely.

The problem as I see it is that, as a field, we continue to view the individual user as the unit of change... or at least operate as if that is the extent of our sphere of influence and/or responsibility with regard to educational technology implementations. We have perpetuated single-loop learning within the educational enterprise by finding ways to "computerize" things as they have always been done in order to attract early adopters who we hope will influence middle adopters who we hope will influence late adopters and eventually lead to scale. This tack works up to a point, but it only temporarily masks the underlying contextual barriers to change and results in a rather quantitative view of being "at scale" (numbers of individuals participating) that quickly disperses after the initiative ends. So, while our discussions about the diffusion of an innovation continue to focus on the conditions that must exist to persuade *individuals* to make changes within their existing contexts, what really impacts substantive and sustainable change from an innovation is more likely the extent to which the *organization* is receptive to new approaches.

Organizational change, therefore, requires more than just sheer numbers of faculty and student participants in the initiative. Instead, as Coburn (2003) has suggested, scaling an innovation may be predicated on other less quantifiable factors including depth, sustainability, spread, and shift in ownership of the need for change. Stated differently, to be "at scale," reforms must effect deep and consequential change in practice—measured qualitatively as well as quantitatively. According to Coburn, this means digging below surface measures of implementation to capture a more nuanced understanding of how the innovation is impacting changes to beliefs, norms, and pedagogical principles as enacted in practice. It means exploring institutional organization and structures to understand how existing business models, policies, and environments are impeding or supporting transformation. It involves watching for the spread of innovation both *across* institutions as well as *within* an institution. And, perhaps most importantly, to be at scale, the reform must finally become self-generative through a shift in ownership of the innovation from the external driver (such as the funder, or a district/system office) to the institutional stakeholders.

While this conceptualization of "scale" emphasizes dimensions that are more challenging to influence and measure, it seems important for us facilitate institutions' double-loop learning if we are to break the current cycle of technology adoption. As a field, we need to take responsibility for understanding and helping to address the organizational cultural factors that will lead to lasting change from the educational technologies we design and develop.

References

Argyris, C., & Schön, D. (1974). *Theory in practice: Increasing professional effectiveness*. San Francisco, CA: Jossey-Bass.

Argyris, C., & Schön, D. (1978).*Organizational learning: A theory of action perspective*, Reading, MA: Addison Wesley.

Coburn, C. (2003). Rethinking scale: Moving beyond numbers to deep and lasting change. *Educational Researcher, 32*(6), 3–12.

REJOINDER BY ROB FOSHAY

Bishop correctly casts the problem of why technological innovations do not go to scale and persist in K-12 within the more general issue of why K-12 innovations of any kind are implemented slowly, incrementally, and imperfectly within the U.S. public education system. She argues that the barriers to change are systemic and require a deep understanding of the beliefs, norms, and pedagogical principles enacted within the schools. It is hard to disagree with this argument; it goes back at least to the groundbreaking work by Matthew Miles (1964).

The question is what are the implications for developers of educational technology. I see at least four lines of opportunity with potential to go to scale:

1. *Develop the kinds of products that meet the requirements outlined above.* These products will probably represent small-scale, nondisruptive enhancements to existing practices, which can be easily understood and implemented within the middle adopter teacher's framework and supported by other stakeholders. Many serious games would fit this strategy, as would electronic "field trips" and use of 1:1 hardware as a reference, creative, and communication tool. Of course, small scale means small effect sizes. Teachers view these as "enrichment" alternatives to existing teaching scripts; if budget cuts eliminate them, the classroom routine would scarcely be affected. Administrators view them as added-cost additions to existing practice.
2. *Develop disruptive and large-scale products designed as part of alternative systems.* The goal in this strategy is "double loop" systemic change of the sort Bishop argues for. The alternative systems are designed to replace or offset large sections of the conventional school structure. Examples include the more comprehensive online high schools (usually statewide, and targeting underserved populations) and some charter schools that represent true alternatives, such as Rocketship (see www.rsed.org). Bishop correctly points out that decisions to adopt these alternatives are often driven by stakeholders outside the conventional school system. I would argue that the most successful education technology innovation to go to scale is an example of this category: *Sesame Street*.
3. *Develop disruptive products that provide alternative learning environments outside the conventional classroom.* Examples include some kinds of "flipped classroom" activities, after-school STEM and enrichment programs, and museum-based and other informal learning programs. Some kinds of personalized instruction systems are examples. This strategy creates learning environments that run outside the conventional classroom and often in parallel with it, and may not have direct involvement of school staff.
4. *Develop products that appeal to administrators by saving cost and time, but without major teacher disruptions.* Examples include computer-based testing, adoption of e-textbooks, or substitution of open-source curriculum materials for textbooks, attendance, and record keeping systems. This strategy emphasizes administrative productivity tools and cost-offset strategies, but instructional innovation is incidental.

The strategic implications of these four lines of opportunity are obvious. As long as schools and funding sources (private and public sector) seek to minimize risk, they will choose the first and fourth options, with limited impact on learning. The second and third options usually demand large investment in research and development, and still larger investment in dissemination. Their very disruptiveness increases their risk, especially if the goal is large-scale disruptive change. There is hope that these disruptive strategies can minimize risk by starting small and growing over time as they gain acceptance. Success with them will require product designers to work with a wide range of stakeholders, using collaborative design methodology.

Reference

Miles, M. B. (Ed.) (1964). *Innovation in education.* New York: Teachers College Press, Columbia University.

Chapter 20

For the Foreseeable Future, Instructional Technology Devices and Products—No Matter How Well Designed—Will Not Eliminate the Need for Human Teachers

Ward Mitchell Cates and Thomas C. Hammond

There can be no question: instructional technology has advanced incredibly over the years. In 1965, Moore projected the density of circuits in computers would double roughly every two years, effectively doubling the processing power of computers; this has since come to be known as Moore's Law. Such circuit density and use of new materials and technologies have also produced remarkable advances in accessible memory and storage devices (Princess Megabyte, 2012; Cocilova, 2013). As a result, computers became both more powerful and smaller, enabling mobile and wearable computers, such as smartwatches, smartglasses, and other Internet-compatible devices.[1] Robotics is a field focusing on using computer technologies to create thinking machines, increasingly in the form of mobile and independent robots.[2] It explores how such robots might take on various responsibilities previously handled by humans. While use of robots has made great inroads in industrial settings (Wallén, 2008), researchers are now exploring how "sociable" robots might be utilized in interactive settings with humans, a research area known as "human-robot interaction" (HRI; see Kidd, 2003). HRI researchers report substantial progress in helping robots relate to humans and humans relate to robots, focusing on robots' evidencing and recognizing facial expressions, receiving and giving touch, using and recognizing gestures, and employing and recognizing speech and intonation (see, for example, Ho & MacDorman, 2010; Mubin et al., 2010; Al Moubayed, Beskow, Skantze & Granström, 2012; Zlotowski, Proudfoot & Bartneck, 2013). HRI applications currently being explored include handling childcare/eldercare and serving in teaching situations (Fridin, 2014).

Dowling (2002) stated, "Arguably the most obvious choice of interactive role for an agent [or robot] would be that of teacher" (p. 3). This is not a new idea. Expanding on his 1973 proposal, Heinich (1991, p. 240) suggested certifying technology products, instead of people, affording such products the same professional status granted teachers. In 1993, Perelman claimed that we already had "the technology today to enable virtually anyone who is not severely handicapped to learn anything, at a 'grade A' level, anywhere, anytime" (p. 23). The idea that technology can and should replace teachers is still being debated today.[3] But what exactly do effective teachers do that we seek to have social robots replace?

Computers are excellent problem solvers, hence the name. They can store more data and calculate far more rapidly than any human brain (Fischetti, 2011). However, not all problems are the same. Rittel and Webber (1973) differentiated between "wicked" problems and "tame" problems. Tame problems can be complex, but they have a clear end goal—for example, mapping a genome or developing a vaccine. Wicked problems, in contrast, have no clear end goal or stopping rule; their outcomes cannot be judged solely as a success or failure but rather as better, worse, or good enough. No two wicked problems are the same, limiting generalizability.

Teaching—or, rather, teaching *well*—is a wicked problem. In fact, Koehler and Mishra (2008) spoke of wicked problems in describing their construct, Technological Pedagogical Content Knowledge (TPACK). TPACK addresses the interaction of major variables in skilled teachers' instructional planning: the curricular content or skill under instruction, the pedagogical method chosen, and the selected technologies to be used by the teacher and/or students as they interact with elements of the setting, such as student interest or aptitude. Teachers' instructional planning is a wicked problem because it is complex. The nearly unlimited, nested details of the curricular content are multiplied by the nuances of the many possible instructional methods and multiplied again by the technological options available. Students' interactions with the instruction are further varied by their strengths and weaknesses with the content, method, and technology. In addition to the complexity of these myriad permutations, the variables are in constant flux. Last year's students may have responded well to one set of strategies for *The Scarlet Letter* and another set for *The Great Gatsby*, but this year's students may not. Or perhaps the curriculum has changed, and the teacher now has to teach Chinua Achebe's *Things Fall Apart* for the first time; what contextual information will students need? Can the teacher use the same strategies for contextualizing colonial Nigeria as for colonial New England? Finally, the aims of teaching encompass not just Koehler and Mishra's cognitive outcomes but the *whole learner*, addressing Bloom's affective and psychomotor domains (Krathwohl, 2002) in order to help develop in students what Mann (1849) termed "character."

Skilled teachers consistently find productive solutions to the wicked problems of instruction, working across the full spectrum of cognitive, affective, and behavioral issues that intersect in the classroom (Cornelius-White, 2007). One student is glowing from a teacher's compliment in the previous period; another is glowering over that same teacher's perceived disrespect. One student is distracted by an upcoming audition for a play; another, by a confrontation at the bus stop that morning. One student is disruptive after being assigned to group work with a social rival; another student is in a group with a close friend and is, therefore, completely off-task. These social and emotional factors are critical to student learning (Wubbels, den Brock, Tartwijk & Levy, 2012). Good teachers, therefore, choose among different tactics—humor, authoritativeness, mentoring, self-deprecation, nagging, friendliness—and teachers work across different time frames. For example, deciding to ignore student A for today and tackle the issue if it recurs tomorrow; to talk to student B outside of class; to immediately confront student C if the problem behavior emerges; but to try to deflect student D—she has oppositional defiant disorder and may erupt if directly confronted. Furthermore, each of these decisions is informed by many other variables: gender, age, culture/ethnicity, religious background, and the like, as well as by the teacher's own identity (for example, Day & Lee, 2011).

Historically, schools' responsibilities regarding students' social and emotional well-being have increased. Since the 1950s, law school has brought greater sensitivity to issues of race (see Simpson, 2014), gender (U.S. Department of Justice, 2012), disability (Aron & Loprest, 2012), and more. Given this trend, the social problems of teaching are likely to grow ever more wicked.

Despite the great advances in computing and robots, substantial barriers to using technology to replace the classroom teacher still exist. Some are technological barriers, such as the practical limitations on chip manufacturing that threaten to slow the continued fulfillment of Moore's Law (Shankland, 2012; Courtland, 2013; Crothers, 2013), or the access and bandwidth issues similarly experienced by wearable computers (Starner, 2001a, 2001b). Others barriers, however, relate directly to the challenges in creating a "theory of mind" from which a robot can relate to humans dynamically and adaptively (Sharkey & Sharkey, 2010, p. 13)—making the connections Palmer (2010) suggested were the heart of what good teachers provide in the place "where intellect and emotion and spirit . . . converge in the human self" (p. 3).

Without such capabilities, a robot would be unable in real-time to analyze the diversity of inputs faced in the classroom and to generate appropriate responses—that is, to handle the wicked problems of teaching. For these reasons, most social robotics development concentrates on having robots serve as assistants and partners, not replacements (DiSalvo, Gemperle, Forlizzi & Kiesler, 2002; Kahn et al., 2012). As Knight (2014) concluded, "Human partnership with robots is the best of both worlds—deep access to information and mechanical capability, as well as higher-level systems thinking, ability to deal with novel or unexpected phenomena, and knowledge of human salience" (p. 18). While one could envision a future in which robots would cross the threshold into full social and intellectual capability, even robotics researchers suggest such a future may be quite distant (see, for example, Jacob & Karn, 2003; Poole & Ball, 2006; Partridge & Bartneck, 2013).

The impetus for wishing to use technology to replace teachers may actually be a financial one. For example, Gingrich (2014) contended that employing technology would likely be less expensive than human teachers. As Sharkey and Sharkey argued, however, there is potential for "widespread use of the technology in situations where there is a shortage of funding, and where what is actually needed is more staff and better regulation" (2010, p. 16). But, as many have noted before, the claims of technology's superiority and its ability to enhance or radically alter teaching have been with us for over a century (Cuban, 2001).

Thus, until technology can respond to learner needs in dynamic, flexible, and creative ways and connect with learners on an emotional and motivational level, human teachers are here to stay. Alternatively, we could reduce the wicked—but incredibly richer—problem of teaching to what a robot or other computer might be able to handle. This approach, however, would change teaching to its lesser cousin, what technology will *permit* us to deliver. To our way of thinking, such a restricted version would not be effective teaching but rather be a pale technological imitation.

Notes

1. "Wearable computer," Wikipedia entry. Web.
2. "History of the Robotics Institute," The Robotics Institute, Carnegie Mellon University. Web.
3. For example, see: "Will technology replace teachers?" Debate.org. Web.

References

Al Moubayed, S., Beskow, J., Skantze, G., & Granström, B. (2012). Furhat: A back-projected human-like robot head for multiparty human-machine interaction. In A. Esposito, A.M. Esposito, A. Vinciarelli, R. Hoffman, & V.C. Muller (Eds.), *Cognitive behavioural systems: COST 2102 International Training School, Dresden, Germany, February 21–26, 2011, Revised selected papers* (pp. 114–130). Berlin: Springer-Verlag.

Aron, L., & Loprest, P. (2012). Disability and the education system. *Future of Children, 22*(1), 97–122.

Cocilova, A. (September 12, 2013). The astounding evolution of the hard drive. *PCWorld*.

Cornelius-White, J. (2007). Learner-centered teacher-student relationships are effective: A meta-analysis. *Review of Educational Research, 77*, 113–143.

Courtland, R. (2013, October 28). The status of Moore's Law: It's complicated. *IEEE Spectrum*.

Crothers, B. (2013, Aug. 28). End of Moore's Law: It's not just about physics. *CNET*.

Cuban, L. (2001). *Oversold and underused: Computers in the classroom*. Cambridge, MA: Harvard University Press.

Day, C., & Lee, J. C.-K. (Eds.) (2011). *New understandings of teacher's work: Emotions and educational change*. Dordrecht: Springer.

DiSalvo, C.F, Gemperle, F., Forlizzi, J., & Kiesler, S. (2002). All robots are not created equal: The design and perception of humanoid robot heads. *DIS2002: Proceedings of the 4th Conference on Designing Interactive Systems: Processes, Practices, Methods and Techniques* (pp. 321–326). New York: Association for Computing Machinery.

Dowling, C. (2002). Agent technologies in the electronic classroom: Some pedagogical issues. *Proceedings of the Ed-MEDIA World Conference on Educational Multimedia, Hypermedia and Telecommunications*, Denver CO, 14, 1–7.

Fischetti, M. (2011, Oct.12). Computers versus brains. *Scientific American*. Web.

Fridin, M. (2014). Kindergarten social assistive robot: First meeting and ethical issues. *Computers in Human Behavior, 30*, 262–272.

Gingrich, N. (2014, Aug. 1). Get schools out of the 1890s. CNN. Web.

Heinich, R. (1991). Restructuring, technology, and instructional productivity. In G. Anglin (Ed.), *Instructional technology: Past, present, and future* (pp. 236–243). Englewood, CO: Libraries Unlimited.

Ho, C.-C., & MacDorman, K. F. (2010). Revisiting the uncanny valley theory: Developing and validating an alternative to the Godspeed indices. *Computers in Human Behavior, 26*, 1508–1518.

Jacob, R. J. K., & Karn, K. S. (2003). Eye tracking in human-computer interaction and usability research: Ready to deliver the promises. In J. Hyönä, R. Radach, & H. Deubel (Eds.), *The mind's eye: Cognitive and applied aspects of eye movement research* (pp. 573–605). Oxford: Elsevier.

Kahn, P. H., Kanda, T., Ishiguro, H., Freier, N., Severson, R. L., Gill, B. T., Ruckert, J. H., & Shen, S. (2012). "Robovie, you'll have to go into the closet now": Children's social and moral relationships with a humanoid robot. *Developmental Psychology, 48*, 303–314.

Kidd, C. D. (2003). *Human-robot interaction: Recent experiments and future work*. Invited paper and talk at the University of Pennsylvania Department of Communications Digital Media Conference, Oct. 31—Nov. 1.

Knight, H. (2014, July). *How humans respond to robots: Building public policy through good design*. Pittsburg, PA: Carnegie Mellon University Robotics Institute.

Koehler, M., & Mishra, P. (2008). Introducing TPCK. In AACTE Committee on Innovation and Technology (Eds.), *The handbook of technological pedagogical content knowledge for teaching and teacher educators* (pp. 3–29). Mahwah, NJ: Lawrence Erlbaum.

Krathwohl, D. R. (2002). A revision of Bloom's taxonomy: An overview. *Theory Into Practice, 41*(4), 212–218.

Mann, H. (1849). *Twelfth annual report of the board of education together with the twelfth annual report of the secretary of the board*. Boston, MA: Dutton & Wentworth.

Moore, G. (1965). Cramming more components onto integrated circuits. *Electronics, 38*(8), 114–117.

Mubin, O., Shahid, S., van de Sande, E., Krahmer, E., Swerts, M., Bartneck, C., & Feijs, L. (2010). Using child-robot interaction to investigate the user acceptance of constrained and artificial languages. *19th IEEE International Symposium on Robot and Human Interactive Communication*, Principe di Piemonte, Viareggio, Italy (pp. 588–593). doi: 10.1109/ROMAN.2010.5598731

Palmer, P. (2010, Mar.25). The heart of a teacher: Identity and integrity in teaching. *Change: The Magazine of Higher Learning*.

Partridge, M., & Bartneck, C. (2013). The invisible naked guy: An exploration of a minimalistic robot. *Proceedings of The First International Conference on Human-Agent Interaction*, Saporo, Japan, Aug. 7–9 (pp. II-2-2).

Perelman, L. J. (1993). *School's out: A radical new formula for the revitalization of America's educational system*. New York: Avon Books.

Poole, A., & Ball, L. J. (2006). Eye tracking in human-computer interaction and usability research: Current status and future prospects. In C. Ghaoui (Ed.), *Encyclopedia of human computer interaction* (pp. 211–219). Hershey, PA: Idea Group Reference.

Princess Megabyte. (2012, July 11). The evolution of computer memory (Educational). YouTube.

Rittel, H. W. J., & Webber, M. M. (1973). Dilemmas in a general theory of planning. *Policy Sciences, 4*(2), 155–169.

Shankland, S. (2012, Oct. 15). Moore's Law: The rule that really matters in tech. *CNET.*
Sharkey, N., & Sharkey, A. C. (2010). The crying shame of robot nannies: An ethical appraisal. *Interaction Studies, 11*(2), 161–190.
Simpson, D. (2014). Exclusion, punishment, racism and our schools: A critical race theory perspective on school discipline. *UCLA Law Review, 61,* 506–563.
Starner, T. (2001a). The challenges of wearable computing: Part 1. *IEEE Micro, 21*(4), 44–52.
Starner, T. (2001b). The challenges of wearable computing: Part 2. *IEEE Micro, 21*(4), 54–67.
U.S. Department of Justice. (2012). Equal *Access to Education:* Forty years of Title IX.
Wallén, J. (2008, May). *The history of the industrial robot* [Technical report]. Linköping, Sweden: Linköpings Universitet.
Wubbels, T., den Brock, P., Tartwijk, J., & Levy, J. (Eds.) (2012). *Interpersonal relationships in education: An overview of contemporary research.* Rotterdam: Sense.
Zlotowski, J., Proudfoot, D., & Bartneck, C. (2013). More human than human: Does the Uncanny Curve really matter? *Proceedings of the HRI2013 Workshop on Design of Humanlikeness in HRI: From Uncanny Valley to minimal design,* Tokyo (pp. 7–13).

RESPONSE BY SUGATA MITRA

1. The "position" statement above and the contents seem a bit different. While the position statement talks about eliminating the need for teachers, the article emphasizes the replacement of teachers by robots and how difficult that would be. Replacing a teacher with a robot would be very difficult, and quite unnecessary. It is like making a calculator that looks like a human being, sits at a table, and does long-hand arithmetic with pen and paper. Quite unnecessary.
2. Can we eliminate the need for teachers, using technology? It would be progressive if we could. Like eliminating the need for a maid to wash our clothes. Using a washing machine. Of course we can eliminate teachers; we are doing so all the time. We do not need a teacher to learn how to tell the time of day by looking at the sun and stars. We used to. Now we have replaced that teacher by using watches. We used to need teachers to learn cursive handwriting. Now we do not need those teachers because we almost never write cursively on paper. We used to need teachers to learn how to work out the square root of a number by hand, paper, and pencil. We do not need that teacher anymore, because square roots are done by machines. I could go on and on.
3. The article talks a lot about teaching, but it does not say too much about learning. It is learning that is changing—mostly because of the Internet. People, particularly children in groups, can learn anything by themselves, using the Internet.
4. When the horse and carriage was replaced by the automobile, there could have been a discussion about whether a robot can replace the coachman. An unnecessary discussion, because the passengers became the drivers. When learning happens on the Internet instead of in the school, the learners will learn to drive that activity. The teacher's role would then end. Like the coachman's did.

REJOINDER BY WARD MITCHELL CATES AND THOMAS C. HAMMOND

Dr. Mitra's response employs a debater's device, *reductio ad absurdum*, in which a logical premise ("Technology, even through artificial intelligent robotics, is insufficient to replace human teachers") is taken to an illogical conclusion ("a calculator that looks like a human being, sits at a table, and does long-hand arithmetic with pen and paper"). He has devalued our position, based on a very broad claim: "People . . . can learn anything by themselves, using the Internet." Naturally, we considered the Internet's potential, but we cannot support his claim because we see three main preconditions to its realization: ubiquitous and equitable access to Internet content, availability of suitable content on the Internet, and curricular coherence and integrity.

While many focus on Internet access and bandwidth in developed nations, our position statement was predicated on what we believed would happen worldwide. According to the United Nations' International Telecommunication Union (2015), developed nations have seen dramatic increases in the number of Internet users since 2000, and access is in many places near-ubiquitous, while developing countries have substantially less access, offering access to only about one-in-three. In the least developed countries, one in ten have access. Even among those with access, however, is there equity? For example, 13 percent of posts on Chinese social media services were censored (King, Pan & Roberts, 2013), and a learner in Saudi Arabia researching *encryption*, *astrology*, or even *swimwear* (let alone, human rights reporting) encounters a filter message. Even if every citizen in China or Saudi Arabia (or Iran or Eritrea or North Korea or Ethiopia) had ubiquitous access, they would not be able to view the full Internet without serious risk.

Internet content often appears because individuals or groups are highly interested in that content. In other cases, there is a profit motive; content is added in order to make money or promote a product. In yet other instances, proponents of political, religious, or social causes add content to attract new followers. While some adding content are highly knowledgeable, many are not; while some adding content have good intentions, others do not. Thus, not all Internet content may be educationally suitable for all learners. Unfortunately, not all learners may recognize the inaccuracies and subtle distortions made by those adding content (see, for instance, the insidious, White supremacist site http://martinlutherking.org).

Curriculum is the logically organized sequence of appropriately leveled learning content and activities, designed to assure learners have appropriate foundational knowledge and skills before attempting more sophisticated learning calling for those prerequisites. Curricula are typically tailored to the needs of learners, often with specific accommodations for learners with special needs. Curricular content and organization is known as *scope and sequence*. While we can locate some Internet curricula with specified scope and sequence (for example, Khan Academy's work in selected content-areas, and some of the work done by various medical schools), there are few comprehensive K-16 curricula online. Without such curricula, not all learners are equally served; for example, learners for whom English is a second language and learners with other special needs are almost certainly less well served. Without clear scope and sequence, one cannot assure that learners find what they need, when they need it, in the form they need it.

What would it take to fulfill our three global preconditions? Access and equity are thorny financial and political problems. It is difficult to imagine how these would be solved when we have not yet been able to assure safe drinking water around the world. It is unclear where the profit that often drives technological development would come from. Similarly, assuring that suitable content were available online is a social, political, and financial challenge. Even if all could agree on what is socially acceptable content and appropriate for learners, who would fund creation and maintenance of such content? Most Internet researchers can report the demise of strong online educational resources, usually for lack of support. And creating appropriate national/international curricula requires massive political will and resource allocation, both of which seem to be missing in most developed countries, let alone the rest of the world. If we had seen evidence that at least one of our preconditions was being well addressed now, we might have been more optimistic. We did not, and we do not foresee a future in which all three preconditions will be met. We, therefore, stand by our statement.

References

International Telecommunication Union. (2015). ICT facts & figures: The world in 2015.

King, G., Pan, J., & Roberts, M.E. (2013). How censorship in China allows government criticism but silences collective expression. *American Political Science Review*, *107*, 326–343.

Chapter 21

What's Next for E-learning?

John Savery

Toffler (1970) defined the term *future shock* as a perception by individuals and entire societies of "too much change in too short a period of time." He predicted that the rapid rate of change in a postindustrial society (now called the Information Age) would lead to social fragmentation, increased specialization, and increased differentiation within the society through an exponential growth of information (information overload). Since 1970, increased automation in industry has reduced the demand for low-skill jobs while the increased complexity in other employment areas has raised the skill level needed for most jobs. The net effect has been a rapid demand for educational opportunities to support lifelong learning as adults need to reskill to get jobs. Lifelong learning has become THE survival skill across the entire employment spectrum—there are few cases where one's knowledge and skills are complete.

> We are living in exponential times. We are currently preparing students for jobs that don't exist yet using technologies that have not been invented in order to solve problems we don't even know are problems yet.
>
> (Fisch & McLeod, 2007)

In the forty-four years since *Future Shock* was published, two generations have come of age—Gen X and Millennials. Their children are now entering an education system that has demonstrated a remarkable ability to maintain the status quo. The *Did You Know; Shift Happens* video reinforces the critical importance of an educational environment that is flexible and able to adapt to changes in the society it serves.

There are many significant trends in education that will converge in the near future to create a new learning ecosystem to support the 77 million Millennials (Taylor & Keeter, 2010) and their children. Three trends that may gain acceptance are (1) a lifelong learning record system, (2) a highly personalized learning environment, and (3) expanded learner control of time, place, and pace of instruction.

1. Data on learner performance has become the most valuable commodity in education. Textbook publishers, learning management system companies, educational record keeping systems, classroom teachers, online teachers, and school systems at every level are collecting data on "their" students. This data is currently proprietary and disconnected. The to-be-developed lifelong learning record-keeping system would aggregate information from multiple sources over time into a user-controlled account. Since lifelong learning occurs in many different contexts, the ability to consolidate and reflect on learning in a personal record is critical. There are many serious questions to be addressed before this personal learning record will become more widely adopted. The data has only one owner—the individual learner—and the systems that are developed

will need to accommodate this singular truth. With appropriate privacy controls in place it would be possible for all learners to have unique identification codes that would protect access to their life-long learning portfolios. With equally strict privacy controls, anonymous aggregated data could be mined from this system. A person's education record must become as detailed and protected as his or her lifelong health record. Consider how useful it would be to teachers and learners when attempting to diagnose a learner's needs to have access to a record of prior learning events—competencies acquired, scores on psychometric tests, standardized tests, observations by previous teachers, and more. The ecosystem that is developing around the ideal of preventative health care should serve as a model for the design and development of an educational care system.

2. Personalized learning environments (PLE) are the next iteration of learning management systems. With the inclusion of data analytics and adaptive learning technologies, these environments will continue to evolve from content storage systems to learning environments able to provide millions of adult learners with the instruction needed to achieve a desired level of mastery. These sophisticated systems will incorporate tools already developed to assess prior knowledge through formal or informal learning experiences. As learner goals are refined, the system will identify gaps between the individual learners' current knowledge/skills and the target competencies needed for the chosen career. The system will manage the individual learners' progress toward learning goals by presenting specific instructional content based on identified learner characteristics and confirm achievement/mastery through adaptive assessments. The role of the teacher/tutor will shift from providing information to facilitating learning and will leverage the data provided by the PLE in the same manner as doctors and engineers incorporate diagnostic information. Detailed transcripts provided by the PLE that identify the competencies achieved will become the "resume" that employers value when hiring skilled workers. It is expected/required that the information about the learners gathered by the PLE would be exported into their lifelong learning record.

3. Increased learner control of time, place, and pace of instruction has been supported by developments in communication technology. Mass public education has historically associated place with learning—thus, we go to a school to learn. While there is much value in social learning through interactions with others, the content (knowledge, skills, attitudes) can be obtained independent of social gatherings. E-learning has substituted a physical place for learning with a virtual place for learning. As is often the case with innovations in education (see SAMR model; Puentedura, 2014), the initial efforts in online learning attempted to replicate classroom teaching with distance teaching. Early iterations of online learning were simply electronic versions of a correspondence course. With current social media tools and improved instructional systems, learners have an opportunity to engage with fellow students and the instructor in ways that did not exist previously. Students in general and adult learners in particular crave self-paced learning in technologically rich online learning environments especially when coupled with practical, measurable instruction, which adaptive learning technologies will surely facilitate—Thus, the exponential growth and acceptance by learners of open/free learning providers like the Khan Academy or Sophia Learning, the expanding use by instructors and students of Open Educational Resource repositories, and the rapid growth of competency-based programs such as Western Governors University, Southern New Hampshire University, Northern Arizona University, and the University of Wisconsin Flex degree. There will always be a place for the top-tier universities and the thousands of other universities with specialized curriculums

whether it be liberal arts or something in the science, technology, engineering, and medicine (STEM) field.

Where Toffler predicted a more fragmented society, the opposite has become the norm in many areas. Many of the social barriers—class, race, gender, ethnicity, religion, age, etc.—that existed in the 1970s have lost their influence as people connect and communicate through electronic channels and as information is available to counter fear of the unknown. We are living in the world of future shock, and e-learning will continue to be an important component in maintaining a more connected world.

References

Fisch, K. & McLeod, S. (2007). *Did You Know; Shift Happens–Globalization and the Information Age*. (Video). Available from https://www.youtube.com/watch?v=ljbI-363A2Q

Puentedura, R. (2014). *Learning, Technology, and the SAMR Model: Goals, Processes, and Practice*. Available from http://www.hippasus.com/rrpweblog/archives/2014/06/29/LearningTechnologySAMRModel.pdf

Taylor, P., & Keeter, S. (Eds). (2010). *MILLENNIALS: Confident, Connected, Open to Change*. Pew Research Center. Available from http://www.pewsocialtrends.org/files/2010/10/millennials-confident-connected-open-to-change.pdf

Toffler, A. (1970). *Future Shock*. New York: Penguin Random House. Print.

RESPONSE BY CLARK QUINN

John Savery has written an intriguing proposal for the future of eLearning, describing three significant trends: (1) a lifelong learning record system, (2) a highly personalized learning environment, and (3) expanded learner control of time, place, and pace of instruction. While I agree, I want to extend these with two further trends that I think are as important or more: (4) the integration of meta-learning skills and (5) the breakdown of the barrier between formal learning and lifelong learning.

Savery's first two points are already being seen. The ability to collect and leverage data to facilitate learning is being seen, for example, in the Predictive Analytics Reporting Framework by Ellen Wagner and colleagues (Wagner & Davis, 2013). PAR is an example of how data is providing the ability to intervene on a variety of emergent factors in learning. Also, companies like Degreed (Degreed.com) are already realizing the call for an aggregated lifelong learning record. Similarly, the individually adaptive learning system has been in development for over a decade (e.g., Shute & Towle, 2003) and is currently being seen in environments such as Knewton (Knewton.com) and Smart Sparrow (smartsparrow.com). The ability to use preassessments and inferred information about the learner to determine a reasonable next course of action is now possible and desirable.

His third point, the rise of learners taking control of their own learning experience, has a caveat. While there are companies providing new alternative resources as he documents, there is an underlying expectation that learners are capable self-learners, and that should not be taken for granted. Learning to learn skills has been touted as valuable, but while there is much promise (Resnick, 1987), there is little reason to assume that schools develop and that learners possess these capabilities.

The opportunity is to not just focus on domain-specific skills but also start layering on "learning to learn" (aka meta-learning). The so-called 21st Century Skills (Partnership for 21st Century Learning, 2015) that define the new workplace competencies are not learned separately, but instead need to be wrapped around other meaningful endeavors. An approach is instead to iterate the competency across other learning—for instance, requiring some form of document creation task at various times, and assessing the quality of the document as well as the content, layering on the meta-skills across other learning goals. The underlying issue is to not trust that these skills will develop but separately assess and foster them.

Beyond meta-learning, my concern is that the discussion is tied to an existing "school" model. In that sense, Savery is demonstrating the ability to go beyond the problems Warschauer (2011) found with schools (curricula, pedagogy, and the use of technology). However, there are ways in which we can transcend schools that I think are going to become important elements of an online learning experience, specifically beginning to leverage life events instead of just ones that we have defined.

The desire is to stop relying on learning experiences that are created and start leveraging the ones that already exist. Learners are engaged with many activities in their lives, but it has been hard to identify and support them. However, with the ubiquity of mobile devices, the sensors they increasingly possess, and processing power, we can go beyond separating the learner from the world to provide learning experiences and start delivering learning *around* learner actions (Quinn, 2012). So, for example, we can know a learner is in a particular context and connect that context to one of that learner's learning goals. Alternatively, we can know what the learner is doing (e.g., from his or her calendar) and provide some pre-, in-, and post-activity scaffolding specific to the learner's goals and the context to turn that from a performance situation to a learning opportunity.

To break down the barriers between life and learning and to scaffold the development of meta-learning, we need a new learning design (Quinn, 2013). We need to look at activities, not content, as curricula, and we need to start looking at the development of the individual as an extended relationship.

The ability to learn in context on one's own should be the goal of our learning system. For that to happen, we need to break down the walls between school and life. To use Savery's favored source, another Alvin Toffler quote is: "The illiterate of the 21st century will not be those who cannot read and write, but those who cannot learn, unlearn, and relearn." Our systems must help learners become those who *can* do so.

References

Framework for 21st Century Learning. Partnership for 21st Century Learning (2015). Web.
Quinn, C. N. (2012). *The mobile academy: mLearning for higher education*. San Francisco, CA: Jossey-Bass.
Quinn, C. N. (2013). Redesigning learning design. *Proceedings of the 3rd International Conference in e-Learning and Distance Learning*, Riyadh, Saudi Arabia.
Resnick, L. B. (1987). *Education and learning to think*. Washington, DC: National Academy Press.
Shute, V. J., & Towle, B. (2003). Adaptive e-learning. *Educational Psychologist*, 38(2), 105–114.
Wagner, E., & Davis, B. (2013). The Predictive Analytics Reporting (PAR) Framework, WCET. *Educause Review Online*.
Warschauer, M. (2011). *Learning in the cloud: How (and why) to transform schools with digital media*. New York: Teachers College Press.

REJOINDER BY JOHN SAVERY

Clark Quinn is correct that my first two forecasts—(1) a lifelong learning record system and (2) a highly personalized learning environment—are becoming more established. Proposing a personalized learning system is not nearly as difficult as actually building one. Multiple competing systems are being implemented, but we are still many years away from effective adoption. Concerning the forecast for a lifelong learning record keeping system, it was intended that the system be a student-centered repository that aggregated all learning accomplishments. Official records such as transcripts and scores generated by standardized tests will contribute a portion of the data. The challenge is aggregating all of the unofficial data. Electronic portfolio products have become more sophisticated (and accepted) and will provide learners with a toolset for maintaining their personal record keeping system and also to share aspects with potential employers. Finally, there continues to be debate about who owns this student data, the validity of the data, and ultimately what value this record of learning accomplishments will have with future employers.

In the area of adaptive learning environments, the major LMS providers are certainly touting their PLE capabilities. Developing these environments is a significant investment by these vendors and their systems will improve over time. As Quinn notes, the idea of adaptive systems is not new, but significant technical (and human) challenges remain, including the inertia of the existing educational system to adopt/change. Significant grant funding for research that expands our understanding of the critical success factors within personalized learning initiatives is beginning to provide positive results (Vogt, 2015). There is still much to be done to make either of these possible futures a reality for learners at all points on their educational continuum.

Quinn agrees with the third identified trend—expanded learner control of time, place, and pace of instruction—and adds two extensions: (4) the integration of meta-learning skills and (5) the breakdown of the barrier between formal learning and lifelong learning. Regarding meta-learning skills, he is correct that there is no guarantee that, when learners have more control over the time and pace of instruction, they will actually perform as we intended. Ironically, becoming a self-aware, self-regulated, and self-directed learner is the intended learning outcome of most competency-based models of instruction. The instructional challenge with CBE systems is to find the balance between humans and machines and optimize the set of capabilities each brings to the learning situation. In the face-to-face and blended classroom environment, the teacher-centric model is gradually losing ground to the project or problem-based approaches. Teaching—or providing learning opportunities—that incorporate 21st Century Skills necessarily means adjusting how learners engage with the subject matter and establishing quality standards. Subject/discipline specific areas will continue to exist, but interdisciplinary studies should see greater growth.

Lastly, Quinn proposes a new design for merging/blending formal and informal learning that leverages/integrates learner activities with ubiquitous technologies. While I concur that mobile technologies have dramatically expanded the idea of "classroom," I also believe that these capabilities need to be used in the context of authentic learning experiences. For example, students using mobile technologies visited a mitigated wetlands (Downing, 2012) to collect data (audio, video, GPS location, date/time) and by using extension devices (i.e., probes) a host of other data—water/air temperature, PH, wind speed/direction, and much more. The mobile devices facilitated the collection and sharing of data, and the instructional tasks (problem/projects/guiding questions) focused the analysis of the data and ultimately the realization of the intended (and some unintended) learning outcomes.

I agree with Quinn that for some students the line between in-school and out-of-school has become increasingly blurred. Similarly, as working adults, we are increasingly connected to our work responsibilities beyond the forty hours per week associated with our job descriptions. As an instructor I would proceed with great caution when imposing on learners outside of the "classroom" with pre-post instructional information just because I happen to know their location. This would definitely require learner agreement and that it be project specific and be limited in scope. It is not clear if or how this strategy would scale. From a completely different perspective, the same or more sophisticated technologies—mobile, GPS, proximity detectors, search engines, communications, etc.—are currently being used by soldiers in combat. The intended outcomes for soldiers are obviously much different—but perhaps these technologies could be used to create a tightly connected virtual class with clearly specified instructional outcome.

References

Downing, B. "Copley wetland created by two brothers goes to UA." 10 Jan. 2012. Ohio.com. Web.

Vogt, K. "Personalized learning is (still) promising." 4 Dec. 2015. Next Gen Learning Blog, Next Gen Learning. Web.

Chapter 22

Any Time, Any Place, Any Pace . . .

Kathryn Kennedy and Joseph R. Freidhoff

Any time, any place, any pace . . . it is an addictive, short, sweet phrase commonly used to promote K-12 online learning. Though well intentioned and theoretically defensible, the laissez-faire mindset this phrase evokes undermines the importance that time, place, and pace have in the learning process and results in suboptimal experiences for novice online learners. If the absence of structure continues to be as pervasive as it has been despite clear findings proving this unstructured environment works, we see the onset of true disadvantage for K-12 student success in digital learning environments.

To illustrate the pervasiveness of this catchy phrase of "Any Time, Any Place, Any Pace," we offer a few references. The beginning of the United States Department of Education's definition of competency-based education[1] declares: "Transitioning away from seat time, in favor of a structure that creates flexibility, allows students to progress as they demonstrate mastery of academic content, *regardless of time, place, or pace of learning*." Milton Chen's 2012 book *Education Nation: Six Leading Edges of Innovation in Our Schools*[2] includes a chapter titled "The *Time/Place* Edge: Learning *Any Time, Anywhere*." In our own state of Michigan, Governor Rick Snyder announced an education reform movement in 2011 calling for an "*Any Time, Any Place, Any Way, Any Pace*" learning model."[3] And the International Association for K-12 Online and Blended Learning (iNACOL)[4] has used the phrase "*anytime, anywhere* online and blended learning" in its advocacy efforts. The precise wording and meanings among these examples and others like them vary, but the simplification or essential message is the notion that structured approaches to times, places, and paces are not in the best interest of student learning. In the rest of this discussion, we outline reasons why this phrase is dangerous to PK-12 learning in particular. To put it into perspective, we draw upon examples from our own research and experiences.

Time

The "time" reference in the phrase establishes a sense of flexibility that students can work any time that they would like to—like never. Unfortunately, without the external time impositions, many students procrastinate and fall too far behind to be successful or at least to learn as much as they should from their courses. What we have found in our own research is that students do best when they establish routines and structure for when they do their online work. In case studies and a mentoring guide[5] developed by our team, mentor teachers who support online learners have shared that when a time structure is not externally imposed, many students repeatedly miss deadlines and do not develop a sense of time management from learning, an important attribute of being college/career ready. For students who cannot self-regulate, absence of a time structure is dangerous because they tend to underestimate the time it will take them to complete their courses or to fail to understand how time on task is related to deeper learning. Our mentor teachers have mentioned that they suggest to students how much time they should spend in their online course as well as how often they should visit their courses. When students become better at managing their time, when they have shown a pattern of behavior that is successful in their online courses, only then do mentor teachers offer students the opportunity of heightened flexibility in their learning. Examination of course data at the *Michigan Virtual School*, a state-supported supplemental online learning program, shows a strong correlation between the frequency with which students access their online courses and their overall final grades. Put simply, more time working in the course tends to yield higher learning outcomes. Unfortunately, many online learners spend less time in online courses than they do in traditional courses. Is it because of this idea of "Any Time . . ."?

Place

The idea of "place" in the phrase has to do with students being able to learn wherever they are. Consider an adult learning example. EdX, governed by MIT and Harvard, uses the following response to an FAQ about who can take an EdX course: "EdX courses are open to everyone. All you need is *access to a computer* with a current browser, *an Internet connection*, and, of course, a desire to learn."[6] The idea that students can learn anywhere they have Internet access reduces, if not entirely dismisses, the importance of other environmental characteristics. Even if we set aside access and equity issues[7] that are tied to place (which is a huge concern), where students work on their online courses matters. *Michigan Virtual School* data suggest schools that require their students to attend adult-facilitated virtual learning labs on a regular basis have students who perform above average in their online courses. When students work off-site, good mentors help students identify characteristics of the best places to learn and help students set up their remote "offices." This structured approach that is proving successful in our research is far from the idea of "Any Place . . ."

Pace

Another element of this popular phrase regards the "pace" of student learning. According to our data visualization research, there is a strong correlation between how frequently students access their course and their performance. Pace and, more importantly, consistent pace matters. The theory that pace is a student's choice is limited by the idea of cognitive maximum versus soft-skill minimum. The theory of moving at your own pace is based on the assumption that students are progressing at the fastest rate possible for them. In practice, too many proceed at the slowest rate they can get away with.

Additionally, if there is no pacing guide or pace structure, can all students keep up, especially those who are not as focused as those who are the type of students that online learning programs are typically geared to—those who are self-motivated, self-regulated, independent learners? Unfortunately, the lack of pacing structure in many PK-12 online learning programs reinforces a selection process that benefits those students who are self-motivated, self-regulated, and independent. When pacing is a suggestion—not enforced through a cohort-model such as those used in traditional education—students move at considerably different rates. Without pacing requirements like due dates, students give greater priority to those things in their life that do have those time boundaries. This has serious implications for equity.

A Telling Dichotomy

A telling dichotomy exists when you compare this phrase to the recommendations we make for teleworkers (as a side note, one of the authors of this piece is a full-time teleworker). For this part of the discussion, we examined two resources, including a *LinkedIn Pulse* article about the "10 Commandments for Remote Working" by Jonathan Sharp[8] as well as Microsoft Office 365's document on "Remote Working Etiquette."[9] For the purposes of this exercise, we included those bulleted points from these documents that are important to the question we pose here: *if we have recommendations for adults on how to work successfully in remote/online environments, why are there not similar recommendations for our PK-12 online learners?*

From "10 Commandments for Remote Working," here are "some tips to help you stay focused":

- Define your spaces.... Separate work from home. Have a room dedicated to working—one that is removed as much as possible from potential distractions. That way, when you enter it, you know it's time to work. This approach helps you change your state of mind from "I'm at home" to "I'm at work." The best option is to use a room with a door for added privacy. [Place matters]
- Stay online as much as possible. If you are not online, it is likely that people may think you are not working—even if you are. Respond quickly to e-mail, and your colleagues will know you are being productive. [Time matters]
- Be assertive. Don't always wait for people to contact you. Ask for information if you don't believe you have received it. [Pace matters]
- Establish a schedule. Keep home work hours similar to those you would keep at an office. Your manager, coworkers, and customers appreciate knowing when you are available. [Pace and time matter]
- Be present. Check in with your team regularly throughout the day and be responsive to their questions and comments. [Pace and time matter]
- Take breaks. Plan time to get up and move around. Consider going for a walk or a run during your lunch break to keep your mind fresh. [Pace and time matter]

And from Microsoft Office 365's "Remote Working Etiquette":

- Be disciplined with your time. [Time matters]
- Communicate your presence (or absence). [Place matters]
- Take a shower and get dressed daily. [Place matters]

Final Statement

"Any time, any place, any pace" has painted the challenge of online learning as a policy problem or a technology access issue and suggests that once impediments are removed, student learning will expand. This wishful thinking is not what is playing out in practice. Many online learners, especially PK-12 online learners, are needlessly struggling because the importance of time, place, and pace have been discounted, and the external supports that ought to be in place to help students succeed are being seen as impediments to learning. The degree of intentionality that is needed around time, place, and pace is the antithesis of the "anys" and may never be well captured in a catchy slogan. Too bad, so sad.

Notes

1. U.S. Department of Education, "Competency-based learning or personalized learning."
2. Chen (2012).
3. Wurfel (2011).
4. iNACOL (2012).
5. Michigan Virtual Learning Research Institute (2014).
6. EdX Help Center.
7. iNACOL (2014).
8. Sharp (2014).
9. Microsoft Office 365, *Remote working etiquette*.

References

Chen, M. (2012). *Education nation*. San Francisco: Jossey-Bass.
EdX. *EdX Help Center*. Web.
International Association for K-12 Online Learning (iNACOL). (2012). Statement of principles for model legislation in states. Web.
International Association for K-12 Online Learning (iNACOL). (2014). Access and equity for all learners in blended and online education. Web.
Michigan Virtual Learning Research Institute. (2014). *Mentoring online learners*, Version 1. Web.
Microsoft Office 365. *Remote working etiquette*.
Sharp, J. (2014). 10 Commandments for remote working. *LinkedIn Pulse*.
U.S. Department of Education. "Competency-based learning or personalized learning." Web.
Wurfel, S. (2011, April 27). Snyder unveils plan to reinvent Michigan's educational system. *Michigan.gov*. Web.

RESPONSE BY VICTORIA RAISH

The notion of any time, any place, any space is synonymous with online learning. Kennedy and Freidhoff caution against the use of these words as they lead to unstructured environments for K-12 online learners. These unstructured environments without empirical evidence providing support for the any time, any place, any pace can lead to "true disadvantage for K-12 student success in digital learning environments." While they focus on what this phrase can mean to the student, I believe that this phrase can convey the benefits of online learning. My reasoning behind this is that online education was a disruptive innovation (Christensen, Horn & Johnson, 2008). At that time, it was necessary to create a diffusion effort that succinctly captured the attributes, relative advantage, compatibility, trialability, and reduction in complexity of that innovation (Rogers, 1995). This phrase is catchy and makes online learning appealing. However, words have multiple meanings, and these words are no different. A clarification on what is meant by these terms and how students can be supported in this learning environment needs to happen for the sake of all students engaged with K-12 online learning. I believe that a failure to look at all users of the system—including students—is what has led to a dangerous use of this phrase.

Huerta, Gonzalez and d'Entremont (2006) urge defining seat time in cybercharter schools. Kenney and Freidhoff include a reference from the United States Department of Education on the competency-based movement away from seat time. One of the perceived advantages of online schooling is that it embraces innovative pedagogical ideas such as competency-based education (Bellefeuille, Martin & Buck, 2005). This takes the conversation away from time and moves it toward learning outcomes. This idea of time is not going to be the one that students consider. Another idea of time in online learning is that for students who have other commitments or unique schedules, it allows them to complete their schooling in nontraditional hours and access recordings to watch the lesson. For the "traditional" online students, they can maintain the same school hours as a student in a brick-and-mortar charter school. Mincemoyer and Raish (2015) asked students in a survey on their communicative practices in cybercharter schools what their average time spent on schoolwork was. The sample size for the survey was small at n = 20 middle school students, and thus the study lacks generalizable significance, but it still provides interesting results. Four students reported spending less than three hours a day on their schoolwork, while four students reported spending over six hours a day on their schoolwork. The cybercharter school these students attended had a recommendation that students spend four to six hours a day on schoolwork. The lack of empirical studies showing time spent on schoolwork suggest students need clear guidelines on how much time they should be spending in school and what they should be doing. This is especially crucial for those students who have not achieved self-regulation. While online school is frequently any time in the sense that it can occur at any time, it is not any time in the sense that students can spend any amount of time they feel like on their work.

There are multiple ways to think about place. There is the macro idea of place that students are not kept in the same physical location and the micro idea of place as the space that students choose to work. Any place implies that geographic barriers no longer exist toward getting education. This is true in states like Pennsylvania where all students can attend a cybercharter school regardless of where they live. Learning spaces, as micro places, that are well-designed for learning support students provide them with the resources they need, and minimize distractions. As Montgomery (2008) says, "space matters" with regard to learning goals and the space impacts success of those goals. From my experience working in a hybrid charter school, students only earned the privilege of working from home if they were able to maintain their grades without the support of the learning center. Students who needed that support came to a *place* that gave them support and guidance in their schooling. This is in agreement with the recommendations that the Michigan Virtual School gives to students. From currently ongoing research on preferences that college students find in a learning space, multiple students even suggested using social media blocking software to minimize distractions so that they can focus on their work. Students should be given guidelines on creating a space that supports, rather than hinders, their learning, while they are still offered choice in their learning space.

The final piece of the "any" puzzle is any pace. I believe that the intentions of this term were to imply that competency-based education sense that students no longer had to work all at the same pace at the same time. Teachers can more easily differentiate their instruction (Tomlinson, 1999) and modify the sequences of material for students. This is similar to a coach who requires all the athletes to train the same or one who modifies the training program for that individual athlete. Therefore, the idea of any pace is a noble one. However, it is easy to see how students can view "any pace" as the idea that there is no path to achieve the learning outcomes. Expecting students to be able to regulate the pace of their learning requires them to have metacognition so that they know what they know and where they need to go (Griffith & Ruan, 2008). I think that any pace is a notion that teachers can take to heart. These teachers know that students may have different learning paces. However, for students any pace needs to be modified to structure their preferred learning pace. The due dates that Kennedy and Freidhoff propose as external pacing requirements are important, but flexibility still needs to be given to allow students to work in a defined range beyond or behind those due dates.

It is my hope that through these ideas and opinions I have put forth we can have open communication on what the meaning is behind these terms and how we can provide structure to students who may misconstrue the meaning of these terms. Ideally, this could happen through conversations and engagements with students on their perception of the phrase "any time, any place, any pace" and what it means for their schooling.

References

Bellefeuille, G., Martin, R. R., & Buck, M. P. (2005). From pedagogy to technagogy in social work education: A constructivist approach to instructional design in an online, competency-based child welfare practice course. *Child and Youth Care Forum, 34*(5), 371–389. doi: 10.1007/s10566-005-5909-2

Christensen, C. M., Horn, M. B., & Johnson, C. W. (2008). *Disrupting class: How disruptive innovation will change the way the world learns* (Vol. 98). New York: McGraw-Hill.

Griffith, P. L., & Ruan, J. (2008). What is metacognition and what should be its role in literacy instruction? In S. E. Israel, C. C. Block, K. L. Bauserman & K. Kinnucan-Welsch (Eds.), *Metacognition in literacy learning: Theory, assessment, instruction, and professional development* (pp. 3–18). Mahwah, NJ: Taylor & Francis e-Library.

Huerta, L. A., Gonzalez, M.-F., & d'Entremont, C. (2006). Cyber and home school charter schools: Adopting policy to new forms of public schooling. *Peabody Journal of Education, 81*(1), 103–139. doi: 10.1207/S15327930pje8101_6

Mincemoyer, H., & Raish, V. (2015). Collaboration practices and attitudes for students in cyber charter classrooms. *Proceedings from SITE '15: Society for Information Technology & Teacher Education International Conference.* Chesapeake, VA: Association for the Advancement of Computing in Education.

Montgomery, T. (2008). Space matters: Experiences of managing static formal learning spaces. *Active Learning in Higher Education, 9*(2), 122–138. doi: 10.1177/1469787408090839

Rogers, E. M. (1995). *Diffusion of innovation.* New York: The Free Press.

Tomlinson, C. A. (1999). Mapping a route toward differentiated instruction. *Educational Leadership, 57*(1), 12–16.

REJOINDER BY KATHRYN KENNEDY AND
JOSEPH R. FREIDHOFF

In her response Raish argues that we chose to "focus on what this phrase can mean to the student, [but she feels] this phrase can convey the benefits of online learning . . . [and that it] was necessary to create a diffusion effort." This juxtaposition between advocacy and practice is exactly the tension we sought to expose. At the core, our concern is that the reductionary rhetoric used to grow online learning and tout its benefits at the same time undermines implementing online learning with the fidelity necessary to attain those benefits. Like Raish, we assign good intentions to most of those promoting online learning through this phrasing. The dangers, however, are significant for those new to the field and those who inadvertently implement without meaningfully planning for the much-needed structural support for students.

We agree with Raish that flexibility of time in online learning is a great way for students who have other commitments or health concerns. Support structures are especially important for students who are juggling other pressing commitments, but what we have seen in practice is that students who display consistency with both the frequency and time of day in which they access their online courses tend to outperform those who access their coursework any time of day. While we support the concept of moving away from "time" as the measure of student learning and instead moving toward student learning outcomes, we caution that issues of time will likely become even more important—not less—with such a move, and that differences in students' self-regulatory skills to manage themselves and their time will be key contributors to achievement gaps, making adult oversight and support paramount.

Space in the way that Raish describes it is a good point. We believe that a space needs to be designated for learning for students so that they, like teleworkers, have a dedicated area that is conducive to their learning needs and style. A graduated trust system with students who are achieving makes sense as well. However, how this plays out from one system to another is very different and is typically inconsistent in quality. In the examples shared by Raish, she promotes giving students choice in their learning space. We support that idea, as long as students are provided with guidance and the resources they need to determine what space would most benefit their learning as well as strategies for ongoing monitoring and reflection about what is working and what could be changed to more optimize the learning environment.

"Any pace" still is concerning to us because it encourages the idea that any pace that students choose will make them be successful at learning a given concept. In our experience and research, studies have shown that pacing guides that scaffold student learning help greatly. These pacing guides can help teachers but also help students stay on track to meeting their learning goals. If there is no pace structure, students typically choose to procrastinate or do not do anything at all. Additionally, students who take only one or two online courses often find themselves with immediate demands from their face-to-face courses. When facing concrete deadlines on almost a daily basis in their face-to-face courses, work that can be deferred such as that in self-paced online courses can tend to receive a lower priority and is done "when there is time." Our data show that many online students dig themselves too deep of a hole by not getting started early enough or quickly enough in a course and are unable to recover. Consequently, some miss out on earning credit for the course, and most of them who display such patterns do not get the most out of the learning opportunity.

For us, the true misconstruing of meaning of these terms typically happens at the stakeholder level and not at the student level. Catchy phrases consisting of ill-defined and ambiguous terms can cause misinterpretation, misinformation, and unsuccessful implementation.

The open conversations that need to be happening should be around what is working and what is not working at the implementation level rather than these kitschy phrases that help move the field further faster on the policy advocacy circuit.

At this stage, we have plenty of data points and momentum, and the most likely scenario of killing that momentum is the lack of performance. The initial utility of this phrase has served its purpose, and now it should be retired, and a new phrase should be instated that aligns more with what is working around online learning and student achievement.

Part 5

Learning Science

INTRODUCTION TO PART 5

Perhaps among the most volatile and exciting dialogues in our field currently is the nature of the relationship between the traditional instructional design field and the learning sciences field, which have recently had a few inroads into true collaboration (Carr-Chellman, 2015, 2016). This section will be most useful to those academics in the field who are interested in deeper understandings of the connections and lack of connections between these closely aligned fields.

Gibbons starts our exploration of these fields by describing the historical split between educational technology and learning sciences, illustrated by the divergent views of two key figures, Robert Gagné and Robert Glaser. Gibbons calls for building bridges across the two communities perhaps through an emerging industry of education. Yip agrees that the two communities would benefit from closer ties but sees those developing around design rather than an education industry.

Rowland extends this same thread by agreeing that design would be a logical connection but also by asserting that a method often adopted by learning scientists—that of design-based research—rarely includes design expertise or produces outcomes that are useful to designers. Zimmerman disagrees and points to partnerships in designing useful outcomes in the form of design principles.

Yip further expands the dialogue by introducing the potential for participatory design. Extending the considerations of partnerships under this concept, Yip suggests that involving end-users as active participants in design processes will produce benefits that far exceed the risks. Reeves agrees and states that instructional designers are often too insular in their work.

References

Carr-Chellman, A. A. (2015). Positing the future: The future of "our" field. *Tech Trends, 59*(4), 4.
Carr-Chellman, A. A. (2016). Emerging marriage: One story of learning sciences and instructional systems as a possible revisioned future. *Educational Technology Magazine, 56*(1), 32–35.

Chapter 23

Points of Contact
Educational Technology and the Learning Sciences

Andrew S. Gibbons

Introduction

During the 1960s and 1970s, leading educational researchers were charting divergent paths with their changing views on instruction, learning, and design. One path led to today's field of educational technology; another led to the learning sciences. Neither of these can be termed a discipline in the traditional academic sense. Rather, they represent gravitational centers typical of modern applied fields such as computer science, medicine, business, and law, which share a body of questions and methodologies that unite them more than divide them.

By studying the interests of two key figures—once-close colleagues whose worldviews slowly diverged—it may be possible to see how educational technology and the learning sciences began to separate. By studying the common goals they initially shared, it may be possible to identify points of contact to guide future research and practice that draws together their common and divergent interests. Their fundamental goals of improving learning and instruction provide a firm foundation for such an effort.

Two Key Figures: Robert Gagné and Robert Glaser

In 1965, in *The Conditions of Learning*, Robert Gagné (1965) proposed a basic pattern of nine events for instruction and a formula for configuring instructional strategy details based on a taxonomy of learning objective types. This pattern of nine events was later used to organize headings of a literature review that Gagné and coauthor William D. Rohwer titled "Instructional Psychology" for the 1969 *Annual Review of Psychology*—the first of a series of chapters by the same title subsequently published in the *Annual Review* (Gagné & Rohwer, 1969).

Three years after the Gagné-Rohwer chapter, Robert Glaser and Lauren Resnick (1972) used a fundamentally different pattern of headings for their "Instructional Psychology" chapter for the *Annual Review*. Glaser and Resnick structured their review in terms of (1) the analysis of tasks to specify the content of learning, (2) the diagnosis of learner characteristics, (3) the design of instructional environments, and (4) the evaluation of learning outcomes.

The juxtaposition of these reviews highlights a basic paradigmatic difference in the minds of the authors that presaged two futures for instructional design and instructional research. The Gagné-Rohwer review emphasized the enacted aspects of instruction, while the Glaser-Resnick review emphasized the importance of the interaction of the learner's cognition with designed instructional artifacts.

Growth Apart

The Gagné-Rohwer and Glaser-Resnick reviews serve as bookends or anchor points in a scholarly discussion that has continued for nearly fifty years. It has resulted in the evolution of two major research communities centered on learning and the design of instruction.

On one hand is the Educational Technology community, which focuses on the application of technological devices and processes for the improvement of instruction. Educational Technology has for most of the time accepted the premises of Gagné and some of his predecessors that categories and formulas can be found that lead to appropriate instructional treatments. Objectives can be typed, and the typing can lead to appropriate instructional strategy choices.

On the other hand is the Learning Sciences community, which focuses on matching the nuances of the learning process with appropriate experience and support for knowledge building. The learning sciences accept the premise that studying the learning process will lead to insights about how the instructional process can be made responsive to the momentary needs of the learner and how the learner can be given greater responsibility for personal learning.

Neither of these positions is capable of supporting commercial industrial activity in an increasingly entrepreneurial education and training world. Both positions live in traditions laid down decades ago, represented by the influence of theorists like Glaser and Gagné. Each of them has grown over the years into a community of research, theory building, and practice. Hoadley observed of them: "there are two very active communities that both study more or less the same area, but these communities hardly talk to one another. . . . How can this be?" (p. 6).

A major question in many minds is whether a resolution or reconciliation can or should be made between the interests and worldviews of these two communities to combine the powerful insights of each into a more coherent, comprehensive, and productive worldview for the design of instructional experiences that can attain industrial-strength volumes, speeds, and quality.

Some bridges between LS and ET are being built through:

- Collaborative projects such as the recent *Handbook of Design in Educational Technology* (Luckin et al., 2013).
- The repositioning and renaming of academic programs to cover topics and skills in both educational technology and the learning sciences.

This essay is concerned with how to construct stronger bridges and more touch points of common research and development interest. My recommendation would require some alteration in the goals adopted by researchers and designers from both communities.

Growth within Separate Communities

The trajectories of the learning sciences and educational technology diverged in a relatively short period of time as cognitivist doctrines gained ascendancy and interest in behaviorism waned. Glaser was a leader in advancing the cognitivist cause. A major point of inflection in his path was the establishment of the well-funded Learning Research and Development Center (LRDC) at the University of Pittsburg under his direction in 1963 and an increase in internationalism. The LRDC was conceived as an interdisciplinary laboratory established to take ideas all the way from research through to implementation in schools.

The LRDC employed a diverse staff as a means of bringing multiple viewpoints to bear on both theoretical and practical problems. The range of backgrounds brought together included psycholinguistics, computer science, sociology, teaching, law, artificial intelligence, anthropology, psychology, educational policy, and eventually cognitive neuroscience.

The path taken by Gagné went in a different direction, as he and his associates at Florida State University increased their focus on schoolteachers and eventually on practicing instructional designers as a community. The point of inflection in this case was less dramatic, as it resulted from the emphasis on technological means greatly amplified by Skinner's teaching machines. Though the machines proved not to be the active ingredient of programmed instruction, the computer picked up its momentum, and questions about the balance between technology and the classroom teacher began to trouble Gagné's associate Leslie Briggs. In 1967 Briggs published a media selection process that in 1970 was followed by the publication of the first instructional design model to call itself by that name. Gagné's own direction was shaped by his wartime experience with the development of large human-machine systems, and this influenced his thinking in a systematic, analytic, and procedural direction. Years of large-scale system development left their imprint on his later work, and behaviorism continued to tug at his theoretical preferences even after he fell under the influence of information-processing psychology and even later when he accepted the value of cognitivism.

Briggs' design model initiated and gave authority to an outpouring of instructional design models and instructional strategy formulas that for many years dominated the attention of what became the educational technology community (Gibbons, Boling & Smith, 2014). Government and military interest in formulaic approaches remained high, and so there was a ready market for these ideas. A stream of publications for the teacher-government-military audience was the result, many of which are still used for teaching basic instructional design using instructional design models. Many of these have gone through multiple editions, giving evidence that there is a demand for explicit design support for the everyday, perhaps untrained, instructional designer.

The Underlying Causes of Separation

Glaser (1982) describes a historical precedent by which education and psychology became separated academic worlds in the early twentieth century, each field becoming uninterested for the most part in the work of the other. In both fields, the cross-pollination of ideas that could have produced knowledge through the practical application of theoretical principles (and learning new questions from the results) was lost. Research publication and theory development in the abstract became ends in themselves. Getting one's hands dirty with practical applications became low-status.

By ignoring each other, Glaser concludes, education and psychology were harming themselves by wasting an opportunity to join forces to change the nature of everyday educational practice and theory at the same time. The observation has been made recently that the same situation exists between the learning sciences and educational technology, as evidenced by the general lack of cross-communication between the two communities (Spector, personal communication, 2014).

Hoadley (2004) suggests several basic factors that distinguish research communities and tend to set them apart from each other. These include differences in scope and goals, theoretical commitments, epistemology and methods, and history. This essay began with mentioning some of the forces of history personified by two theorists whose differences in all of these respects characterize the situation between the two design communities today.

With regard to the remaining areas, Hoadley identifies similarities that may exert more gravitational pull than the differences.

However, at present, an analysis of article cross-referencing (Kirby, Hoadley & Carr-Chellman, 2005) shows the imbalance of interest between the separate communities. This leads to the conclusion that though one community (educational technology) finds some interest in the enterprise of the other (learning sciences), there is little reciprocation. This separation is ironic, because one of the founding goals of the learning sciences was to create Dewey's "bridging science" between scientific research, design, development, and instructional practice (Glaser, 1982; see also Glaser & Resnick, 1972). Educational technology specializes in development, but the learning sciences have not embraced their body of knowledge. Possibly this is because that development process knowledge has not shown significant advancements through research for decades. New views of the design process are needed and are emerging.

Bringing the educational technology and learning sciences communities into a closer working relationship will not become a priority until their goals, theoretical commitments, and methods—as well as their incentives—come into alignment in some way. Changing economic forces may provide the right conditions.

Points of Contact

A shift is underway in the financing and organization of education and training. Public schools at all levels are facing pressures from multiple competitors that Christensen, Anthony, and Roth (2004, see Chapter 5) describe as disruptive. Corporate education and training, once relegated to the training department where careers went to die, are being pulled into central positions in the fabric of organizations as a competitive tool for retaining employees, preserving organizational knowledge, and nurturing careers. Both corporations and higher education are placing emphasis on executives who function as chief learning officers. Universities especially are testing new business plans to keep them relevant and solvent within a new economic landscape (Gibbons, 2014, pp. 401–404).

I believe that educational technology and the learning sciences should expand their views to comprehend a larger enterprise, which is to feed sound principles into a growing an increasingly commercial education and training market. The larger view is the new *industry* of education, which at one time may have been an oxymoron but now is rapidly becoming a fact, even for government-supported educational institutions.

Both the learning science and educational technology communities have existed within and been supported by the context of higher education and grants. Virtually all research and development on instructional design comes from this context, which is one of the reasons that advances within the well-funded learning sciences community have been more rapid than those in the educational technology community, whose once generous external academic funding for technology enhancement (read: devices) has long since been diverted to other educational purposes.

Despite the imbalance in funding, these fields have in common goals that were formed in 1957, when Sputnik awakened education from its siloed slumber. Gagné and Glaser were energized by the goals that were set at the time, even though they took different approaches to reaching them. Gagné's framing of the problem was:

> To understand how learning operates in everyday situations of the school is a most valuable kind of understanding. But it does not unlock the mysteries of education.

What it can do is illuminate some of the activities of the curriculum planner, the course designer, and the instructor.

(Gagné, 1965, p. 24)

Glaser framed it this way:

If it can be agreed that the science of psychology must supply the knowledge for the precepts of instruction, then it follows that the translation of scientific knowledge into practice requires technological development. However, at this point in time, an entity known as the educational technologist or an instructional designer hardly exists in our society. If such a person did exist, a framework could be suggested in which he might carry out his job.

(Glaser, 1966, p. 433)

Gagné and his future work drifted in the direction of "everyday situations": a practical view focused on factors external to the learner that was interested in the study of external conditions to support learning. Gagné's experience with large-scale system design was also a preoccupation, leading to emphasis of systematic design procedures. Glaser's future work concentrated on the "science of psychology": the inner workings of the mind during learning. For Glaser, this was not a departure from the past. Even in behaviorist times, he had maintained an interest in mental processes because of his early work in measurement and assessment.

Separate communities developed around the interests and questions of these and other great leaders in what became a larger, very diverse community of "instructional design." Glaser's "if such a person did exist" became "this person now comprises a vast community of professional and technical designers."

The two communities of educational technology and the learning sciences that were once joined by a common interest now need to come together more closely and cooperatively in a common project they may not be fully aware they share: the project of remaining relevant in the emerging industry of education.

These communities each have unique strengths to contribute to a closer relationship. Designers in the learning sciences have traditionally not been concerned with the design process per se. Their focus has been on exploring the learning process and charting the relationships among complex variables given less detailed attention by educational technology. Designers in educational technology have dealt with the industrial implications of design using engineering process models (Gibbons et al., 2014). However, a new generation of designers is exploring alternative interpretations of design that the learning sciences have not had the opportunity of exploring themselves because of their more theoretical focus (Hokanson & Gibbons, 2014; see also Rowland, 1993, 2008; Boling & Smith, 2010).

Other more mature and industrially linked R&D communities from many disciplines have made themselves relevant not only because of government-funded research but also by forming ties with industrial sponsors with real problems to solve. Engineering, for example, is divided into several subcommunities with specialized interests (e.g., chemical, civil, electrical, etc.) and distinct industrial ties—and therefore industrial-sized incentives for ideas brought to commercial fruition.

Engineering disciplines have grounding in theory and enjoy sophisticated tools for measurement, research, and development. The term "research and development" is an expression of the industry-orientation of these subcommunities and "applied" subcommunities related to a number of other disciplines (e.g., biology, genetics, computer science, business, etc.).

Because most people have access to high-powered digital development tools, and because the tools make compelling surface effects easy to create, a vast army of media and technical professionals dabble in instructional design. The majority of these are untrained in the architectures and operations of instructional experiences. When everyone is a designer, there is no incentive to consult a professional. Therefore, the instructional designer tends to be a service professional, more like the nurse than the doctor.

Instructional design has remained largely a craft, rather than evolving into a profession along the lines of engineering, law, and medicine. These professions have firm theoretical and research bases growing out of years of research and development, combined with practical experience.

Often the practitioners of instructional design who do have industrial ambitions are business people—amateurs and entrepreneurs—rather than professional instructional designers. Because instructional design has been trivialized by the amateur, the commercialization of education and training has been in the hands of the untrained, who use intuitive methods that present shiny surfaces to the user. This has left academics largely in the dust.

The accumulated theoretical knowledge of the instructional design communities is ready for commercial application, but there is no leadership in that direction. I do not believe that leadership coming from only one of the communities I have been describing will be capable of making a convincing argument to industry that they have the substance to form productive industrial ties. I recommend, therefore, that leaders in both the educational technology and the learning science communities look for points of contact and encourage greater cooperation to build the instructional design community of the future—capable in theory, and capable in industrial-scale design.

Progress is both constructive and destructive. Old ways, old allegiances, old ideas make way for new ones. Guided by the hands of many stakeholders, change over time can be constructive, and it can allow healthy adaptation to new circumstances, new priorities. Just as the traditional silos of educational and psychological research have evolved toward multidisciplinary cognitive studies and design-based research, these new concepts will before long themselves superseded by even newer ideas. By considering improved sharing of new goals, theoretical views, methods, and a willingness to cross-communicate the educational technology and learning science communities can ensure their continued relevance in a future history that they helped to narrate.

Note: I want to thank Dr. Mike Spector of the University of North Texas for his constructive comments on the draft of this essay. I assume full responsibility for any errors or wrongheaded conclusions in the final version.

References

Boling, E., & Smith, K. M. (2010). *Intensive studio experience in a non-studio masters program: Student activities and thinking across levels of design.* Montreal: Design Research Society.

Christensen, C. M., Anthony, S. D., & Roth, E. A. (2004). *Seeing what's next: Using theories of innovation to predict industry change.* Cambridge, MA: Harvard Business Review Press.

Gagné, R. M. (1965). *The conditions of learning.* New York: Holt, Rinehart & Winston.

Gagné, R. M., & Rohwer, W. D. (1969). Instructional psychology. *Annual review of psychology, 20*(1), 381–418.

Gibbons, A. S. (2014). *An architectural approach to instructional design.* New York: Routledge.

Gibbons, A. S., Boling, E., & Smith, K. M. (2014). Instructional design models. In J. M. Spector, M. D. Merrill, J. Elen, & M. J. Bishop (Eds.), *Handbook of research on educational communications and technology* (4th ed.). New York: Springer.

Glaser, R. (1966). Psychological bases for instructional design. *Audio-Visual Communication Review*, *14*(4), 433–449.

Glaser, R. (1982). Instructional psychology: Past, present, and future. *American Psychologist*, *37*(3), 292–305.

Glaser, R., & Resnick, L. B. (1972). Instructional psychology. *Annual Review of Psychology*, *23*, 207–276.

Hoadley, C. M. (2004). Learning and design: Why the learning sciences and instructional systems need each other. *Educational technology*, *44*(3), 6–12.

Hokanson, B., & Gibbons, A. S. (Eds.) (2014). *Design in educational technology: Design thinking, design process, and the design studio*. New York: Springer.

Kirby, J., Hoadley, C. M., & Carr-Chellman, A. A. (2005). Instructional systems design and the learning sciences: A citation analysis. *Educational Technology Research and Development*, *53*(1), 37–47.

Luckin, R., Puntambekar, S., Goodyear, P., Grabowski, B. Underwood, J., & Winters, N. (Eds.) (2013). *Handbook of design in educational technology*. New York: Routledge.

Rowland, G. (1993). Designing and instructional design. *Educational Technology Research and Development*, *41*(1), 79–91.

Rowland, G. (2008). Design and research: Partners for educational innovation. *Educational Technology*, *48*(6), 3–9.

RESPONSE BY JASON YIP

I agree with Gibbons that the learning sciences (LS) and educational technology researchers (ET) need to come together to solve practical problems, but I am not sure if focusing on "the industry of education" is the common ground that will unite these two separate communities.

First, I believe the common ground that does connect LS and ET is the commitment to *design*. As Hoadley (2004) points out, boundary crossing is occurring between LS and ET, and design plays a central role in this merging. As learning scientists who create new learning innovations, LS integrates design-based research (DBR) (e.g., Brown, 1992; Collins, 1992) to study learning in real-life environments through design and systematic changes (Barab, 2006). The goal of DBR is to closely examine learning environments through its multiple changes and enactments within naturalistic contexts, so that we may develop new theories, artifacts, technologies, and pedagogical practices for other contexts. As such, design cannot be separated from research on learning. Gibbons writes that "designers in the learning sciences have traditionally not been concerned with the design process per se," but I do not fully agree with this. Understanding how deep learning occurs requires methodologies that involve working closely with schools, teachers, learners, families, and other stakeholders. The process of design in LS tends to focus more on understanding the people's processes of learning through ethnography, ethnomethodology and conversational analysis, quasi-experimental design, and sociocultural psychology (Sawyer, 2006) to inform and make design decisions. Therefore, understanding how learning occurs and in what contexts supports the design process in LS.

Similarly, researchers in the ET community are calling out for stronger connections to research agendas beyond quasi-experimental design methods. Cuban (2001) notes that computers and educational technologies are often integrated into classrooms with low impact to learning and little consideration for the realities of real-life. Reeves (2006) argues that ET needs a better approach toward technological design. Reeves boldly states, "the reality of educational technology research is that isolated researchers primarily conduct one-off quasi experimental studies rarely linked to a robust research agenda, much less concerned with any relationship to practice" (p. 55). However, the common goal of design for authentic learning between ET and LS can make for better partnerships. ET's history of design connects well with LS's focus on understanding deep learning and how technology acts as a facilitator for learning.

Second, I do agree with Gibbons that for too many years, the accumulation of theoretical knowledge, without practical application for learning, leaves much skepticism in both research fields for practitioners. However, I am not sure if the "increasingly commercial education and training market" is the right place for our communities to come together. Learning and education is not the same as medicine, engineering, and computer science, for which theory and commercialization may coexist better. In David Labaree's (1997) seminal work, he contends there are two alternative views of education that compete with the goals of increasing *democratic equality* (e.g., Dewey, 1916). *Social efficiency* focuses on economic well-being and participation in the free market. Schools are responsible for teaching technical skills to learners so that they can get a job and be productive members of the workforce. *Social mobility* approaches focus on education as a commodity, and its only purpose is to help people rise up toward desirable social positions. While social efficiency tends to direct learners' attention away from civic engagement toward the economy, it still focuses on the quality of learning. Social mobility, however, is quite antithetical to democratic schooling, highly individualized and possessive. However, developing education and learning environments solely for efficiency and mobility are ultimately counterintuitive toward increasing equality and democracy.

While our communities are somewhat divided, I do believe our overarching goals as researchers in LS and ET are to create learning innovations that better empower learners and as a democratic society as a whole. However, if LS and ET researchers form ties with industrial sponsors as our common ground, I believe we risk compromising democratic ideals for social efficiency and mobility. For instance, commercial training enterprises often have deadlines and end goals that focus more on market forces. However, LS researchers' commitments to understanding deep learning requires lengthy time and theoretical commitments in both research and design (Sawyer, 2006), which may conflict with commercialization priorities. Overall, while LS and ET need pragmatic solutions for our complex learning problems, Gibbons' suggestion to focus our common goals with the industry of education may also create philosophical paradoxes for both communities. I am not saying that research into commercial education does not have a place in LS for technological design, but I am concerned we need to discuss the possible conflicts in philosophy that will inevitably occur.

References

Barab, S. (2006). Design-based research. In R. Sawyer (Eds.), *The Cambridge handbook of the learning sciences* (pp. 153–169). New York: Cambridge University Press.

Brown, A. L. (1992). Design experiments: Theoretical and methodological challenges in creating complex interventions in classroom settings. *Journal of the Learning Sciences*, 2(2), 141–178.

Collins, A. (1992). Toward a design science of education. In E. Scalon & T. O'Shea (Eds.), *New directions in educational technology* (pp. 15–22). New York: Springer-Verlag.

Cuban, L. (2001). *Oversold and underused: Reforming schools through technology, 1980–2000.* Cambridge, MA: Harvard University Press.

Dewey, J. (1916). *Democracy and education.* New York: Macmillan.

Hoadley, C. M. (2004). Learning and design: Why the learning sciences and instructional systems need each other. *Educational Technology*, 44(3), 6–12.

Labaree, D. F. (1997). Public goods, private goods: The American struggle over educational goals. *American Education Research Journal*, 34(1), 39–81.

Reeves, T. C. (2006). Design research from the technology perspective. In J. V. Akker, K. Gravemeijer, S. McKenney, & N. Nieveen (Eds.), *Educational design research* (pp. 86–109). London: Routledge.

Sawyer, R. (2006). Introduction: The new science of learning. In R. Sawyer (Eds.), *The Cambridge handbook of the learning sciences* (pp. 1–16). New York: Cambridge University Press.

REJOINDER BY ANDREW S. GIBBONS

Thanks, Jason, for a thoughtful response. You said many things that I like very much. In particular, your comment that "design cannot be separated from research on learning" touches the heart of the issue that some people think separates ed tech (hereafter ET) and the learning sciences (hereafter LS). Your statement may be the best bridge between the two.

I should explain my recommendation that "the industry of education" might be the best common ground for the meeting of ET and the LS. I am sure it seemed like an odd recommendation.

My recommendation was based on my own observation of the incredible surge in investment by entrepreneurs who want to provide educational products and services. There exists now a gold rush mentality among many who wish to cash in on the technology-based educational product market. Miners in this case include major publishing companies (Pearson, McGraw-Hill, Wiley), online high schools, charter schools, enterprising online training providers (Khan Academy, Nova Southeastern, Capella, and others), higher education online providers of courses and degrees (ASU, Carnegie-Mellon, EdX, Coursera, and others), online MOOC providers,[1] and even leading personalities like Clayton Christensen and the Christensen Institute, who are offering seminars, literature, and services to public educators and parents.[2] These are not the only miners: hardware and software companies like Apple, Microsoft, and Cisco are learning how to invent themselves into the education and training business.

The commercialization of education is advancing at a faster rate now than ever before, and the gold fever shows no sign of abating. As is typical of a gold rush mentality, the idea is to get there first, not to get there best. As a young designer in the 1970s, I witnessed firsthand this mentality taking over design practice as systematic instructional design models, which, when they were found to have economic value, began to proliferate rapidly. It was the land of opportunity in those days for consultants, each of whom had their own instructional design model, slanted toward a segment of the market they wanted to win as a customer. (Confession and first-person data: I worked for a company and participated in the creation of a hundred-box instructional design model. The customer—a government organization—liked the model so much that it requested a more detailed one. So we built them a two-hundred-box model, which it also liked, and it was useful to the organization.)

Literally hundreds of these models were created (see Goodson & Andrews), 99 percent of them built by an activity splitting and recombination process, representing no more than a metaphorical "rearrangement of the deck chairs," but one it was hoped would have economic advantage. Virtually all of them shared the same engineering/management viewpoint. In my own recent work (Gibbons, 2014), I point out that these were not really "design" models, because in each one there was a box labeled "now design the instruction." That box had, and still has, little in it for the designer, though the models have a lot of content for a project manager.

The lasting impact of that design model gold rush on us today cannot be questioned, because design models are enshrined in the common practices taught to the vast army of instructional designers working in industry, education, and military-government. They exist there as formulaic processes devised in the 1970s (ADDIE/ISD) that are still widely used, especially by novices. Once the "anyone can design" mentality had set in, managers saw the advantage and adopted models as a way of controlling training quality, economics, development timelines, and standardization. Improved quality of instruction was implied, but it was not the main point; economy was.

No one would argue today that these models are the final answer to improving the quality of instruction, that they are based on research, or that they have been validated through any kind of controlled study. They exist because someone said they existed (see Smith & Boling, 2009; Gibbons & Yanchar, 2010; Gibbons, Boling & Smith, 2014).

Here is my point: if instructional designers of any persuasion—whether they are educational technologists or learning scientists—want to be relevant and have long-term impact on instructional design practice and instructional quality in the future, they must begin to make input in an important way to these entrepreneurs, starting now. If they want their new ideas to find acceptance that leads to innovative application in an increasingly commercial and competitive venue, then they must have an open dialogue: not with each other, but with the entrepreneurs, even becoming partners with them in their enterprises.

There is a vast pool of research on learning that has not made it into widespread practice. For us to become participants in change to the designer's paradigms and the delivery paradigm, we must adopt the concept of design-based research in terms of what it really represents—industrial research and development—and begin to practice it in partnership with those who have the funds: seeing that our ideas on learning and design get to the end of the row, not just into the journal. Getting more research grants will not have the long-term impact that a relationship with a vendor will. In principle, what I am recommending is the natural extension of Ann Brown's philosophy of taking research out of the lab and into the real world, in an educational world that is now humming with economic tension.

The audience for educational products and the manner in which they are delivered—the very shape and form of the products themselves—will be governed in the future not by the scientist but by members of multidisciplinary research and development groups funded and directed by the visions of entrepreneurs. Who is better equipped to help them spin that vision than us—together?

Notes

1. "MOOCs: Top 10 Sites for Free Education With Elite Universities." BPDA Detroit Chapter. Web.
2. The Clayton Christensen Institute for Disruptive Innovation. Web.

References

Gibbons, A. S. (2014). *An architectural approach to instructional design*. New York: Routledge.
Gibbons, A. S., Boling, E., & Smith, K. M. (2014). Instructional design models. In J. M. Spector, M. D. Merrill, J. Elen, & M. J. Bishop (Eds.), *Handbook of research on educational communications and technology* (pp. 607–615). New York: Springer.
Gibbons, A. S., & Yanchar, S. C. (2010). An alternative view of the instructional design process: A response to Smith and Boling. *Educational Technology, 50*(4), 16–26.
Smith, K. M., & Boling, E. (2009). What do we make of design? Design as a concept in educational technology. *Educational Technology, 49*(4), 3–17.

Chapter 24

Bring Design to Design-Based Research

Gordon Rowland

Over the past twenty years or so, I have watched the development of Design-Based Research (DBR) with a mixture of curiosity and skepticism. I have not conducted DBR studies myself, but I have read many articles and reports, reviewed a couple manuscripts for journals, attended a dozen or more presentations, and talked about the subject with scholars and practitioners in the learning sciences and instructional design. I find myself repeatedly asking two questions:

- Who brings design expertise to DBR projects?
- For whom are outcomes useful?

I will use these questions to organize a critique below. First, I should clarify what I understand DBR to be, based on sources such as Brown (1992), Design-Based Research Collective (2003), and Barab and Squire (2004).

DBR is a methodology or overall approach to conducting research, more so than a specific method. It involves partnering researchers with practitioners to set research in real contexts and, through an iterative process of conceptualizing and implementing interventions, to create (1) a design that is usable and useful in the specific context and (2) theoretical principles regarding learning, instruction, and design. In the examples I have seen, most of the practitioners involved were teachers, and designs typically employed advanced technologies/media.

On the one hand, DBR appeals to me in comparison to traditional experiments by setting research in real settings and situations. While we have gained much knowledge from studies in the lab, the AOTBE (all other things being equal) caveat has restricted their utility in practice. DBR, at least in idealized descriptions, recognizes the complexity of real settings and attempts to respond with flexibility and adaptation in its methods. I certainly also appreciate the focus on making concrete positive change in learning and instruction.

On the other hand, through the lens I bring from design, and the subfield of instructional design and technology (IDT), the instances of DBR I have seen suggest that the promise of the approach is overstated.

I find myself answering the first question, "Who brings design expertise to DBR projects?" with "no one" or perhaps "not whom they think." For example, researchers partner with teachers and, perhaps because projects involve technologies with which the researchers are more familiar, assume they possess greater design expertise. I suspect the reverse is true. Teachers, whether they have formal training in such or not, engage in curricular and instructional design on a regular basis. In contrast, researchers may have little to no experience in designing.

In fact, I have found it to be the exception when a DBR report suggests true respect for what practitioners/teachers bring to the table. Rather they seem to be treated as necessary participants to gain access to the real setting, dominated by the language associated with research and technology. As one group of proponents described at a recent AERA conference, it was necessary for them to "engage teachers as learners." They—that is, the researchers—were presumably the teachers' teachers. I have even seen and heard researchers (and, unfortunately, educational technologists) use the phrase "teacher-proof," meaning that their designs need to be protected from modification by teachers. Through my lens, that seems arrogant and representative of the privilege that most DBR studies grant to the researcher. It is no wonder that other teachers and schools resist adoption of designs, what DBR proponents lament as a "scaling problem."

There are several other contributing factors to my "no one" answer to the first question: project initiation and framing, the nature of iterations, and the connection of complexity to design. I will describe each below.

Design is conducted for, or better, *with* a client (e.g., Nelson & Stolterman, 2012). This can take the form of a custom product developed through close collaboration, or more of a speculative product intended for mass distribution. DBR seems to claim the former but simultaneously want the latter. Consequently, what I hear (secondhand) from teachers is a frustration that researchers promise collaborative problem identification and framing but arrive with specific intentions and desires, essentially a solution to which the problem will be fit.

DBR critics ask how the iterations of conceptualization and implementation differ from formative evaluation. The response tends to be something along the lines of "they are similar, but DBR iterations are more rigorous and more open to new ideas." That is true. They are more rigorous and open than the most primitive form of formative evaluation that a novice learns in his or her first course—a stage after development in a linear model, in which one attempts to "test quality into" a design. However, that form bears little resemblance to how skilled designers evaluate their ideas and partial-products. Rather, they constantly evaluate and constantly look for new ideas to improve their designs throughout the process, and they use a wide variety of methods that are every bit as rigorous as DBR experiments. In fact, while the DBR experiment focuses on testing theory, often doing so through what IDT would recognize as media comparison (which we have known for decades is problematic), design evaluation methods are focused on improving the design. Maybe the two goals are incompatible?

The third factor concerns complexity. A driving force for the development of DBR was the recognition that settings are complex, and research that isolates variables outside those settings misses complex dynamics and interdependencies. In a sense, it sees trees but misses the forest. However, by definition complex systems are unique, nonlinear, and unpredictable. Beyond the most common sense and general, they defy prescription. DBR seems to recognize the paradox in suggesting that principles represent "local theory," but (setting aside the issue of what is and is not theory) for whom is such theory useful?

That question is half of the larger second question, "For whom are the outcomes useful?" Those outcomes, the design, and the theory appear to have two potential user groups, and both are problematic. First, as I mentioned above, there are repeated statements of dissatisfaction from researchers that designs are not widely adopted. That is not the least bit surprising for designs that are based primarily on researchers' desires and views of what teachers should want. Second, the theory outcome betrays a fundamental misunderstanding of what designers do and what knowledge they rely on in designing. A novice may rely on basic principles in a simple situation; an expert working in a complex situation relies on judgments in the moment based more on case experience and precedent. The principles I have seen that were derived from DBR do not go beyond what experienced designers would consider common sense.

If I am off base with these statements, one way to demonstrate it would be to cite principles that (a) significantly advance our knowledge, representing something skilled designers do not already know, and (b) have been applied to significantly enhance another design in a different context.

If that proves difficult, I suggest two things that might shift DBR in more productive directions: (1) involve designers, and (2) produce outcomes that experienced designers can use. The first is a suggestion to be more conscious of privilege, give greater respect to teachers, and bring greater design expertise into the process—to recognize that being skilled at research and savvy with technology by themselves give someone zero design capability. Exceptions to the typical DBR studies I have seen are projects conducted by Joke Voogt and her colleagues in the Netherlands who have partnered researchers with curriculum *designers*, and demonstrated concern for teacher-participants' roles. Great!

The second is a suggestion to align outcomes with how designers work and the tools they use—for example, Nigel Cross' (2011) work on design thinking and Erik Stolterman's (Stolterman & Pierce, 2012) work on design tools. The typical DBR report gives only surface-level information about the design and next to no information about the design process (as opposed to the experiments that attempt to test quality in). Design cases such a those documented in the *International Journal of Designs for Learning*, with rich information on both, could be very helpful. Perhaps an evolution from Design-Based Research to Design-AND-Research (Rowland, 2008) would help us all.

References

Barab, S., & Squire, K. (2004). Design-based research: Putting a stake in the ground. *The Journal of the Learning Sciences, 13*(1), 1–14.

Brown, A. L. (1992). Design experiments: Theoretical and methodological challenges in creating complex interventions in classroom settings. *The Journal of the Learning Sciences, 2*(2), 141–178.

Cross, N. (2011). *Design thinking: Understanding how designers think and work.* Berg: Oxford.

Design-Based Research Collective. (2003). Design-based research: An emerging paradigm for educational inquiry. *Educational Researcher, 32*(1), 5–8.

Nelson, H., & Stolterman, E. (2012). *The design way: Intentional change in an unpredictable world* (2nd ed.). Cambridge, MA: MIT Press.

Rowland, G. (2008, November–December). Design and research: Partners for educational innovation. *Educational Technology, 48*, 3–9.

Stolterman, E., & Pierce, J. (2012). Design tools in practice: Studying the designer-tool relationship in interaction design. *DIS 2012 • In the Wild.* June 11–15, Newcastle, UK.

RESPONSE BY HEATHER TOOMEY ZIMMERMAN

Like Gordon Rowland, I was drawn to design-based research (DBR) as it as an inquiry tool that can be used to conduct learning research in situ; however, Rowland and I disagree on the utility of DBR. I intend to use our points of disagreement to start a discussion about when and how DBR is an appropriate methodological perspective.

My understanding of DBR was developed from reading seminal papers by DBR researchers such as Brown (1992), Barab and Squire (2004), Bell (2004), and Collins, Joseph, and Bielaczyc (2004). My understanding of design and DBR was enhanced as I came to work on DBR projects set within formal and informal settings. I was and am part of teams working on the development of a culturally and personally relevant science curriculum, the design of tools for summer camps to connect home and family settings, and the creation of tools for out-of-school sites to use to support intergenerational learning in the outdoors. I also have followed recent discussions that are advancing the DBR methodology (e.g., Sandoval, 2014) or suggesting other forms of DBR to the field of education, such as design-based implementation research (DBIR) (Penuel, Fishman, Cheng & Sabelli, 2011) and educational design research (McKenney & Reeves, 2013). Through these experiences, I have come to think deeply about the role of a distributed design process in DBR and how design principles are valued outcomes of a DBR study.

Distributed Design Work in DBR

Throughout my participation in these projects (as well as reading methodological perspectives), I have come to understand DBR is a perspective on the development and study of interventions in educational settings (workplaces, schools, museums, and more) with two related goals. The one goal is improving theory about learning and design, and the other goal is improving the tools that support teaching and learning in ways that will make a meaningful difference in the lives of people. As such a partnership to support DBR activities has to include team members who are familiar with the educational setting, familiar with the design of educational tools, familiar with research methodologies sensitive enough to investigate learning in situ, and familiar with the full system in which the educational tools shall be used. Within this description, I purposely did not use the term "expert" in research, design, setting, or theory because in a design-based research study, the expertise is distributed across the team.

Rowland asserts a weakness of many DBR efforts is not having one specific person identified as the design expert on the team; this is the first point in which we disagree. DBR, and its relative DBIR, is not a business-as-usual research method where a team is assembled with subject matter experts, educators, computer programmers or curriculum designers, and researchers. Instead, a central tenet of DBR is that the research and development efforts should include collaborations between research and practice. The educators then are not clients, as Rowland suggests, but partners. Within the ethos of collaborative research-practice partnerships, an idea in DBR has evolved that all team members' contributions should be empowered (Engle, 2008). Acknowledging the whole team is important in DBR because of DBR's goals to improve theory and educational practice in ways that make the team's educational innovation sustainable within the researched education setting as well as the full educational system in which the innovation is embedded. With this goal, the expertise to design a tool (whether it is a technology, a curriculum, a teaching strategy, or a new form of engagement for learners) requires design input from multiple vantage points. Identifying one person as "the designer" does not reflect the participatory nature, with the needed shifts in authority and accountability, required to conduct high-quality DBR and DBIR work.

While it is true that a large, well-funded team may place a person in the formal role of developer or designer (as Rowland points out in his paper), if a team is truly taking DBR perspective, then the designer's job entails bringing in others' perspectives of what effective design looks like within that setting and system on equal footing to his or her knowledge of design models and techniques. If a partnership has not been achieved, one could argue then that the team is not conducting a DBR study. Perhaps the problem that Rowland identifies is not a problem with DBR as a method but in an overapplication of the term.

That said, while most DBR researchers with whom I affiliate start their research in partnership with practitioners and situate their research in problems of practice, a researcher or university faculty member should not presume that he or she knows best how and when educators should participate in a DBR project. Just as research participants have the right to opt in and opt out of any and all study activities, all partners do too. Negotiations and discussions are the best tools to guide who does what task, when they complete the task, and how much involvement they should have—not someone external to the situation who makes the presumption about who has how much design expertise. There cannot be a one-size-fits-all formula to a DBR, education design research, or DBIR project because the development of educational interventions that address local concerns and global theory are derived from the intersection of learning principles and lived experience.

Design Principles as One Useful Outcome in DBR

At the end of his commentary, Rowland suggests that DBR does not have useful outcomes to other projects and people. He asks when have the outcomes of DBR been applied to other projects and when have design principles been identified as something that skilled designers do not know. While it could be that a handful of skilled designers have noticed that one design choice is more effective with learner outcomes than another design choice, this is not the same as saying DBR research is not valuable or is just common sense. Because research is an empirical enterprise that seeks to develop systematic knowledge, the role of research is to show to whom, in what circumstances, and in what system design principles apply. Designers need to know not just something works, but they need to know which learners benefit from these approaches, in what range of educational settings do the principles work more fully, and in what sequence and how often should the principles be applied.

As far as the utility of a design-based research project, there are multiple frameworks of design (a set of linked design principles) that are published, which provide the basis for new research in design. For example, there are multiple DBR projects that work together to expand and enrich the concept of scaffolding. In the journals *Journal of the Learning Sciences* and *Educational Technology Research and Development*, there are articles that list design principles and frameworks that have been cited hundreds of times—demonstrating how researchers use the prior work to justify their decisions in new interventions. In my own most recent DBR project on science learning outdoors with mobile computers (Land & Zimmerman, 2015), we include a chart of how the prior research influenced our design choice made to support youth and families. At one point, a group of educational researchers came together to promote a design principles database (Kali, 2008), and perhaps the best solution to Rowland's critique is for researchers conducting DBR and DBIR to come together again to advance a more coherent, synthetic set of principles that show what DBR can offer to the field of educational design.

References

Barab, S., & Squire, K. (2004). Design-based research: Putting a stake in the ground. *The Journal of the Learning Sciences, 13*(1), 1–14.

Bell, P. (2004). On the theoretical breadth of design-based research in education. *Educational Psychologist, 39*(4), 243–253.

Brown, A. L. (1992). Design experiments: Theoretical and methodological challenges in creating complex interventions in classroom settings. *The Journal of the Learning Sciences, 2*(2), 141–178.

Collins, A., Joseph, D., & Bielaczyc, K. (2004). Design research: Theoretical and methodological issues. *The Journal of the Learning Sciences, 13*(1), 15–42.

Engle, R. A. (2008). Establishing collaborations in design-based research projects: Insights from the origins of the MMAP project. *Proceedings of the 8th International Conference on International Conference for the Learning Sciences-Volume 1* (pp. 216–223).

Kali, Y. (2008). The Design Principles Database as means for promoting design-based research. In A. E. Kelly, R. A. Lesh, & J. Y. Baek (Eds.), *Handbook of design research methods in education* (pp. 423–438). New York: Taylor & Francis Group.

Land, S. M., & Zimmerman, H. T. (2015). Socio-technical dimensions of an outdoor mobile learning environment: A three-phase design-based research investigation. *Educational Technology Research & Development, 63*(2), 229–255.

McKenney, S., & Reeves, T. C. (2013). *Conducting educational design research*. Chicago: Routledge.

Penuel, W. R., Fishman, B. J., Cheng, B. H., & Sabelli, N. (2011). Organizing research and development at the intersection of learning, implementation, and design. *Educational Researcher, 40*(7), 331–337.

Sandoval, W. (2014). Conjecture mapping: An approach to systematic educational design research, *The Journal of the Learning Sciences, 23*(1), 18–36. doi: 10.1080/10508406.2013.778204

REJOINDER BY GORDON ROWLAND

I welcome the opportunity to comment on Zimmermann's response to my position paper.

I agree with Zimmermann in many areas—for example, the value of collaborative partnerships, on how distributed work can lead to improved outcomes, on the importance of gaining input from multiple vantage points, and on negotiating and discussing who does what and how much involvement individuals will have. Those are a few basic characteristics of effective design practice. Her argument regarding single designers, however, is based on a misunderstanding.

I suppose one might infer from a couple things I stated that I felt it was necessary to include someone with the title and responsibilities of *designer*. That is not what I intended or, in all other areas, stated. Rather, I argued for the value of inclusion of *design expertise*, whether centered or distributed. Learning scientists would likely bristle at the notion of a DBR study conducted with limited expertise in research—say one participant having taken an undergraduate course in research methods—but they appear to think that little more than the intention to make something and actions taken to do so constitute sufficient design expertise to not only produce effective designs but develop design principles.

In contrast, I believe design is a special form of inquiry on par with scientific research, equally grounded in theory and demanding in practice. Design is not an applied science. Learning scientists seem to treat it as merely an activity through which they can conduct *in situ* studies. One reasonable test that I suggested in my paper was that of outcomes. I asked to see principles that (a) significantly advance our knowledge, representing something skilled designers do not already know, and (b) have been applied to significantly enhance another design in a different context.

Zimmermann responds with a reference to "articles that list design principles and frameworks that have been cited hundreds of times" and refers to a principles database (Kali, 2008). Trying to be open to the possibility that my statements were uninformed, I examined the database.

In the database's Browse Mode I found that it includes (at least in parts that are open to the public), thirty-four "pragmatic principles" linked to four "meta-principles." The meta-principles include help students learn from each other; make contents accessible; make thinking visible; and promote autonomous lifelong learning. To give a flavor, the first ten of the pragmatic principles are build on student ideas; communicate the rich diversity of inquiry; connect to personally relevant contexts; create a clear and engaging flow of activities; create a cognitive conflict; design prompts for planning and monitoring; employ multiple social activity structures; enable manipulation of factors in models and simulation; enable multiples ways to participate in online discussions; and enable students to relate between micro and macro levels of phenomena.

A couple observations come immediately to mind. First, aside from some terms associated with recent technologies, the pragmatic principles (or instructional tactics) have been known and applied for decades. To find no works in the reference lists from the body of research on instructional message design, for example (e.g., Fleming & Levie, 1978, 1993), is telling and unfortunate.

Second, the database includes a Design Mode, and this is equally illustrative. Here the database developers adopt the ADDIE model to guide the user through the application of principles to cases. One familiar with the design and design expertise literatures would immediately recognize this as a linear, waterfall approach that is typical of novice behavior and effective in only simple circumstances.

Perhaps there is more to gain from the links to features and the connections to conditions and contexts of application, as Zimmermann argues. However, what leads it to be reasonable to ignore the decades of work that preceded the learning sciences and to adopt an especially primitive conception of design escapes me.

Zimmermann's response caused me to explore the database and to examine the contexts and outcomes of many DBR studies. For that I am grateful. I continue to believe, however, that the learning sciences—perhaps as a consequence of alignment with science—have devalued design and, therefore, design expertise. Also, my own field of educational technology has a long history of reinventing the wheel, and it is unfortunate to see the learning sciences now taking a turn. I continue to believe that bringing more design to design-based research would be a good idea.

References

Fleming, M., & Levie, W. H. (1978). *Instructional message design*. Englewood Cliffs, NJ: Educational Technology Publications.

Fleming, M., & Levie, W. H. (1993). *Instructional message design* (2nd ed.). Englewood Cliffs, NJ: Educational Technology Publications.

Kali, Y. (2008). The design principles database as means for promoting design-based research. In A. E. Kelly, R. A. Lesh, & J. Y. Baek (Eds.), *Handbook of design research methods in education* (pp. 423–438). New York: Taylor & Francis Group.

Chapter 25

Participatory Design

Jason Yip

In *The Simpsons* season 2, episode 15, the main oafish patriarch, Homer Simpson, is asked by his wealthy brother to design a car for the average man. Although hesitant at first, Homer eventually dictates to the car designers to build in strange features, such as a bubble dome, tail fins, and several car horns. The car design team reluctantly follows through with this plan and creates a monstrous and hideous car. The public unveiling of this car is disastrous, and ultimately Homer's user-design bankrupts his brother's company.

I begin this argument with this fictitious vignette to demonstrate some of the fears researchers may have about *participatory design* (PD) in the development of learning environments. As experts in the field of the learning sciences and instructional design, we may have some uncomforting reservations about giving stakeholders key access to developing new learning innovations and environments. For instance, a number of studies indicate that learners do not always know what strategies are best for their own learning (Kirschner & van Merriënboer, 2013). As a result, this may lead to concerns of the Homer Simpson PD situation for instructional designers—that is, developing learning environments that do not meet our end learning goals because learners themselves do not have a grasp of learning theories and strategies for design. However, a number of researchers in the learning sciences are using PD as part of designing new environments and learning technologies (see Bonsignore et al., 2013 for more details).

At its core, PD is a set of theories, practices, and methodologies that involve end-users as active participants in the design process (Schuler & Namioka, 1993; Muller, 2008). In the mid-1970s, the Scandinavian trade union democracy movement focused on giving union workers the opportunity to make an impact in the design of computer-based tools in the workplace (Bødker, Ehn, Sjögren & Sundblad, 2000). Since then, PD has transitioned from a sociopolitical movement with adults to a design philosophy that has had impact on user populations such as child with special needs (Frauenberger, Good & Keay-Bright, 2011; Foss et al., 2013) and older adults (Ellis & Kurniawan, 2000).

In the mid-1990s, PD researchers began working together with children to develop new innovations for youth. Here children take on various roles at different points to support design. Druin (2002) noted four roles of children, from minimally involved to full partnership: user, tester, informant, and partner. Users and testers are the least involved; children try out the innovations and provide feedback but have little investment into the design. Informants provide direct feedback and input at different stages of the design, but not continuously so there is still less investment from the users. Cooperative Inquiry (co-design) is a method of PD in which children can act as full design partners and work alongside together with design researchers to solve a problem (Druin, 2002). Designers use specific design techniques to support equal partnership (Walsh, Foss, Yip & Druin, 2013), such as using art supplies and crafts for children to communicate their ideas. Adults play an active role in helping children articulate, generate, and synthesize their ideas. Adults can also generate their own ideas and work with children to further a design.

As more involved methods of PD have increased in children's technology design, the learning sciences may be more receptive toward this design process. For instance, Quest Atlantis (QA) (Barab, Dodge, Thomas, Jackson & Tuzun, 2007), a multiuser virtual environment used to support science inquiry, employed critical ethnographies and worked together with children in PD to design mockups and propose design trajectories. The team also worked with teachers to make sure their professional needs could be met. The QA team commented that their success in developing a collaborative virtual space was in part from the development of "rich relationships with [children] we came to regard not simply as 'participants' but as 'collaborators'" (Barab et al., 2007, p. 280). More recently, researchers at the Human-Computer Interaction Lab (Bonsignore et al., 2013) have utilized co-design methods to build *ScienceKit* (Clegg et al., 2014; Yip et al., 2014) and *SciDentity* (Ahn et al., 2014). In these two projects to support science learning, co-design partnerships with children allowed us the advantage of understanding what youth seek out in terms of learning and design. In these three co-design projects (and many others), we did not meet the same fate as Homer Simpson and his ill-designed car. I outline three ways in which PD can be used fruitfully for learning environments and instructional design.

First, the learning sciences approach to learner centered design (LCD) and design-based research (DBR) is complementary to PD. In LCD, the learner is the central figure in the design process (Soloway, Guzdial & Hay, 1994); design is focused on helping the learner develop expertise. In DBR, the focus is on developing and testing theories in complex and unpredictable real-word settings, which means constantly engaging with participants in their own contexts (Collins, Joseph & Bielaczyc, 2004). As DiSalvo and DiSalvo (2014) note, these two approaches in the learning sciences are complementary to PD because of the focus on the learner in real-world settings. Working together with learners in the design of learning environments helps us understand learners and their contexts. In short, PD already fits well within the scope of methods of design and evaluation in the learning sciences.

Second, PD does not mean that design researchers only listen to user designers and ignore educational research and learning theories. One misconception of PD is that researchers only listen to the opinions of the users. However, a true partnership means that opinions are taken seriously from multiple stakeholders. Leveraging learner interest and ideas into meaningful design is not easy. For example, learners may ask for gamification or edutainment, but this may only "candy coat learning" (Disalvo & Disalvo, 2014, p. 794) and not address the deeper issues in learning. Therefore, researchers in learning and instructional design still need to utilize their own expertise into the design but be able to listen and work with learners. Working together with learners also supports ideation in context (Godden & Baddeley, 1980), the notion that knowledge and design is better done in the presence of the authentic context.

Third, PD addresses the issue of power and authenticity through partnerships. Why bother with PD and co-design then if adult researchers are ultimately going to pick what they want? The key to meaningful PD is relationship building and member checking. Member checking (Lincoln & Guba, 1986) is a method in qualitative research in which researchers check with the participants of a study the quality, credibility, and validity of an account. Creswell and Miller (2000) note that better member checking data occurs when (1) researchers spend prolonged engagement in the field and (2) close collaborations occur between participants and researchers. Similarly, in co-design partnerships, researchers constantly member check with stakeholders over a period of time to see if the design of the learning environment matches their needs. Power dynamics are already an issue when adults interview children learners (individually and in focus groups); this is especially true when the children do not trust the adults (Eder & Fingerson, 2002; Morgan, Gibbs, Maxwell & Britten, 2002). In co-design, because the children and learners work closely with the adults over a given time, the learners are more prone to being honest. PD methods that allow for close and prolonged contact between learners and researchers help both parties develop stronger relationships that allow for both criticisms and idea generation. Indeed, in my own research with Kidsteam, a group of children who co-design with adults on a weekly basis for several years, the children are known to be quite honest and tell adults exactly when a design is poor (e.g., "This is boring!" "I don't like this!") (Yip et al., 2013).

In general, utilizing PD for instructional design can be fruitful when careful considerations take place. However, the debate over PD in design in general is not over; it is impossible to ever "prove" that PD is a better design process than a centralized design by expert instructional designers. By no means is my short argument going to solve that debate. That being said, we know that design thinking is good for learners to develop problem solving skills, interest-driven learning, and agency (Kafai, 1996; Kafai, Fields & Searle, 2012). Design thinking is an integral part of co-design for all participants and has been shown to be beneficial for child design partners (Guha, 2010). In the larger scheme, PD is an attempt at democratic design. If our education strives toward democracy (Dewey, 1903), then our methods of designing curricula and learning environments need democratic processes. If we can develop learning environments through democratic means, increase design thinking in our designers, and still develop learning environments that have shown potential for increased learning, we in the learning sciences need to consider PD more as a viable process for design.

References

Ahn, J., Subramaniam, M., Bonsignore, E., Pellicone, A., Waugh, A., & Yip, J. C. (2014). "I want to be a game designer or scientist": Connected learning and developing identities with urban, African-American youth. *Proceedings of the 11th International Conference of the Learning Sciences (ICLS 2014)*.

Barab, S., Dodge, T., Thomas, M. K., Jackson, C., & Tuzun, H. (2007). Our designs and the social agendas they carry. *Journal of the Learning Sciences, 16*(2), 263–305.

Bødker, S., Ehn, P., Sjögren, D., & Sundblad, Y. (2000). Co-operative Design—perspectives on 20 years with "the Scandinavian IT Design Model." *Proceedings NordiCHI 2000* (pp. 1–9). Stockholm, Sweden.

Bonsignore, E., Ahn, J., Clegg, T., Guha, M. L., Yip, J., Druin, A., & Hourcade, J. P. (2013). Embedding participatory design into designs for learning: An untapped interdisciplinary resource. *Proc., Computer-Supported Cooperative Learning Conf. (CSCL 2013)*.

Clegg, T. L., Bonsignore, E., Ahn, J., Yip, J. C., Pauw, D., & Gubbels, M. (2014). Capturing personal and social science: Technology for integrating the building blocks of disposition. *Proceedings of the 11th International Conference of the Learning Sciences (ICLS 2014)*.

Collins, A., Joseph, D., & Bielaczyc, K. (2004). Design research: Theoretical and methodological issues. *The Journal of the Learning Sciences, 13*(1), 15–42.

Creswell, J. W., & Miller, D. L. (2000). Determining validity in qualitative inquiry. *Theory into Practice, 39*(3), 124–130.

Dewey, J. (1903). Democracy in education. *The Elementary School Teacher, 4*(4), 193–204.

DiSalvo, B., & DiSalvo, C. (2014). Designing for democracy in education: Participatory design and the learning sciences. *Proceedings of the International Conference of the Learning Sciences* (Vol. 1, pp. 793–800).

Druin, A. (2002). The role of children in the design of new technology. *Behaviour and Information Technology, 21*(1), 1–25.

Eder, D., & Fingerson, L. (2002). Interviewing children and adolescents. In J. F. Gubrium & Holstein (Eds.), *Handbook of interview research: Context and method* (Vol. 1, pp. 181–203). Thousand Oaks, CA: Sage.

Ellis, R. D., & Kurniawan, S. H. (2000). Increasing the usability of online information for older users: A case study in participatory design. *International Journal of Human-Computer Interaction*, 12(2), 263–276. doi:10.1207/S15327590IJHC1202_6

Foss, E., Guha, M. L., Panagis, P., Clegg, T., Yip, J., & Walsh, G. (2013). Cooperative Inquiry extended: Creating technology with middle school students with learning differences. *Journal of Special Education Technology*, 28(3), 33–46.

Frauenberger, C., Good, J., & Keay-Bright, W. (2011). Designing technology for children with special needs—Bridging perspectives through participatory design. *CoDesign: International Journal of CoCreation in Design and the Arts*, 7(1), 1–28.

Godden, D., & Baddeley, A. (1980). When does context influence recognition memory? *British Journal of Psychology*, 71(1), 99–104.

Guha, M. L. (2010). Understanding the social and cognitive experiences of children involved in technology design processes (3443561). University of Maryland—College Park, College Park, MD. Retrieved from ProQuest Dissertations & Theses (PQDT). (855814381)

Kafai, Y. (1996). Learning design by making games. In Y. Kafai & M. Resnick (Eds.), *Constructionism in practice: Designing, thinking and learning in a digital world* (pp. 71–96). New York: Routledge.

Kafai, Y., Fields, D. A., & Searle, K. A. (2012). Making technology visible: Connecting the learning of crafts, circuitry and coding in youth e-Textile designs. In J. van Aalst, K. Thompson, & P. Reimann (Eds.), *Proceedings of the Tenth International Conference of the Learning Sciences (ICLS)* (Vol. 1, pp. 188–195). Mahwah, NJ: Erlbaum.

Kirschner, P. A., & van Merriënboer, J. J. G. (2013). Do learners really know best? Urban legends in education. *Educational Psychologist*, 48(3), 169–183.

Lincoln, Y. S., & Guba, E. G. (1986). But is it rigorous? Trustworthiness and authenticity in naturalistic evaluation. *New Directions for Program Evaluation*, 1986(30), 73–84.

Morgan, M., Gibbs, S., Maxwell, K., & Britten, N. (2002). Hearing children's voices: methodological issues in conducting focus groups with children aged 7–11 years. *Qualitative Research*, 2(1), 5–20.

Muller, M. J. (2008). Participatory design: The third space in HCI. In A. Sears & J. Jacko (Eds.), *The human-computer interaction handbook* (2nd ed., pp. 165–186). New York: L. Erlbaum Associates.

Schuler, D., & Namioka, A. (1993). *Participatory design: Principles and practices*. Hillsdale, NJ: L. Erlbaum Associates.

Soloway, E., Guzdial, M., & Hay, K. E. (1994). Learner-centered design: The challenge for HCI in the 21st century. *Interactions*, 1(2), 36–48.

Walsh, G., Foss, E., Yip, J. C., & Druin, A. (2013). FACIT PD: Framework for analysis and creation of intergenerational techniques for participatory design. *Proceedings of the SIGCHI Conference on Human Factors in Computing Systems (CHI '13)* (pp. 2893–2902). New York: ACM.

Yip, J. C., Ahn, J., Clegg, T. L., Bonsignore, E., Pauw, D., & Gubbels, M. (2014). "It helped me do my science." A case of designing social media technologies for children in science learning. *Proceedings of the 13th International Conference on Interaction Design and Children (IDC '14)*. New York: ACM.

Yip, J. C., Clegg, T. L., Bonsignore, E., Gelderblom, H., Rhodes, E., & Druin, A. (2013). Brownies or bags-of-stuff? Domain expertise in cooperative inquiry with children. *Proceedings of the 12th International Conference on Interaction Design and Children (IDC 2013)* (pp. 201–210). New York: ACM.

RESPONSE BY THOMAS C. REEVES

This was a difficult response to compose, primarily because I agree with virtually every word of Jason Yip's excellent explanation of the value of *participatory design* (PD) in the process of designing effective learning environments. Truth be told, I could sum up my overall response to Yip's piece in two words.... "Right on."

Interestingly, the benefits of PD that Yip highlights in his chapter are highly aligned with the benefits of the kinds of formative evaluation and design-based research activities that have been recommended to the educational technology community for many years. For example, my colleague John Hedberg and I have long argued that education and training developers should invest in more intensive formative evaluation throughout the instructional design process than they normally do (cf. Reeves & Hedberg, 2003). Indeed, when asked, I usually recommend that seventy-five to ninety cents of every dollar spent on evaluation be expended on formative activities because formative evaluation has the largest return-on-investment of all the six primary evaluation functions—i.e., Review, Needs Assessment, Formative Evaluation, Effectiveness Evaluation, Impact Evaluation, and Maintenance Evaluation.

For more than two decades, I have worked with colleagues such as Jan Herrington, Susan McKenney, and others to promote the idea that educational technologists should move away from research focused on comparing the differential effects of educational media vehicles with so-called "traditional instruction" and engage more fully in design-based research (also known as "educational design research") that is intended to yield robust interventions as well as enhanced design principles (cf. McKenney & Reeves, 2012; Reeves, McKenney & Herrington, 2011). In short, we need to move from research that seeks to answer the question "what works?" to educational design research that addresses the question "how can we make this work?"

With my strong endorsement of Yip's chapter in mind, my response seeks to address any readers who still might be skeptical about the value of PD within the context of instructional design. Although I agree with Kirschner and van Merriënboer (2013) that learners do not always know what strategies are best for their own learning, this conclusion concerns interactive learning environments that have been designed to give a learner false choices such as the option of deciding not to engage in additional practice even when the learner's previous interactions clearly indicate that the learner requires such practice. If representative learners had been involved in the participatory design of that environment, it most likely would have been designed to eliminate such a misleading option.

Will the set of concepts and tools that PD brings to the instructional design table guarantee success? Unfortunately not. In searching for more information about PD, I found several sites describing how PD is being applied to the design of aircraft cabins in ways that dramatically enhance passenger comfort. Have you noticed these new seats on your flights? I have not either . . . at least not in the coach section where I normally am. This is probably because the people who ultimately make the decisions about putting airplane seats in airplanes are much more concerned about capacity and profits than customer comfort. Similarly, the potential of systematic instructional design to maximize the effectiveness of learning environments is rarely realized because of numerous external factors such as budget, time, and the reluctance of administrators, practitioners, and even learners to stray very far from traditional approaches. Consider the negligible budget for formative evaluation designated for most federally funded educational innovation projects compared with the much greater resources available to conduct randomized controlled trials of these "innovations" despite the fact that they have rarely been optimized through either rigorous formative evaluation or design-based research.

To conclude, I concur with Jason Yip that those "in the learning sciences need to consider PD more as a viable process for design." But I think this admonition is even more important for instructional designers. I cannot imagine learning scientists conducting their work without close engagement with teachers and students, but instructional designers all too often carry out their professional activities in ways that are far too insulated from their ultimate audiences. We continue to design education and training environments that have not sought to realize the enormous benefits of participatory design. This must change.

References

Kirschner, P. A., & van Merriënboer, J. J. G. (2013). Do learners really know best? Urban legends in education. *Educational Psychologist, 48*(3), 169–183.

McKenney, S. E., & Reeves, T. C. (2012). *Conducting educational design research.* New York: Routledge.

Reeves, T. C., & Hedberg, J. G. (2003). *Interactive learning systems evaluation.* Englewood Cliffs, NJ: Educational Technology Publications.

Reeves, T. C., McKenney, S. E, & Herrington, J. (2011). Publishing and perishing: The critical importance of educational design research. *Australasian Journal of Educational Technology, 27*(1), 55–65.

REJOINDER BY JASON YIP

Thomas Reeves' response to my stance on participatory design (PD) and the learning sciences and instructional design has a lot of very nuanced aspects I would like to expand upon. In short, Dr. Reeves has brought up critical issues for researchers considering the use of PD in their own practices.

First, Dr. Reeves comments on the notion of "representative learners" and their involvement in PD and designing learning environments. This is an important aspect to clarify and expand—that is, who is a representative learner for PD, and what contributions can he or she make? In my own research (Yip et al., 2013), we were interested in designing new learning tools for an informal learning environment called Kitchen Chemistry, which focuses on science learning through cooking. In that study, we worked with two groups of children. The first group of children were the design domain experts, an intergenerational design group called Kidsteam. Kidsteam is composed of researchers at the University of Maryland and a group of children ages seven to eleven. We classified Kidsteam as design domain experts because they were well versed in PD techniques. These children came twice a week to the lab for at least a year, with some children involved in PD projects for three years. The second group of children were the subject domain experts. They were the children from the Kitchen Chemistry informal science program. These children spent several weeks with my research group involved in cooking science investigations, and we worked with them only briefly (three design sessions) using PD to develop new learning technologies for Kitchen Chemistry.

Briefly, this study showed that subject domain experts and design domain experts had different ideas about design. The Kidsteam (design experts) had little understanding of Kitchen Chemistry but came up with open-ended and more creative ideas for the learning technologies. The Kitchen Chemistry children (subject experts) knew more about KC, but kept their ideas mostly on the pragmatic level. The question I am posing with this study is, who is the representative learner in a particular learning environment? For this study, a reader might conclude that the subject expert children are the designers we needed to consult because of their knowledge of the Kitchen Chemistry learning environment. But, as PD researchers, we also wanted the creative ideas from the design expert children. Ultimately, we concluded that both sets of children were valuable in their own right. However, many researchers may not have access to design expert children for practical and logistical reasons. Our takeaway is that in working with "representative learners" (whether subject or design experts), it is overall important to develop strong relationships with children to develop understanding of design for learning environments.

Second, Thomas is absolutely right that adherence to PD does not guarantee success without major support. His airplane seat analogy is an appropriate comparison to the tension between innovation and limitations. If PD is to be taken serious as a philosophy and method for instructional design, it must be valued at all levels of decision making. Although Dr. Reeves provides a pessimistic example, I offer a counter real-life example to Thomas' airplane analogy, in which there is an innovative design of airplane cabins through PD, but no follow through from decision makers. At the University of Maryland, we worked with user experience researchers at *Nickelodeon* to develop a new website interface for the company homepage.[1] The children in Kidsteam developed the "Do Not Touch" button, a website button that when you clicked on it, random, silly, and fun animations would happen on the website. From the beginning, we had buy-in from all levels at the PD process, from the user-experience designers to the leadership involved in the online distribution. As a result of this PD process from the beginning to the end, the Do

Not Touch button has been a key design feature on the Nickelodeon website and mobile app and has won the company an Emmy design media award in 2014.[2]

Currently, PD in instructional design is in the airplane analogy Dr. Reeves uses, but what if the use of PD could be the Nickelodeon's Do Not Touch button case? What if PD were the standard in creation of learning technologies and environment and championed by all levels, from designers to decision makers? This is the vision I am hoping to lead in the learning sciences and instructional design, that PD would be a pervasive design philosophy and supported throughout the entire process of learning and instructional design.

Notes

1. For more information, see "2014 SandboxSummit: A co-design journey: Random + Ridiculous = Fun."
2. See "Nickelodeon launches new Nick.com with unique horizontal layout, edge-to-edge design, TV everywhere and slate of original, digital-only series."

References

"2014 SandboxSummit: A co-design journey: Random + Ridiculous = Fun." YouTube.

"Nickelodeon launches new Nick.com with unique horizontal layout, edge-to-edge design, TV everywhere and slate of original, digital-only series." (2014, August 4). *Business Wire*. Web.

Yip, J. C., Clegg, T., Bonsignore, E., Gelderblom, H., Rhodes, E., & Druin, A. (2013). Brownies or bags of stuff: Domain expertise in cooperative inquiry with children. *Proceedings of the 12th International Conference on Interaction Design and Children (IDC 2013)* (pp. 201–210). New York: ACM.

Conclusion

We are hopeful that these dialogues have created for the field a starting point for further discussion and development. While we agree that compendia of encyclopedic or research reviews in handbooks are of great value to the field, in this text we have taken a different approach. Here our hope was that by asking authors to go directly to a potentially controversial position, with responses and rejoinders, we would be able to truly engage the field in significant development and further advance the parameters of the field overall.

The five sections in this book have covered a great deal of ground. From the foundations of the nature of design and instructional designer preparation, to contexts and technology use, all the way to comparing fields between traditional instructional design and the learning sciences, this series of dialogues has attempted to introduce complex issues with depth and positionality. By asking authors to take up and explicate specific positions with strong support for their opinions, rather than writing more expositional text describing or theorizing about these same topics, we have encouraged the authors, and you, our readers, to go into deeper reflection on these topics, granted within a potentially more narrow focus.

Where do these dialogues leave us now? At this point we have strong statements, in many cases supported by responses, and in some cases rejected or refined by the responses. Rejoinders further clarify the original position vis-à-vis the response and help to support the positions. We believe that each is significant and that the reception of the text over time by readers will help to sort out which of these dialogues will have lasting effect in which subfields of the broader discipline.

Index

abduction 22–3, 24
academia 40, 44
academic journals 27
academic tenure system 26
accumulation of disadvantage 128
achievement gap 112, 114, 179
activity format 150, 151, 153, 154
activity systems 31
ADDIE models *see* analyze, design, develop, implement, and evaluate (ADDIE) models
advancing knowledge 27
aggrandizing design 8, 10
Agrarian Age 111
Ainslie, George 117
ambiguity 8, 58
analyze, design, develop, implement, and evaluate (ADDIE) models 40, 86, 87, 98, 192, 200
"A Nation at Risk" 110
Annual Review of Psychology 183
"Any Time, Any Place, Any Way, Any Pace" learning model 173–80; final statement 175; pace 174; place 174; telling dichotomy 175; time 173–4
Apple 118, 126, 192
apprenticeship 44, 104
Archer's design model 81
Argondizza, Thomas 44, 46–7
Argyris, C. 154
art connected to instructional design 8–9, 13, 15, 16
assessment for and of student learning 133, 135
Association for Educational Communications and Technology (AECT) 62, 94
Association for Talent Development (ATD) 62, 94
assumptions, in design education 65–6; counter-productive practices 66; hidden 65
ATD Research 92
attainment-based student progress 133–6
attainment-based system 133–4
attitude 29, 30–1, 74, 106, 150

Bannan, Brenda 18–25
bastardization 28

B Corporations 118
behavioral level of design 58
behavioral psychology 40
Bishop, M. J. 131, 154, 156
black box model 44–5, 46
Bloom's Taxonomy 33, 159
Boling, Elizabeth 55, 60–1, 62, 81–2, 84, 86–7
Branch, Robert Maribe 48–9, 50, 51, 53–4
Briggs' design model 185
Briggs, Leslie 185

"Can the Adjective Instructional Modify the Noun Science?" (Merrill) 88
Carr-Chellman, Alison 45
Cates, Ward Mitchell 131, 158–60, 164–5
change/adoption theories 31
Chen, Milton 173
Christensen, Clayton 192
Christensen Institute 192
Chronicle of Higher Education 145
Clark/Kozma debates 32
Classic Dialogues (Savenye) 148
closed-access journals 142
cognitive skills 29, 86, 96
Cohen, Jonathan 117
collaboration: appeal to emotions through 58; content knowledge and 35, 37, 38; in Design-Based Research 195, 197, 200; in design education 68, 69; in design teams 96; in developing design expertise 58; in educational design research 143; between instructional science and technology 89; in instructional systems development 39; between LS and ET 184, 190; for paradigm change 112; in participatory design 203; to preparing instructional designers 96, 98; in professional design practice 20; between science, art, and design 17; in task-based learning 134; on virtual patient simulation 68; *see also* partnerships
communities: change within 31; growth within 184–5
competency-based assessment *see* attainment-based student progress
competency-based design model 101, 171

competency-based education 173, 177, 178
complex design problems 81, 85, 96
complex systems, definition of 195
computer-based tools 152, 202
Computing Research Association 128
Conditions of Learning, The (Gagné) 183
constructivism 41
contact, points of 186–8
content agnosticism 2, 33, 35
content in instructional design, role of 32–8
core judgment 60, 62
corporate systems 117–23
counter-productive practices 66
creative design: benefits in pursuing 71; psychological conditions found to inhibit and catalyze creativity 69; risk associated with 72; safe place for exploring, while mitigating risks 72; value-added provided by 71
criterion-referenced testing 46–7, 112, 134; *see also* attainment-based student progress
Cross, N. 57–8
curriculum script 150, 151, 153, 154

data on learner performance 166–7, 169
Davidson, Richard 117
Degreed 169
De Re Militari (Vegetius) 46
design, definition of 2, 8, 33
design-based research (DBR) 194–201; design principles as useful outcome in 198; distributed design work in 197–8
design character 86
design education: assessment 75–6, 78; assumptions 65–6; classrooms 104, 106, 143, 145, 150, 190; collaboration in 68, 69; conclusion 67; contexts of learning, design, and technology 101; curriculum, scheduling of 75, 78; design steps in 73, 74; disciplinary definitions 64–5; for educating disciplines 64–72; graduate programs 88, 89, 91, 95–6; implications 66; instructional technology, future of 88–94; issues in 103–9; master's programs 90–1, 93; paradigm change 110–15; project-led, as educational model 73–4, 77–8; research skills and design skills, importance of 75, 78; scaffolding supervising 74–5, 78; science of instruction and technology of instructional design 88–90, 92; simple-to-complex approach 81–7; sociopolitical part of 73; students as partners in learning process 74, 78; substantive part of 73; technical part of 73; T-shaped professionals 73, 77; undergraduate programs 88, 92
designer identity 77, 96
designerly ways of knowing 58, 98
designers-by-assignment (DBA) 91
design expertise: developing 57–63; requirements for 48–54

design inquiry 13, 14, 15, 24
design precedents 78, 95–6
design process, definition of 10–11
design skills, importance of 75, 78
design steps in design education 73, 74
design theory 19, 81–2, 86
design thinking: in design-based research 196; in developing design expertise 57, 62, 65; in educating T-shaped professionals 77; in learning by doing and reflecting 73–4, 77–8; in participatory design 204; in preparing instructional designers 56, 95–6, 98; to understand nature of design 18, 24
Design Thinking Research Symposium 79
Dewey, John 10–11, 60, 186
digital immersion learning 145
direct instruction 142, 146
Dirksen, J. 58
disciplinary definitions 64–5
dissertation studies 41
distance education 145
doing, learning by 73–4, 77–8
double-loop learning 131, 154, 155
Dousay, Tonia A. 56, 92–3, 94
Drucker, Peter 119, 120
DuBois, W. E. B. 99

economic value, definition of 120, 122
Edison, Thomas 143
education, defining success in 32
educational design research 142–3, 149, 197, 206
educational reform 110–15, 137
educational technologies: ICT products 150–3; learning sciences and 183–93; lines of opportunity with potential to go to scale 156; in schools, building to scale 150–7; women in 124–9; *see also* instructional technology
educational technologist 48–9, 50, 54, 193, 195, 206
Educational Technology Research and Development 198
Education Nation: Six Leading Edges of Innovation in Our Schools (Chen) 173
e-learning 166–72
eLearning Guild 62
eLife 142
Eliot, Charles 103
Ellson, Douglas 41
emotional design 58
empirical qualities of ISD 40
end-users as active participants in design processes 181, 202
engineering design, models for 81, 187
espoused theory 154
ethics 120, 122–3
Everyday Cognition (Lave and Rogoff) 22
evidence, range of 30

Index

experts, thoughts on instructional design 64–9, 72
exploration, education through 145

Facebook 125, 126, 128
factory model of schools 111, 112
First Principles of Instruction (Merrill) 88
Fortney, Kathleen 55, 57–9, 60, 62–3
Foshay, Rob 101, 122–3, 131, 150–3, 154, 156
free-choice learning 145
Freidhoff, Joseph R. 131, 173–5, 177, 178, 179–80
full immersion learning 145
future shock, defined 166
Future Shock (Toffler) 166

Gagné, Robert 181, 183–7
Gagné-Rohwer review 183, 184
Gale, Walter H. 148
Gen X 166
Gibbons, Andrew S. 19, 22–3, 24–5, 60, 181, 183–8, 190, 191, 192–3
Glaser, Robert 181, 183–7
Glaser-Resnick review 183, 184
Glimcher, Paul 122
Google 108, 125, 126, 128
Google+ 125
graduate programs 88, 89, 91, 95–6
"Green Book, The" (Reigeluth, Myers and Beatty) 139
groupthink 122
growth in learning sciences: growth apart 184; growth within separate communities 184–5; separation, underlying causes of 185–6
guarantor of design 81
guerrilla design 26–31

Haidt, Jonathon 122
Hammond, Thomas C. 131, 158–60, 164–5
Handbook of Design in Educational Technology (Luckin) 184
harassment 124–6
Harmon, Stephen W. 131, 137–8, 139
Harvard curriculum 103–4
heuristic qualities of ISD 40
hidden curriculum 110, 112
Hirumi, Atsusi 55, 68, 71, 72
Hoadley, C.M. 184, 185–6
Hokanson, Brad 32–4, 35, 37–8, 56, 98–9, 100
Human Performance Improvement (HPI) 117–23
human-robot interaction (HRI) 158
Hunting-and-Gathering Age 111
hyperbolic discounting 117

ICT products 150–3
ideas, synthesizing and generating 33, 203
ill-structured domains (ISDs) 142

#ILookLikeAnEngineer grassroots campaign 129
Industrial Age 110, 111, 112, 133, 137, 139
Information Age 110, 111–12, 115, 133, 137, 138, 139, 166
information retention 32, 37
innovation, definition of 28
Innovators (Isaacson) 124
inputs, black box 44
inquiry, focus on process of 12–13
Institute of Education Sciences (IES) 148
instructional design (ID): aggrandizing design 8, 10; appreciation of, raising 7–11; art connected to 8–9, 13, 15, 16; content in, role of 32–8; design inquiry 13, 14, 15, 24; design process, defined 10–11; expertise required to practice 48–54; guerrilla design and 26–31; how novices and experts think about ID 64–9, 72; inquiry and outcome, focus on process of 12–13, 16–17; models (*see* instructional design models); natural order, aligning with 9; nature of 18–25; performance-based 41, 112; phases 10; rational inquiry and action, chasm between 13; reflective practice of 7, 51, 54; relationship of, to other design disciplines 7–17; science-based approach to 12–13, 15, 16, 88–90; studio approach to teaching 82, 84, 86; *see also* instructional systems development (ISD)
instructional design and technology (IDT) 26, 30–1, 194, 195
instructional designers: design expertise, developing 57–63; design expertise, requirements for 48–54; preparing 55–6, 95–100; *see also* design education
instructional design models: "*Any Time, Any Place, Any Way, Any Pace*" 173–80; Archer's 81; Briggs' 185; in commercialization of education 192–3; competency-based 101, 171; in design-based research 198, 200; in education of instructional designers 55–6, 57, 59, 60, 62, 63; for engineering design 81, 187; factory model of schools 111, 112; in future of instructional technology 88, 89, 92; in guerrilla design 26, 28; hyperbolic discounting 117; inadequacy of 19; mathematical 39; mental model of learning 141; need for variety of new and competing 106; for planned change 28, 30; prescriptive 18, 20; project-led education as educational model 73–4, 77–8; science-based 88–9; simplistic, reliance on 18, 19, 20; systematic 22; in *Systematic Design of Instruction* 88; teacher-centric 171; for teaching complex performance of instructional design 81, 82, 84–7; in undergraduate programs 88, 92; for use in college instruction 40; of value of ICT product in teaching 151–2; *see also*

instructional systems development (ISD) models
instructional methods: comparison studies of 41; in learner-centered paradigm of instruction 134–5; level of 41
"Instructional Psychology" (Gagné and Rohwer) 183
instructional science 89–90, 99; see also science-based approach to ID
instructional strategies 31, 41–2, 69, 84, 86, 89, 90, 134, 139
instructional superstructure 133–4; attainment-based system 133–4; personal learning plan 134
instructional systems development (ISD) 39–47; academia 40, 44; behavioral psychology 40; critiques from corporate practice 42; essential qualities of 40; evolution through real-world testing 40; models (see instructional systems development (ISD) models); roots of 39–40; strengths of 39–42; supported by experts 41; supported by formal research 41; theoretical challenges 41–2; universities in 40, 44, 46; in U.S. military 39, 44, 45, 46; vocational education or training in 40, 44, 46, 47
instructional systems development (ISD) models 48–54; ADDIE 40, 86, 87, 98, 192, 200; attributes of 49; black box 44–5, 46; complexity contained within 48; comprehensiveness and usability of 41; contextual adaptations of 40; IPISD 39; level of detail depicted in 42, 45, 47; Pebble-in-the-Pond 84, 86, 87; SAM 42, 45, 84, 86–7; see also instructional design models
instructional technology: "Any Time, Any Place, Any Way, Any Pace" learning model 173–80; devices and products 158–65; e-learning 166–72; future of 55, 56, 88–94; master's programs 90–1, 93; science of instruction and 88–90, 92; undergraduate programs 88, 92
instruction for student learning 133, 135
integrated student assessment 135
intelligent tutoring system 142
International Association for K-12 Online and Blended Learning (iNACOL) 173
International Board of Standards for Training, Performance and Instruction (IBSTPI) 41, 49, 50–1
International Society for Performance Improvement (ISPI) 62
Internet technologies 124–6
Interservice Procedures for Instructional Systems Development (IPISD) model 39
"in-the-wild" cognition 24–5
intrinsic motivation 112, 134, 137
IPISD model see Interservice Procedures for Instructional Systems Development (IPISD) model

Isaacson, Walter 124, 129
iterative qualities of ISD 40
It's a Wonderful Life (film) 118

James, William 46
Jefferson, Thomas 46
JIT instruction see just-in-time (JIT) instruction
Journal of the Learning Sciences 198
just-in-time (JIT) instruction 133, 134–5

Kafkaesque example 118
Kahneman, Daniel 118
Kane, T. J. 148–9
Kaufman, R. 120
Kennedy, Kathryn 131, 173–5, 177, 178, 179–80
Kidsteam 204, 208–9
Kitchen Chemistry 208
Knewton 169
"knowing-how" 98, 99, 100
"knowing-what" 98, 99, 100
knowledge, advancing 27
Knowledge Age 137, 139; see also Information Age
Koehler, M. 159

Laibson, David 117
learner-centered paradigm of instruction 133–9; instructional methods 134–5; instructional superstructure 133–4; integrated student assessment 135; just-in-time (JIT) instruction 133, 134–5; technology functions 135–6
learner control of time, place, and pace of instruction 167–8, 169
learner performance, data on 166–7, 169
learning, definition of 37, 141–2, 145
Learning Research and Development Center (LRDC) 184–5
learning sciences (LS): Design-Based Research 194–201; educational technology and 183–93; educational technology researchers and 190–1; Gagné and Glasser 183–8; growth apart 184; growth within separate communities 184–5; introduction to 181; participatory design 202–9; points of contact 186–8; separation, underlying causes of 185–6
learning theory 26, 45, 79
levels of design 58, 64
Lovelace, Ada 124

mansplaining 125
Marker, Anthony 101, 117–19, 120, 122–3
Marra, Rose 101, 128–9
Martin, Barbara L. 28–9, 30
massive open online courses (MOOCs) 103, 107, 125, 141, 145; project-based (pMOOCs) 141
master's programs 90–1, 93

Index   215

mathematical design models 39
math, English, science, and social studies (MESS) 115, 139
McCombs, Barbara 41
media: comparison research 145; definition of 145; learning from and with 141–9
"Men Explain Things to Me" (Solnit) 125
mental model of learning 141
Merrill, M. David 55–6, 81, 82, 84–5, 86, 88–91, 92, 94, 145
MESS see math, English, science, and social studies (MESS)
meta-learning skills 131, 169–70, 171
micro-aggression 125
Miles, Matthew 156
Millennials 166
Mishra, P. 159
Mitra, Sugata 131, 163, 164
Molenda, Michael 39–42, 44, 45, 46–7
MOOCs see massive open online courses (MOOCs)
Moore's Law 158, 159

National Assessment of Educational Progress 110
National Center for Women in Technology 128
National Science Foundation (NSF) 148
nature of design 18–25
Nelson, Harold 8, 9–11, 12–15, 60, 86
neuroscience of intellect *vs.* wisdom 117–23
norm-referenced testing 110, 111, 112
"no-significant differences" 142, 148
novices, thoughts on instructional design 64–9, 72

online learning 107, 131, 145, 167, 169, 173–5, 177, 179, 180
open adaptive systems 31
Orbis Sensualium Pictus (Comenius) 47
Organisation for Economic Co-operation and Development (OECD) 110, 114
organizational culture 31
organization learning 31
outcome, focus on process of 12–13, 16–17
outputs, black box 44

pace of instruction: in "*Any Time, Any Place, Any Way, Any Pace*" learning model 174; learner control of 167–8, 169
pacing guides 150, 151, 174, 179
paradigm change 110–15; introduction 110; position statement 111–13
Parrish, Patrick 7–11, 16–17, 60
participatory design (PD) 202–9
partnerships: benefits of 35, 62–3, 181, 200; co-design partnerships with children 203; collaborative research-practice 197; complications in 35; between LS and ET researchers 190; power dynamics and 203–4; see also collaboration
Patagonia 118–19
Pebble-in-the-Pond model 84, 86, 87
Peck, Kyle 101, 106–7, 108
peer-reviewed open-access publications 142, 143
performance-based instructional design 41
personalized learning environments (PLE) 167, 169
personal learning plan 134
piecemeal reforms 110, 112, 113, 115
PISA test 110, 114, 115
place of instruction: in "*Any Time, Any Place, Any Way, Any Pace*" learning model 174; learner control of 167–8, 169
planning for student learning 133, 135
pMOOCs see massive open online courses (MOOCs), project-based (pMOOCs)
points of contact 186–8
political activism 31
political affiliation 31
position statement 1–2
Predictive Analytics Reporting (PAR) Framework 169
Prensky, Mark 139
prescriptive design models 18, 20
prespecified design process 46
pressure politics 31
principled resistance 26, 28
problem framing 30, 31
problem solving 19, 39, 54, 57, 72, 73, 77, 86, 112, 117, 141; skills 68, 84, 85, 94, 110, 204
professional identity development 78
programs, for advancing knowledge 27
progressive pedagogies 26–7
project-based massive open online courses (pMOOCs) 141
project-led design education, as educational model 73–4, 77–8

Quinn, Clark 131, 169–70, 171, 172

radical ideas 28–9
Raish, Victoria 131, 177–8, 179
real-world testing 40
"Reclaiming Instructional Design" (Merrill, Drake, Lacey, Pratt, and ID2 Research Group) 89
recordkeeping for student learning 133, 135, 139
Reeves, Thomas C. 131, 141–3, 145–6, 148–9, 181, 190, 206–7, 208–9
reflecting, learning by 73–4, 77–8
reflective level of design 58
reflective practice of instructional design 7, 51, 54
Reigeluth, Charles M. 45, 101, 110–13, 114, 115, 131, 133–6, 137–8, 139

Reinventing Schools: It's Time to Break the Mold (Reigeluth and Karnopp) 111, 112, 113
religious affiliation 31
"Remote Working Etiquette" (Microsoft Office 365 document) 175
research, ISD supported by 41
research and development 186, 187–8
research skills, importance of 75, 78
Resnick, Lauren 183
resource system 150, 151, 154
Rieber, Lloyd P. 50–1, 53
risk associated with creative design 72
robotics 158–60, 164
Rohwer, William D. 183
Roman education 47
Rowland, Gordon 57, 181, 194–6, 197, 198, 200–1
Ruthven, Ken 150, 151, 152, 154

SAM *see* Successive Approximation Model (SAM)
Savenye, Wilhelmina C. 131, 145–6, 148
Savery, John 131, 166–8, 169, 170, 171–2
scaffolding 78, 169, 198
Schank, Roger C. 103–5, 108–9, 114
scheduling curriculum 75, 78
Schekman, Randy 142–3
Schön, D. 58, 154
Schwartz, Barry 118
science-based approach to ID 12–13, 15, 16; importance of 89–90; technology and, relationship among components of 89–90, 99; *see also* learning sciences (LS)
science-based design models 88–9
science in ethics 120, 122–3
"science of design" 20, 23, 24
science, technology, engineering, and mathematics (STEM) 142, 156, 168
scope and sequence curriculum 150, 164
self-directed learning 133, 134, 137, 171
separation, underlying causes of 185–6
Silber, K. H. 57
simple-to-complex approach 81–7
single-loop learning 154
Skinner, B. F. 40, 45, 185
Smart Sparrow 169
Smith, Kennon M. 64–7, 68, 69, 71–2
social/emotional factors 159
social movements 31
sociopolitical part of design education 73
Solnit, Rebecca 125
Spector, Mike 188
STEM *see* science, technology, engineering, and mathematics (STEM)
Stolterman, E. 8, 9–11, 60, 86
"straw man" proposition 146
studio approach to teaching 82, 84, 86
substantive part of design education 73

Successive Approximation Model (SAM) 42, 45, 84, 86–7
supervising, scaffolding 74–5, 78
systematic design models 22
Systematic Design of Instruction, The (Dick, Carey, and Carey) 88
systematic development process 46, 47
systematic qualities of ISD 40
systemic qualities of ISD 40
systemic/transformational change 31
systems approach 39–47; *see also* instructional systems development (ISD)

task-based learning (TBL) 133, 134–5
task-centered organization 133
teacher-centered instruction 112, 133, 134, 139
teacher-centric design model 171
teamwork 68, 73, 77
technical part of design education 73
Technological Pedagogical Content Knowledge (TPACK) 159
technology: barriers to using 159, 164–5; introduction to 131; learner-centered paradigm of instruction 133–9; learning from and with 141–9; relationship among components of instructional science and 89–90, 99
technology functions, learner-centered paradigm of instruction 135–6
"10 Commandments for Remote Working" (Sharp) 175
Ten Steps to Complex Learning (van Merriënboer and Kirschner) 88
theories, in design education 73–4, 75, 79, 80
theory-in-use 154
Thorndike, Edward L. 47
time, concept of moving away from 179
time-based student progress 111, 112, 133, 136
time economy 150, 151, 154
time of instruction: in "*Any Time, Any Place, Any Way, Any Pace*" learning model 173–4; learner control of 167–8, 169
Toffler, Alvin 111, 112–13, 139, 166, 168, 170
Tracey, Monica W. 55–6, 77–8, 79, 80, 95–6, 98–9, 100
traditional instructional design 96, 181, 206, 210
T-shaped professionals 55, 73, 77
Tumblr 125
21st Century Skills 169, 171
Twitter 125, 126

undergraduate programs 88, 92
United Nations' International Telecommunication Union 164
University of al-Qarawiyyin 44
U.S. military 39, 44, 45, 46

Valian, Virginia 128
value, definition of 120, 122
value-added provided by creative design 71
virtual patient simulation 68
visceral level of design 58
Visscher-Voerman, Irene 55, 73–6, 77, 78, 79–80
Vygotsky, L. S. 134

Wagner, Ellen 169
Wardrip, Peter Samuelson 35
Warschauer, M. 169
Watters, Audrey 101, 124–6, 128
well-structured domains (WSDs) 142

"what works?" questions 142, 149, 206
whole learner 159
wicked problems 55, 86, 131, 158–60
Wilson, Brent 26–7, 28, 30–1
wisdom, neuroscience of intellect *vs.* 117–23
women in educational technology 124–9
work environment 128, 150–1
World War II 39, 44, 45, 46

Yip, Jason 181, 190–1, 202–4, 206, 207, 208–9

Zimmerman, Heather Toomey 181, 197–8, 200, 201
zone of proximal development 134